DATE DUE

			PRINTED IN U.S.A.

CLARIBEL ALEGRÍA, 1990. (Courtesy Mel Rosenthal)

CLARIBEL ALEGRIA AND CENTRAL AMERICAN LITERATURE

Critical Essays

edited by
Sandra M. Boschetto-Sandoval
and
Marcia Phillips McGowan

Ohio University Center for International Studies
Monographs in International Studies

Latin American Series Number 21
Athens, Ohio 1994

Library of Congress Cataloging-in-Publication Data

Claribel Alegría and Central American literature : critical
  essays / edited by Sandra M. Boschetto-Sandoval and
  Marcia P. McGowan.
    p.   cm. – (Monographs in international studies. Latin
  America series ; no. 21)
    Includes bibliographical references.
    ISBN 0-89680-179-9 (pbk.)
    1. Alegría, Claribel–Criticism and interpretation.
  I. Boschetto-Sandoval, Sandra M. II. McGowan,
  Marcia P. (Marcia Phillips) III. Series.
  PQ7539.A47Z594 1993   93-28679
  861–dc20   CIP

CONTENTS

PART ONE
Contextual Conjunctions: Literary Discourse, History, and Cultural Revolution

PART TWO
Feminist Representations

PART THREE
Extraliterary Cartographies

APPENDIXES

ILLUSTRATIONS

ix

FOREWORD

To delve into the vast and varied opera of Claribel Alegría is to connect with one of the most disturbingly beautiful and turbulent regions of present-day Central America. Alegría, whether in her radiant, bold poetry, in her journalistic essays, or, in her testimonial fiction, incorporates the everyday struggles of her own historical journey with those of the oppressed. As she speaks for the absent ones, the downtrodden, the grieving, those who live on the border of words and life, Alegría dedicates herself to providing these other voices with a space, a means of recalling their special relationship to the landscape of the world. More significantly, she teaches us to love them.

Alegría also reflects a turbulent life as traveler, or, better said, as restless wanderer. At nine months of age she had abandoned her birthplace, Esteli in Nicaragua, for El Salvador because of the forced political exile of her father at a time when North American troops were invading Nicaragua. Alegría did not return to her native land until the Sandinistas' prophecy of victory was fulfilled. The spectre of the fierce dictatorship of Somoza, the Matanza of the peasants at Izalco, the small heartrending pueblos of Central America—these do not appear as mere anecdotes or supporting space for her poetry and prose; rather these spaces are transformed into the very shape of her text, into a manner of speaking without subterfuge, formed in the authenticity of her writing, a writing implicated in the political, social, and magical history of the region.

In numerous interviews and personal testimonies, Alegría affirms that she writes "letras de emergencia" or "urgent literature." In fact, to read, for example, *Flores del volcán / Flowers from the Volcano*, *La mujer del río* (The woman of the river), or *Luisa in Realityland* is to share a poetry carved with visceral and concrete images, revealing the history of a people in vital urgency and flux, the history of a people and of a region desperately invoking their autonomy and freedom of expression, creating a ceremonial square which calls for schools and pencils without bombs or mercenary armies. Alegría elaborates in her poetry all of this hallucinatory reality, mingling horror with heartrending tenderness, and grafting both emotions powerfully and expressively onto the page. Alegría tells us of a country of smoke and death:

> In my country
> some time ago
> the soldiers
> began killing children
> bruising the tender flesh
> of children
> tossing babies
> into the air
> on bayonets.
> (*Luisa in Realityland*, 35)

To classify her poetry as strictly a political legacy would be to diminish the aesthetic command of her work. Alegría uses the power of written words to make us feel the cries of the children, their absurd timeless deaths, and to recreate the historical legacy of the people of Central America. As readers of these words, it is possible for us to imagine the bullets and to feel in them the weight of history, in the same way in which Pablo Neruda used to summon forth the Spanish Civil War or the Chilean genocide during the years of Pinochet's dictatorship.

To listen to Alegría recite or converse, or to receive from her a letter-poem, a poem-song, is almost the same thing because Alegría belongs to that alliance of Latin American writers who do not make of their work a fragment separate from life. On the contrary, these writers walk out onto the street and converse with people from every walk of life about everyday experiences. From the color of their children's eyes, from the deprivation of women and men, from those ashes of Izalco is born an irascible and audacious poem. From her commitment to people comes Alegría's definition of political responsibility:

Political commitment, in my view, is seldom a calculated intellectual strategy. It seems to me more like a contagious disease, athlete's foot, let's say or typhoid fever. And if you happen to live in a plague area, the chances are excellent that you will come down with it. Commitment is a visceral reaction to the corner of the world we live in and what it has done to us and to the people we know. ("The Writer's Comment," 308)

The entire artistic creation of Alegría is visceral. Stemming from the very depths of her being, it moves us, it frees us not only to feel, but to think as well. I recall, for example, *Luisa in Reality-land*, the autobiographical collection of prose poems, as a celebration of life, as well as an invocation to the dead. In this and in her other writings, Alegría breaks with every canonical concept of literature and its genres. She dares with characteristic boldness to write an autobiography that combines fragments, that recalls particular sayings, that speaks of her native trees, of the *ceiba* tree, and of the landscape which awakens poetry in the young Luisa, a suffering and irate poetry produced by injustice. *Luisa in Reality-land* represents the story of this wanderer through the labyrinthine spaces of infancy where light and magic commingle with the horrors of war, with the dead who are not invoked in vain:

> Your death congeals you
> you are motionless
> my life in turn
> flows
> carrying me swiftly
> toward our reunion.
> (*Luisa in Realityland*, 127)

Alegría is inexhaustible. She travels through Central American territories and also spends lengthy periods of time in Mallorca reflecting, feeling, writing. She returns to Central America after lecturing at North American universities; with her soft voice, her tender yet penetrating gaze, she transforms the consciences of the young, making them feel responsible by evoking these tormented lands whose histories are so intertwined with that of North America. During her travels, she presents lectures, composes poetry, creates intrinsically beautiful, exceptionally narrated and elaborated novels such as "Family Album" or testimonial works such as *They Won't Take Me Alive.* In order to construct the latter, Alegría interviews family members, recuperates and narrates the spaces through which the extraordinary figure of Eugenia moves, and in this way recreates the complex image of a being submerged in the revolutionary process of her country.

This preface can only reflect traces of Alegría's illuminating and effervescent presence. We recognize in her, as well, an indefatigable strength, patience and goodness. Students in North American universities remember her as always well-disposed to dialogue, whether political or personal. In South America, especially in Chile where she took up residence for several years, people remember her with the same affection, describing her as a tireless cultural activist.

In this collection of essays compiled by varying interpreters of Latin American literature, the reader will enter ever more deeply into the multifaceted work of Alegría, from her testimony to her verse. The reader will not fail to comprehend Alegría's various designs for making literature, but most of all, she will be able to observe unceasing commitment to the voiceless, the historyless, the ones burdened by absence. By means of this woman's furious, fiery, tender and lovesick words, the marginalized, the indigenous recuperate spaces, resuscitate their dead, and celebrate life by defying death. Thanks to Alegría, it is possible to say once again that poetry does not live in vain, that it is dangerous because it is capable of transforming and resurrecting history and the people who struggle to recapture it.

Marjorie Agosín

(Translated by Sandra M. Boschetto-Sandoval)

ACKNOWLEDGMENTS

The two people who have been most central to this project are Alexander (Sandy) Taylor and Judy Doyle, founders and editors of Curbstone Press. Without their special attention, affectionate understanding, and conversation, we most likely would not have encountered the people about whom we speak. It is to Sandy and Judy that we dedicate these essays.

Over the past year many colleagues, students, and friends have kept up animated conversations with us on the lives (public and private), and works (varied and complex) of Claribel and Bud; all of them have wondered why this project has taken as long as it has. In an important sense, this book is also for them.

While we cannot thank individually all those who gave us thoughtful encouragement on this manuscript, we do want to make special mention of a few. To Marc Zimmerman, whose astute and sympathetic guidance in the very preliminary stages provided an important impetus to our work, sincere thanks. We also are indebted to him for his helpful, lucid, and intelligent comments on these essays. To Mel Rosenthal, who extended a photograph of Claribel Alegría, we are most grateful. We are indebted to Margaret Crosby for taking time out from her dissertation to help us compile our bibliography. Special thanks are due also to Jennifer, and to the peerless Constance Campo, Raymond Le Cara, and Ginger LaBeske Dwyer, without whose tireless and careful transcriptions and word processing this manuscript would have taken much longer than it has.

Finally, to those who gave us the privilege of thinking and writing in relative solitude, especially John and Ciro, special thanks are in order. We hope the wear and tear on personal relationships has not been prohibitively high.

INTRODUCTION: AN INITIAL CARTOGRAPHY

Sandra M. Boschetto-Sandoval
and
Marcia Phillips McGowan

In a recent autobiography, Claribel Alegría confesses to always having written her poems "under obsession's spur" (Alegría 1992, 14). Writing, like speaking, becomes compulsive when it takes such possession of the writer that breaking with its daily routine reduces her to the chaos of the world that surrounds her. In "Family Album" (*Family Album*), Claribel Alegría's narrator Ximena determines to free herself from certain family terrors and infantile obsessions. As she awakens finally to a new political consciousness in dialogical confrontation with both real and imaginary selves, Ximena finds the voice to speak against human suffering and injustice, "the stench of the rotting room" (118).

Like Ximena and the mythical figure of Scheherazade, Alegría has had to narrate stories and invent fictions in a desperate race against time and death: the death of identity and desire, the silent deaths of the unnamed she must salvage from disappearance. As Nancy Saporta Sternbach (1991, 94) reminds us, however, unlike the mythical storyteller who makes the word flesh, Alegría makes the flesh word, reinscribing thereby an entirely new writing (and reading) of the body as text. Thus, Alegría's writing reflects a movement toward remembered and rebodied writing that materializes woman's specificity. Like many Latin American women writers in voluntary or forced exile from their homeland, Alegría also has had to write in defiance of a system which imposes anonymity. Writing, therefore, has become her way of prolonging an illusory freedom, of postponing death. Employing vindication and the use of oral history as means by which to frame her narrative, Alegría is a subversive storyteller. Like the oral histories passed from woman to woman, from generation to generation, she is intent on breaking silences, raising consciousness, envisioning a new future, and seeking collective action.

To situate the works of Alegría within its Latin American sociohistoric and political contexts is to retrieve, reconstruct, and recover not only a particular history of oppression and colonial restructuring; it also is to ground reality in a specific historic moment when subjects come to see themselves as integral parts of a collective process of intervention in history. The "struggle for a better world" is what characterizes both the projects of popular historiography and the works of Alegría.

As poet, essayist, journalist, novelist, and writer of quasi-*testimonio*, Alegría functions in a manner very similar to that of a cartographer. Tracing the heights, depths, and contours of her memory, she charts the most recondite and trauma-laden regions of her psyche. The effect is not unlike that of a series of symmetrical mirrors, simultaneously reflecting inward and outward. The maps she draws, however, while subversive, are necessarily anchored in her own discontinuous locations, not only geographical, but historical and personal. The cities of Hammond, Louisiana, and Washington, D.C., the island of Mallorca, Spain, and the countries of Nicaragua, El Salvador, Mexico, Chile, Uruguay, Argentina, and France; all are interrelated markers on the path to self-discovery and renewal. In El Salvador, the turmoil of the region instills the "deep psychic wound that has never healed" (Alegría 1992, 3); she encounters, too, the authors and compositions that play a decisive role in her adolescence: the works of Beethoven, Juan Ramón Jiménez's *Platero y yo*, and Rainer María Rilke's *Letter to a Young Poet*.

In Louisiana, the empty classroom which she occupies from five to six every afternoon in her finishing school becomes the much-awaited "room of her own" for working on poetry. In Washington, her two-year mentorship with Juan Ramón Jiménez results in the publication of her first book of poems, *Anillo de silencio* (Ring of silence) in 1948. In Mexico (1951-53) she writes *Vigilias* (Vigils), a book composed largely of sonnets, but one in which she "hits upon her own poetic voice" (Alegría 1992, 9). In Chile (1953-55), besides working on the anthology of Latin American authors, *New Voices of*

Hispanic America (1962), with her husband, Darwin "Bud" Flakoll, she writes a new book of poems, *Acuario* (Aquarium), in which she begins "to pay more attention to what was happening around [her], rather than gazing at [her] own navel and [her] interior, subjective states" (Alegría 1992, 10).

By the time she arrives in Montevideo, Uruguay (1958), writing has become a compulsion. During her stay, Cuba is liberated from Yankee imperialism, and Alegría acquires a "new attitude" toward current events. In Argentina (1960) she publishes *Vía unica* (One-way traffic), nostalgic poems of lost childhood, love, and death, themes that would become ever more interwoven, central components of her poetry. Four years in Paris (1962-64) result not only in further friendships with several Latin American writers and artists in exile, including Carlos Fuentes, Julio Cortázar, Saul Yurkievich, Mario Benedetti, and Mario Vargas Llosa, but in the writing of *Cenizas de Izalco* (Ashes of Izalco, 1964), among the best books in the Biblioteca Breve competition in Barcelona.

Ten years later *Ashes* is published in El Salvador when the dictator Molina decides to leave office with a "liberal image" (Alegría 1992, 12). The Ministry of Education is ordered to publish works by Salvadoran writers, and, ironically, *Ashes* is one of those chosen. It soon becomes a secondary school text for Salvadoran children.

In 1968 Alegría and Flakoll discover Deyá, Mallorca. These are productive years. *Pagaré a cobrar* (Installment payments) is published in 1973, and *Sobrevivo* (I survive) wins the Casa de las Américas poetry prize in 1978. Alegría also writes three short novels in Deyá: "El detén" (The talisman), published in Barcelona in 1977, "Albúm familiar" (Family album), published in Costa Rica in 1982, and "Pueblo de Dios y de Mandinga" (Village of God and the Devil), published in Mexico in 1985. At the urging of Julio Cortázar and his second wife, Carol Dunlap, to whom Alegría has related many anecdotes of childhood, Alegría writes *Luisa in Realityland*, published in 1987. She also composes an anthology of Robert Graves's poems in Spanish and edits with Darwin Flakoll another anthology, *Nuevas voces de Norteamérica* (New voices of North America), a collection of poems by young U.S. poets.

While extensive, Alegría's cartography is essentially one of struggle. In March of 1980, Monsiñor Oscar Arnulfo Romero, archbishop of San Salvador, is shot in the back by a member of a death squad while saying mass in a hospital chapel. The assassination marks a crossroads in Alegría's life. The death squads eliminated "the voice of the voiceless," but they also stirred others to rise up and denounce the government-sponsored atrocities and terrorism that afflicted the region. Alegría marks this moment as the beginning of her "political career" (Alegría 1992, 14). While historically discursive categories are clearly central sites of political contestation, they must be grounded in and informed by the material politics of everyday life, especially the daily struggles for survival of poor people—those written out of history. In this regard, Alegría's "political career" had begun to take shape long before the assassination of Archbishop Romero.

Despite her upper-middle-class upbringing (her father was a well-known and respected physician and her mother, a member of the Salvadoran oligarchy), Alegría's life and work must be examined from a clearly oppositional location. The contradictions are evident when she speaks of her family:

> And my father was from a very humble background. My father's family were campesinos. They had a ranch. They were not poor, but they were campesinos. And my father was the only one who studied, who had a profession, you see. My mother, on the other hand, was from the very high bourgeoisie from El Salvador, from the Oligarchs; they had lost their money, but she is from very the very high bourgeoisie, and so all my mother's family were very right wing, except my mother (Cl. laughs). She was not, you see. But, of course, I was listening to all kinds of things, and in my house, mostly, people from the bourgeoisie would come, but then my father talked differently, and I went to a beautiful school that was also a school that was run by one of my uncles, but he was also a very intelligent man, and he was against his own class so I was receiving two currents, and many people in my family, they are, right now, right wing. I think I am the only black sheep. (Cl. laughs). (Conversation with Alexander Taylor, Managua, 1987)

A significant anecdote, pertinent to Alegría's autobiographical ebbs and flows, is related in "Family Album" when Ximena inquires of the Indian maid Chus, her imaginary friend from "the other Santa Ana," as to how babies are born and who brings them. Chus replies,

"That depends. Rich people claim their children from the cemetery, poor children wait for parents in the market." Ximena sat still in silence. "And where was I brought from?" she asked after a pause. Chus stopped braiding, sat Ximena on her knees and gave her a kiss. "I'd say that despite coming from a wealthy family, they found you in the market." (Alegría 1991, 85)

Like the sign of Taurus under which she was born and, in the Chinese lunar horoscope, the sign of the rat, Alegría has operated at the crossroads of "two currents," the conventional and the subversive. The oppositional alliance between "cemetery" and "market" is a viable one, particularly when located at the juncture of contests over the meanings of racism, colonialism, gender, and class. It is also a crucial context for delineating Alegría's engagement with Third World feminism. A "mestiza consciousness," as Gloria Anzaldúa (1987) refers to it, is a consciousness of the borderlands. It is a plural consciousness in that it requires understanding multiple, often opposing ideas and knowledges, and negotiating these knowledges, not just taking a simple counterstance. Two axes of myth—one referring to collective history, the other to the individual's history— do not work in isolation. The articulation between them contributes to producing the tension in Alegría's narrative between self and society, making it possible for the speaker to present herself as a social agent, that is, as a subject involved in history. Consciousness in the work of Alegría charts itself as polymorphic, simultaneously singular and plural, male and female, dominant and subaltern, always "on the border" of being. In this respect too, her work displays a poetic cartography of the historical and political location of Third World peoples. Rather than color, racial identification, gender, or class, the common context is struggle.

Alegría's text(s) represent(s), in fact, the intersection of many contradictory discourses and voices and the attempt to invert the polarities, among others, between orality/literacy, theory/practice, and expert knowledge/common knowledge. The works of Alegría suggest, then, an "imagined community" of Third World oppositional struggle. "Imagined" not because it is not "real," but because it suggests potential alliances and collaborations across divisive boundaries; and "community" because in spite of internal and external hierarchies, it nevertheless suggests a significant, deep commitment to horizontal comradeship. Memory is the primary agency for the creation of both comradeship and resistance.

Collective consciousness and resistance are most evident in the revolutionary testimonials of Latin American women and men who speak from *within* rather than *for* their communities. Alegría, too, has contributed, as facilitator, to that collective voice. In her work, memory, history, and storytelling are woven through numerous genres: fictional texts, oral history, poetry, as well as testimonial narratives. The writing/speaking of a multiple consciousness is seen as a necessity for conceptualizing notions of collective selves in resistence to political practices against Third World peoples. Equally significant is the very diversity of genres embraced by Alegría, works which encourage readers to reexamine the role of literature and the conjunction of literature, history, and extraliterary elements from various oppositional locations.

If oppressed groups must be able to speak in many codes, and if no single discourse will be sufficient to their revolutionary situation, then normal categories of literary definition and genre must also mesh, intertwine, become indistinguishable, and finally beg for new definitions and dialectic articulation. Alegría's texts are encountered promiscuously; they pour in on us from all directions in diverse, coexisting genres, and in differently paced flows. Her textual material is complex, multiple, overlapping, coexistent, juxtaposed—in a word, "intertextual." If we use a more agile category like discourse, indicating elements that cut across different texts, we can say that all her works are also "interdiscursive." As readers and critics of her work, we believe it is possible to overhear, in the totality of her works, the stirrings of a dialogue, an allegory of relation and negotiation between "intelligentsia" and subaltern peoples, the search for a more popular, socially extensive literature, not exclusive, nevertheless, of more elite "magical literatures."

Only recently invited to return to her homeland of El Salvador, from which she was exiled by "a heavy boot with foreign hobnails," Alegría has experienced the oppressor's "dash of ice water on the soul" (Alegría 1992, 11). She has translated that suffering into poetry. Rather than political testimony, she prefers to view her work as "love poems" to her people. "I have never sat down to write a poem denouncing something. Speeches, pamphlets and newspaper articles serve for that. But if a situation or event moves me, that emotion can sometimes be translated into poetry, just as love or death or a tranquil evening can be so translated" (Alegría 1992, 14). As contributor Sternbach (1991, 94) has already noted, Alegría often subverts and transforms the literal meaning of "cemetery," to unearth rather than bury the intimacies of heart and mind.

At the same time, the conjunction of love, resistance, and death is always a discursive category of political contestation. As Ileana Rodríguez suggests here, Alegría's works reflect confluences between reflection and action, romanticism and realism, which culminate in "collective revolutionary narratives." To determine the success and/or failure of these narratives is to read/misread the convergence of Alegría's plurality of voices. As Bakhtin himself has made clear, the failure to understand results in a dialogue about interpretive norms. Incomprehensibility creates the space whereby new imaginary forms are engendered.

To read the literary collage of a writer as deeply commited to both incantation and elegy as is Alegría is to learn to look at the world twice, to unveil its transparency, and to penetrate the vague clarity of things, the unmasking possibilities of the mask. To reread Alegría's work is also to share in the politics of survivorship. Survivorship, positively defined, is the project of everyday life, a "life among the ruins," but one that is intensely meaningful because it presents us with critical understandings other than victimization, understandings that raise issues not only of resistance but of healing, both for oneself and for other members of society.

Convinced by the poet Robert Graves that she is indeed a hamadryad, a wood nymph living only for as long as the tree of which she is the spirit and in which she lives, Alegría has herself both denounced and acclaimed translation as "the most difficult of literary tasks." While our intent is to address this book to an English-speaking audience that may still be unfamiliar with her work, we recognize the limitations and dangers inherent in our presumptions. We trust, however, that, despite encumbrances, the "aroma" of the original intent remains intact and that the spirit of Alegría's ineffability is captured in these essays. We hope that our readers will be enlightened by the multiplicity of critical orientations contained herein. Marjorie Agosín's preface comes as close as possible to capturing the warmth, humanity, and ebullience of Alegría, whose presence is indeed "effervescent." Her frequent laughter does not bubble to the surface; it explodes, as the voices of her narrators, long silenced, suddenly erupt on the pages of her texts.

In organizing the book, it seemed best to chart the following cartography. The essays in the first section present sociohistorical, political, and literary contexts which should illuminate for the student of Alegría's work her singular place in the literary history of Central America and in its people's struggle for liberation. The essays contained in the second section engage the reader in a feminist dialogic in which one encounters various critical validations and valorizations of Alegría's many female voices. The third section involves the reader in the pursuit of extratextual or extraliterary resonances in Alegría's work. These headings are not meant as strict categorizations of the essays found herein, which, like the work of Alegría herself, evince a plural consciousness. We regard them as appropriately "interdiscursive," as entering into their own dialectic articulation, as establishing their own brand of "horizontal comradeship." As we hope the reader will discover, we have charted many of these essays (especially those by Rodríguez and Molinaro) as "border crossings" between one path of discourse and the next.

In compiling the bibliography and in conversing with academics from whom we solicited essays for this collection, we were dismayed at the sparse critical attention that Alegría's work has been afforded to date. It is time to acknowledge Alegría's stature as a major contemporary writer. At last, these essays grant Alegría's work the serious critical scrutiny it deserves. The recognition is long overdue.

Like Claribel's "seed book" or journal, our compilation offers a very partial conceptual map: it touches upon certain contexts and foregrounds others. We see this as a map which will of necessity have to be redrawn as the author herself both responds and reemerges with evermore conventional and subversive strategies, and as her readership develops and transforms the ways we understand both her work and our obsessions—reading the Third World woman writer, the convergence of literature and history, of the poetic and the political—which continue to conjoin the literary establishment in a dialogue of voices.

Both of us feel privileged to have worked on this book and to have collaborated with each other. We have been gifted in knowing Alegría and her husband Darwin "Bud" Flakoll. Both writers have confirmed our suspicion that (as Alegría remarks in the interview at the end of the book) magic is "just another way of looking at reality" and that "reality does not have to be circumscribed to just what we are touching and seeing." Our subconscious is not as close to the surface as Alegría's; we cannot fetch it on command. But we can give conscious attention to work that we admire, work that valorizes the voices of those who would otherwise be marginalized. In Alegría's work they are central and strong; perhaps this is her greatest magic.

WORKS CITED

Alegría, Claribel. 1991. *Family Album*. Trans. Amanda Hopkins. Willimantic, Conn.: Curbstone Press.
———. 1992. *Contemporary Authors Autobiography Series* 15. Detroit: Gale Research, 1-14.
Anzaldúa, Gloria. 1987. *Borderlands/La Frontera: The New Mestiza*. San Francisco: Auntlute.
Sternbach, Nancy Saporta. 1991. "Remembering the Dead: Latin American Women's 'Testimonial' Discourse." *Latin American Perspectives* 18/3 (Summer): 91-102.

PART ONE

CONTEXTUAL CONJUNCTIONS: LITERARY DISCOURSE, HISTORY, AND CULTURAL REVOLUTION

Language takes on symbolic meaning as the embodiment of a culture. For Claribel Alegría's readers, knowing the joys as well as the sufferings of her protagonists brings into the American living room the struggles of Central American guerrillas, writers, and actors in the drama of revolution. What has seemed distant, exotic, and political suddenly becomes intimate, familiar, and personal. This is a gift Alegría brings us through language.

The essays in this section provide sociohistorical, political, and literary contexts for the reader of Central American poetry and prose narrative, particularly the texts of Alegría. In displaying his general overview of the variety in Alegría's work, Jorge Ruffinelli reminds us of the simultaneity of the development of Latin American culture with the "political formation of the continent." Ruffinelli observes that Alegría's work finds its origins in "political indignation at abuses of power," as well as in "emotional and intellectual identification with the cause" of the Salvadoran people. In his analysis of *They Won't Take Me Alive* and "Village of God and the Devil," Ruffinelli also recognizes the complementarity of two paths in Alegría's writing, one public (*testimonio*), the other private (literary-poetic).

Arturo Arias provides a crucial Central American literary context for Alegría's work, repositioning *Ashes of Izalco* as key to the generic change in Central American literary discourse from poetry to narrative and to a redefinition of Salvadoran society from the perspective of the Matanza. Arias contends that Alegría (with her husband Darwin Flakoll), in initiating this change, led the transforma-

1

tion of Central American narrative by precipitating the end of social realism's "authoritarian discourse" and the beginning of "cultural dialogism."

Ileana Rodriguez's essay on *They Won't Take Me Alive* takes revolution as its context. Using Gayatri Spivak's *Selected Subaltern Studies* as a theoretical point of reference, Rodriguez shows how Alegría's text "contributes to the study of subalternity, presenting us with a reading of woman as revolutionary subaltern, central to the social text." Rodriguez articulates the tendency of male testimonio to constitute the revolutionary subject as male subject and to "metaphorize" the masses and women as marginal. In Eugenia, who merges masculine and feminine in a "simultaneous representation as woman/man," Rodriguez uncovers a revolutionary, collective maternity. The vulnerability and death of the marginalized guerrilla and masses are "juxtaposed" in Eugenia's essence. In dying, Eugenia occupies the subject position of the masses; she triumphs and is empowered in the text. No longer an image, a *figura* looked to for succor by males in struggle, woman is the "unequivocal center" of Alegría's text.

PUBLIC AND PRIVATE IN CLARIBEL ALEGRÍA'S NARRATIVE

Jorge Ruffinelli

Claribel Alegría: Person and *Persona*

C laribel Alegría was born in Nicaragua in 1924 but lived during the most important periods of childhood and intellectual education in El Salvador. Consequently, she is both a Nicaraguan and a Salvadoran, or, better said, a Latin American. She is the author of unique works of poetry, narrative, and testimony about the war in El Salvador from the point of view of the popular resistance in the recent history of the country. The name "Claribel Alegría" gives value to many books which differ in genre and purpose even though they are related by the same ethical stance.

In her books we find a peculiar quality of narrative language and a mastery of style that has been built through the years. At the same time it is possible to recognize in them the author's natural capacity to write in a very musical language with the rhythm of oral speech and imagination. This literary imagination was born as an experiment: *Cenizas de Izalco* (Ashes of Izalco) (1966) was planned as a novel to be written by four hands, hers and those of her husband, the American journalist and writer Darwin J. Flakoll. Twenty years later, in "Pueblo de Dios y de Mandinza" (Village of God and the Devil) (1985), imagination is even more refined. Even now, when Alegría is still young and productive, one can say that her literature has reached a most superb maturity of expression.

The literature of Alegría contains many lines of development which are various and simultaneous but not convoluted. Poetry comes first because that was the genre in which she started to publish and probably to write. Some of her works were distinguished by international literary awards. One of her first books, *Anillo de silencio* (Ring of silence) (1948), was published when Claribel was twenty-four years old and fairly unknown. It carried a prologue by a celebrated Mexican writer of the time, José Vasconcelos. Other books followed: *Suite* (Suite), *Vigilias* (Vigils), *Acuario* (Aquarium), *Huésped de mi tiempo* (Guest of my time), *Vía unica* (One way), *Aprendizaje* (Apprenticeship), *Pagaré a cobrar* (Charge on delivery), *Sobrevivo* (I survive) which received the Casa de las Américas Prize in 1978, *Suma y sigue* (Add and carry), *Flowers from the Volcano*, *Poesía viva* (Live poetry), *Petit pays* (Small country), *Poema-río* (Poem Fleuve), *Tres cuentos* (Three stories), *Cenizas de Izalco* (Ashes of Izalco), "El detén" (The talisman), "Album familiar" (Family album), *Nicaragua: La revolución sandinista* (Nicaragua: The Sandinista Revolution), *No me agarran viva: La mujer salvadoreña en lucha* (They won't take me alive: The Salvadoran women at war), and *Para romper el silencio, Resistencia y lucha en las cárceles salvadoreñas* (To break the silence: Resistance and struggle in the Salvadoran jails).

There are several ways to consider Alegría's work as a whole. One of these consists in looking for an explanation of its variety, for the reasons that a writer cannot express certain themes and concerns that in a particular genre but can do so in another, as is the case with Alegría. Another question is that of how this choice of a particular genre marks different territories: the personal and the collective, the public and the private. Alegría told the author Elena Urrutia in 1988 of a very significant process through which she felt forced to choose narrative in 1966 to tell a story for which poetry was useless. It is important to recognize how political circumstances imposed themselves upon her writing.

> I started to write during my adolescence. Poetry was and still is my first passion. However, there were certain things that I was not able to write as poetry, like all that horrible massacre in El Salvador in 1932. That event impressed me deeply even when I was only seven years old. I used to tell Bud [my husband] and some other friends episodes which I witnessed.

4

I kept in my memory the stories that I had heard. Martínez ordered all the newspapers of the epoch to be burned, and nobody dared to write about that chilling event. It seemed as if the Salvadoran people had suffered a collective lobotomy. Nobody remembered the horror. At last Bud convinced me to write a novel with him, and that is how *Ashes of Izalco* was born. For me it was an experience of catharsis. (Urrutia 1988, 8)

A second way of examining her writing involves looking at the unity of her work as demonstrated by the character and personality of the writer which transcends it in all of her books, regardless of how different they may be. If her work is diverse, perhaps it is because it reflects the diversity and multiplicity of the very world that it describes and because such a world, in turn, demands diverse forms of expression to reveal its true nature. But the perspective from which this world is described remains constant. The Nicaraguan poet José Coronal Utrecho (1989, 174) expresses this beautifully in a book that attempts to capture the "unity" of Alegría's personality.

The only definition—always different, always the same—of a person is the person itself. That person, Claribel Alegría, the only Claribel Alegría, is simply Claribel Alegría. And for my part, I have not met such a "person" in Central America in a long time, especially one that succeeds in being such a person simply by being one, without doing anything to call attention to oneself. . . . In the person of Claribel Alegría it is impossible to discover the dividing line between person and poet, just as in the poet Claribel Alegría it is impossible to discover the line between poet and person. This gives rise to a series of tautologies and word games regarding her persona. The poet Claribel Alegría cannot be separated from the person Claribel Alegría, and likewise, Claribel Alegría the person cannot be separated from Claribel Alegría the poet. All that is Claribel Alegría is part of her persona. In simpler terms, it is her persona that distinguishes her from all the rest, without any effort on her part to be distinct.

This fragment by Coronel Utrecho, along with the other 260 pages, forms his book *Líneas para un boceto de Claribel Alegría* (Lines for a sketch of Claribel Alegría) (1989). The book, indefinable as Alegría herself, nonetheless reveals the magnetism that she exerts over her readers. This magnetism may be defined as the ability to narrate, capturing the attention of the reader and enriching him or her.

In "The Talisman" (included in *Family Album*, 1991), there appears a notable phrase, uttered by a cynical character named Mark, referring to the effect of this narrative magnetism: "Humanity is divided into two parts: those who are drowsy and naive and who want someone to tell them a story to further put them to sleep, and those who are clever and capable of inventing stories that will take the pants off of the gullible ones." Alegría tells her stories without taking our pants off because she is completely lacking in cynicism; neither does she tell them to put the reader to sleep, but rather to awaken him or her. So it is that her testimonial works are "consciousness-raising." And her novels, similarly, are built on what James Joyce would call "epiphanies," images through which a world is discovered and revealed, be it the world of elements more or less autobiographical, as in "The Talisman," "Family Album," "Village of God and the Devil," (three short novels comprising the 1991 collection *Family Album*), or *Luisa in Realityland* (1987), that is, the world of Santa Ana, El Salvador, or of Deyá, Mallorca; or be it the terrible world of the prisons or the hoped-for world of personal detachment and heroism without wonder. Here one finds indications of a twofold path that leads to both the personal, private and subjective, and the social, with its collective vision, the discovery of the others. The autobiographical vein that characterizes a good part of Alegría's work is obvious, as in the attempt to separate herself from her own person in order to attend to the world of others. Included in this autobiographical vein are the personal "portraits": Carmen in *Ashes of Izalco*, Ximena in "Family Album," Marcia in "Village of God and the Devil," and even—why not?—Karen in "The Talisman." Along with Utrecho, we would say that each one of these is a person and is part of the person of Alegría, since she is the person who has given them literary life, that is to say, the privilege of remaining in the memory of the reader.

Alegría has managed alternative and equally different categories which traditionally remain distinct in writers and which even form the bases of different careers. But just as she has known how to write subjective poetry with subtlety and novels with original fantasy, she has also produced testimonial books in which fantasy and subjective subtlety give way to a direct account, expressively economical, but at the same time full of strength, the strength that a master of narrative and poetic language can apportion to it.

Public and Private, Two Divided Paths

Although common sense provides us with a very clear idea (and feeling) of what is "public" and what is "private," it is important to realize that both the idea and the feeling are of a cultural nature. They have not been the same at all times nor in all places. In fact, there did not always exist such a clear and categorical distinction between "public" and "private." Therefore, without having to define what these terms signify for twentieth-century Western society, it is nevertheless necessary to consider some of their historical meanings. It would seem, for example, that the "private" category came second historically. Barrington Moore, Jr., who has studied the meanings of these terms in the Classic period, in the Old Testament, and in the civilization of ancient China, asks the following:

> Is there a need for privacy? If there is, it can hardly be a compelling one like the need for air, sleep, or nourishment. Every human activity, from working through praying or playing, has been carried out somewhere in the company of other human beings. Nevertheless human beings do not always want to do things that way. In seeking privacy . . . such a person seeks at least temporary escape or surcease from contact and conversation with other human beings because their presence has become overly demanding, oppressive, or simply boring. (Moore 1984, 72)

Thus the social, public, and collective function historically preceded the individual, private, and selfish function, or has at least had a preponderant role in history. This is an interesting point because one of the most notable aspects of Latin American culture has been its simultaneous development with the political formation of the continent. This is seen with even more clarity when in the second decade of the nineteenth century, the independence movements gave birth to what we now know as Latin America, that is, a distinct and formative culture, and one different from others such as the European and the North American.

Politics has been fundamental in many aspects. Perhaps the most interesting is that the relation with the political has resulted in conflict because of the need to move from one culture to another diverse models and paradigms arising from the metropolis. If, on the one hand, the relation with the political has become a means of legitimation for literature, other paradigms have been produced and introduced as well, in the same manner in which historical transformations distance us from the original necessities and, within a "planetary" culture, create other necessities. Among these is the need for privacy, which gave rise to a literature that is intimate or subjective or individualist. And in a strictly literary sense, the most personal and nontransferable (and, consequently, the least capable of being duplicated) is the fantastic, the "original."

In the remainder of this essay, I want to highlight some of the aspects of the "public" function of the work of Alegría, using her book *They Won't Take Me Alive* (No me agarran viva: La mujer salvadoreña en lucha, 1983) as an example, distinguishing it but at the same time reuniting it with the more private element, that of literary fantasy, as in a novel such as "Village of God and the Devil" (Pueblo de Dios, y de Mandinga, 1985). As I will also attempt to show, these two lines of creation and intellectual production are separated only by distinct objectives, which in the end are perfectly complementary, in the same way in which the culture of Latin America is a product as well as a process still in formation.

The existence of two distinct paths, separated by the notion of "public" and "private," is equally if not more evident in the work of Alegría as in that of other writers. One of these paths leads to a realistic literature, one that is documentary and testimonial, while the other is more fictitious and subjective, belonging to the field in which personal remembrances are joined with fictitious longing. This difference is notable above all in the characteristics of the writing style and in the use of fantasy. While in other works of fiction, Alegría does not hesitate to boldly explore the possibilities of the imagination—to the point that one could speak of "magical realism" when characterizing, for example, "Village of God and the Devil"—in her testimonial works, the authorial voice appears willing to pass to another level, and what is more, to stay there.

8

In *Para romper el silencio* (To break the silence), as well as in *They Won't Take Me Alive*, Alegría and Flakoll decide to "make public," to testify, to collect various testimonies and documents about the lives of a series of anonymous civilian combatants in the Salvadoran resistance movement working against an unpopular government. The war, which in 1992 was finally achieving a truce and a political agreement between the government and the combatants, in terms of warriors began in 1970 and cost countless lives. Since the means of mass communication always had been in the hands of government groups, the "other" story, that is, the story of the revolutionaries told by the revolutionaries themselves, has remained unknown, reflected only scarcely in books, pamphlets, and analyses of clandestine or limited circulation. These two books, however, offer an intermediation; given that the authors are public figures who never "passed" into hiding nor into armed conflict, they are able to put themselves in contact with many clandestine combatants and to gather and transcribe their testimonies.

In the Latin American literary production of the last two decades, the testimonial genre has undergone fundamental changes. From being considered a phenomenon akin to journalism, a material of little textual value and only passing interest, it has become a legitimate heir of the great Latin American literary tradition, to the point that in many cases its quality equals or surpasses that of this same Latin American literature. While literature in the 1960s seemed to abandon the original paradigms that identified it with political life, those which were much closer to the cultivation of textuality or pure description (because of the influence of the French *nouveau roman*), the *testimonio* seemed to recover that legacy and transform it to its own advantage. Many explanations of this phenomenon have been offered already; among the most important is the fact that excellent writers (from Elena Poniatowska to Gabriel García Márquez) have employed it to the maximum of their abilities. But this increase in the "fortune" of testimonial literature has, at the same time, generated theoretical problems (Beverley 1987), especially concerning the "place" of the intermediary or negotiator. Poniatowska once defined her use of the testimonio as the "giving of voice to those who have none," in other words, to take advantage of the access that the literate classes have to the means of mass communication and education, as well as of the prestige granted to writers, in order to reflect through all of these elements and "make way" for a voice that

9

otherwise would not reach the same audiences. The negotiator or intermediary, then, is never confused with the subject of the work. The intermediary may have sympathy for the politics or the social class of the subject, but their lives are frequently very different.

Eugenia/Ana María's Story

Of great interest is the estimation made by the author herself of the possibilities of testimonio as a genre. Alegría (and Flakoll) made use of testimonial narrative for a book about Nicaragua.

> When the Sandinista revolution was won, we felt very happy and we thought that the testimonial was the best way of relating contemporary history and that it was worthwhile to do it. We traveled to Nicaragua from Mallorca and wrote *Nicaragua: la revolución sandinista*, published in Mexico in 1983. It is a testimonial, but it is also history. It begins with William Walker, the filibusterer, and ends with the triumph of the revolution. (Moraña 1991)

Nevertheless, the collective history must still take root in individual cases, whose exemplary and dramatic qualities are the necessary secrets of their success. *They Won't Take Me Alive* arose in the midst of the "private" life of Alegría, in Mallorca, the land of her fantasy.

> Being back in Mallorca, I happened to meet a young man from El Salvador who began to tell me of how he had just lost his wife, who belonged to a band of guerrillas and had died in El Salvador. "If I were a writer," he told me with tears in his eyes, "I would write about that." "I'll do it," I responded to him impulsively. I traveled to Nicaragua to interview friends of Eugenia, the guerrilla name of the young woman, who were there in hiding. (Moraña 1991)

The example of *They Won't Take Me Alive* revives the aforementioned problem, but it also includes one aspect that is singular and edifying. There is no doubt that the political sympathies of Alegría lie with her subject, that she (and Flakoll) promote the "public" knowledge of the popular heroism of these stories as

10

implicit but obvious critiques of the system of government and those who administer it. The writing of her two books is itself the result of an emotional and intellectual identification with the "cause" of the Salvadoran people, and, as is seen in an earlier quote by Alegría, in many cases her literature has its origins in political indignation at abuses of power. *They Won't Take Me Alive* is the story of "Eugenia" (nom de guerre), whose real name was Ana María Castillo Rivas, who was born in 1950 and killed in military action when she was in her twenties. The book is a profile of, and an homage to, that woman, and, through her, the many Salvadoran women who have given part (or all) of their lives for the social and political causes of the resistance. What distinguishes Eugenia's story, as it does Alegría's, is that it is the story of a middle-class professional woman with a university education whose political evolution gradually led her to a greater commitment to the revolutionary forces, until she herself became a commander, lived in hiding, and died at the hands of violence. I am interested in emphasizing this process because it is equivalent, on another level, to the intellectual process of the Latin American writer, one who is cultured, educated, successful in the literary profession and who "returns" to the public sphere to offer, in addition, as an intellectual contribution to the same cause, the best of his or her talent, namely, writing.

In Latin American testimonial narrative, one of the main elements is precisely this: the demonstration of an evolution in the character whose life the author has chosen to relate. This is true even in autobiographical testimonies (from the text that "founded" the genre in contemporary terms, namely Ernesto Che Guevara's *Tales of Guerrilla Warfare* [*Relatos de la guerra revolucionaria*], to Omar Cabezas in *Fire in the Mountain* [*La montaña es algo más que una inmensa estepa verde*]). The story directs itself toward the establishment of the paradigm of the revolutionary as a figure who wants to change an unjust social order and therefore makes a commitment to action; for this the narration of a process of personal change becomes fundamental. In nearly all of the examples within the testimonial genre, this change is from a "private" being to a "social" being, from individual subjectivity to collective objectivity. In this respect the testimonial narrative is radically different from the biographical/autobiographical genre. While in the latter, the narrator decides to describe the singularity of the individual, one who stands out and who presumably deserves to be known and admired by the

11

"public," in the testimonial genre the most heroic acts of the individual are "representative" of a greater collectivity (the revolutionary group or "the people"). Therefore it comes as no surprise that the subtitle of *They Won't Take Me Alive* is a generic description: *"The Salvadoran Woman in Struggle for National Liberation,"* that is, a description of not one such woman but all such women. This individual woman, named "Eugenia," represents many others, perhaps all of them.

The evolution that led Ana María Castillo Rivas to become "Eugenia," in other words, that which led her from legality to secrecy, from social aid to armed conflict, is perhaps the most important theme of this book. It is the paradigm of the evolution from private to public. It is suggested numerous times, not only by the intermediary—the writer in the third person singular who organizes the story—but also by the many voices of those gathered and interviewed to give testimony of Ana María/"Eugenia." Among these voices there are many that are important, but the most significant may be those of her sisters and her husband, since they were the people closest to the character who is the subject of the testimonial.

The Clandestine Heroine

In her college years, Ana María was a well-to-do middle-class young woman with a promising future like that of so many professionals. However, one feature she shared with some of her fellow students but not with others was a preoccupation with helping those most in need in order to collaborate in the construction of a country with dignity. She attempted to do this by studying sociology (so that she might understand better the reality of her country) and by affiliating herself with a social welfare group called University Catholic Action (ACUS). Because of bureaucratic problems, her sociology career was cut short, and consequently, in order not to distance herself too much from her original concerns, she chose social psychology. Neither one nor the other—neither Catholic Action nor her career—was satisfactory. Her husband Javier testified that the change in Ana María began with her reading.

At university she began to obtain access to a lot of books and this helped her gain in understanding. She began to worry

12

herself about arriving at a more scientific comprehension of the problem. She began to get to know how capitalism works, the issue of class struggle, not only in terms of rich and poor but of capitalist exploitation, and that our countries are dependencies of North American imperialism. This was going on throughout her university career. Our comrade took a decisive step forward. She abandoned ACUS and joined a movement called the University Socialist Movement. (52-53)

The theme of the "evolution" of Ana María appears various times, but since the book is not about a singular individual, it is not unusual to find it in the testimonies of other characters as well. Thus, for example, Commander "Marcial," the most important figure in the Salvadoran resistance at the time, is quoted referring to the same juncture of decision to change in order to confront completely new conditions. The passage is worth citing for its clarity of expression and because it is not merely incidental but rather quite significant within the story of Ana María.

So it became essential to uncover our capacity for advancing along this path, and whether we as individuals were capable of transforming ourselves in order to follow it—if we were able to acquire the necessary political context, realise the necessary sacrifices, renounce normal life and exchange it for secrecy and the total compartmentalisation of one's existence. (54)

Ana María succeeded in doing it, and upon transforming herself into "Eugenia" and maintaining a permanent desire for that transformation, she also became the subject of the admiration of her colleagues. The book emphasizes this change: "Eugenia underwent a process of proletarianization, though hardly a romantic one" (60). "Her work in the field was extraordinary. She distinguished herself from the first moment as an organizer" (40); "Eugenia initiated and deepened a process of proletarianization that would, in time, become one of her most notable characteristics" (67); "Eugenia never stagnated, never stayed the same. She was always in a process of unfolding" (75); "Commander Ricardo also stressed this process of growing maturity that transformed Eugenia, a girl of bourgeois origins, into a militant revolutionary" (82). The capture of her husband was a huge blow for Eugenia, but nevertheless she "capitalized" on it to achieve an internal change: "I think it must have been a period when our comrade gained greatly in her proletarian understanding. The organization plainly perceived Eugenia's new level of development," notes Javier himself (87).

Raised to a schematic level, the life of a clandestine member of the resistance is one of constant tension. Although she may be hidden behind a pseudonym or nom de guerre, the passage into secrecy requires that the real person be left behind, and that person then becomes the object of persecution by the authorities, the police and the military. It is clear, in all of the "voices" in this book, that the clandestine life is not "normal" life but rather the opposite. For this reason, one of the most interesting aspects of *They Won't Take Me Alive* consists in reevaluating how a "normal" life is established and developed within the "secret" life, that is, how solutions are discovered for problems such as the necessities of affection, love, and family when the political cause necessarily comes first. In this sense, not only the specific story of Eugenia but also the "voices" of the other women interviewed for the book are interesting, as they draw attention to the drama of a contradiction without solutions between the "private" necessity and the "public" service of the same persons.

Eugenia and Javier meet, work together, fall in love, marry, and have a daughter. All of this could be normal, as in any middle-class life, but with the essential difference that in this case "normal" life is found within an "extraordinary" life. In the case of this couple, they run the risks of separation, of imprisonment (Javier), or even the death of one of them (Eugenia). The case of the children is perhaps the most dramatic that the book describes, because these children, whether it be by circumstances or by choice, almost always pass into a "normal," secure life, that is, into the trauma of separation and de facto orphanhood. When this does not occur, that is, when there is physical security for the couple with children, the historically positive outcome is shared responsibility. In this sense, the book presents numerous testimonies of how the awakening of political conscious-ness can overcome problems of gender in relation to the occupation and education of children. According to all of the references collected here, within an organization like the one to which Eugenia belonged, the traditional masculine hegemony disappears and is replaced by a concept and a practice of equality. Although there are no objective data to affirm this phenomenon of relations between men and women, at least the story of Ana María is a testimony in this sense.

The drama of these lives threatened by danger, marginalized from "normal" social life, and admirable for the level of human abnegation that they demonstrate, seems to exclude some aspects easily found in the literary works of Alegría. Humor and fantasy, for instance, find no comfortable place from which to express themselves. The style itself is different: plain, unadorned, and without value judgments, essayistic tendencies, or interpretive zeal. The intention is to organize the story so that the actions speak for themselves and so that they themselves give the reader the possibility of interpretation. Or the intention may be to allow the collective "voices" that the main character represents to express themselves as directly as possible. Thus the "intermediary" of the testimony ultimately disappears from the text, as the book transforms testimonial narrative into documentary, publishing letters recovered from Eugenia. And it goes even further: the book reproduces an actual copy of one of these letters, thereby allowing the voice of Eugenia to reach the reader through her own writing.

Through her dedication to a popular and not a personal cause, Eugenia the combatant is transformed into a "public" figure upon her unfortunate death, since the book could not have been written had she remained alive. Yet what is most exceptional is the "private" character of the letter that appears on pages 138 and 139, for it is a love letter. Also exceptional, and also sufficient in some way for justifying its inclusion, is that this love letter is found in a revolutionary context, and that in it the references to the political struggle are equally if not more abundant than the expressions of love. It is left as a document with a theme that remains to be studied: love in the time of war.

Village of God and the Devil

"Pueblo de Dios, y de Mandinza" (Village of God and the Devil) (1985) fulfills a function very different from that of the testimonial and in it is realized a notably unique style. At the same time, it accomplishes a literary feat worth mentioning: it destroys the myth that defines "magical realism" as a phenomenon and style specifically Latin American, by illustrating that in ancient Europe,

15

precisely in Mediterranean Mallorca where the story takes place, "strange things" also happen and that the fantasy of the location nourishes and fertilizes a restless and creative imagination such as Alegría's. If I take this story as an example of her "private" literature, it is because in it there is reproduced an "autobiographic" structure that also can be found in other works. For example, the characters live in Mallorca and are friends of Robert Graves, exactly like the real people, Alegría and her husband Darwin J. Flakoll.

But the private category also includes the use of fantasy, that is, the subjective and individual response of the person (Marcia/ Claribel) to the stimuli of the environment. This response, with such large doses of the fantastic, would be inconceivable in a testimonio. Here lies the great difference between these two discursive practices, which I have tried to distinguish, indicating the oppositional or complementary elements of private and public, in order to show how the discourse that "represents" others leaves itself very little room for fantasy, and this, in turn, is richly and infinitely reproduced in the literary discourse that is concerned with actions not involving society but rather a specific group of people or sometimes a single person.

The story told in "Village of God and the Devil" is apparently very simple. Slim and Marcia, a foreign couple, live in Deyá, one of the three towns in Mallorca, in which appeared Mandinga (the Devil). They live there as if they were in paradise, ever since Slim, who is ill and receives electroshock treatments, suffers (or enjoys) a vision, one that is cosmic and cataclysmic, apocalyptic, and entirely metaphysical. Contemplating the effects of a nuclear catastrophe, he reaches the following conclusion:

> When, in the blink of an eye, the poles have toppled to create a new Equator, the meltdown will raise the water level of the world's oceans by approximately sixty feet. One can also reckon on earthquakes, tidal waves, and cyclonic storms as the planet tilts violently and seeks its new axis. Given all this, we'll need to look for a spot at least a hundred feet above sea level, and accumulate a stock of food sufficient to meet our needs for a year, just like the Mormons do. (140)

For Slim, that ideal place is Deyá, Mallorca; that is why he and Marcia come to the island. While for months (and probably years)

Slim prepares himself to write the "definitive" novel about Deyá, Marcia (or her alter ego Alegría) writes that novel, and she does it beautifully. Her view of people and things is above all poetic, one would say slightly *piantada*, or eccentric, if speaking in the language of Cortázar, although the most familiar atmosphere would be that of Lewis Carroll. The world of Deyá is absurdly fantastic, fantastically absurd. And this fantasy touches everything; every step of the story is hallucinatory. When Marcia goes to buy herbs or vegetables for dinner, she passes don Antonio on the stairway and notices that he looks tired. Later, reflecting on this, she will recall that don Antonio died several months earlier. One could say that this is a ghost town, like that of Comala in Juan Rulfo's *Pedro Páramo*, but with the condition that these ghosts are recognized with humor, a "vital" humor that validates the paradox.

"Strange things took place in the village," says the narrator at one point, and this is the constant slogan of the novel. Thus it is a novel of ghosts and apparitions, in which the tradition that these two foreigners come across during their stay, as if it were the historic annals of the village or the "raw material" of which Slim will probably never write, is transformed alchemically into fragments, a series of histories, episodes symbolic of one thing: the unusual.

In the end, a real character presides over the story, although he is barely "present": Robert Graves, the famous British poet, essayist, and novelist, author of *I, Claudius, The White Goddess, Good-bye to All That, The Greek Myths*. The extraordinary writer, who during the last years of his life spent part of the year in Deyá, is the protagonist by reference in one of the novel's most attractive episodes: his dialogue with Raimundo Lulio, who inherits the philosopher's stone, a frightful "black hole." The story of the black hole and its infinite voracity constitutes a tale that will go down in history as one of the most enjoyable chapters of our literature. It occupies the ending like a sort of hallucinatory history which touches upon if not the confines of the universe and of horror, then at least the confines of a humor full of subtlety, charm, and imagination.

The novel begins by describing the everyday life of the couple, and it proceeds with the gradual creation of a fantastic atmosphere which, however, never abandons reality but rather cultivates it, uses it as a ballast, and thus makes even the most incredible seem credible. Here lies the interior magic of this novel. In any case, its artistry comes secondhand from the sum of extravagantly horrifying stories developed around characters with some very peculiar tendencies: for instance, Anabel and the guru of the seventh estate, Elliot and his attraction to accidents, the Manuela who is ultimately revealed as a Manuel. These and many others constitute the "local legends" that Marcia records in her notebook. It is not difficult to see in them a true freshness of imagination, and in others a slipping into ancient motifs (the girl who is born without arms as well as the story of Ben Austin, the pornographer, and his death by decapitation).

Deyá is a place full of history and legend. Graves was not the only one to spend time there every year. "According to the Mallorcans," notes Alegría, "Cagliostro lived there while he was searching for the manuscripts of Raimundo Lulio to further his alchemical researches. They claimed that Picasso also lived there incognito, not to mention Salvador Dali and don Santiago Rusinol" (Moraña 1991, 146). Culture, alchemy, poetry, and metaphysics: a grave combination that weighs much more heavily in this place than do the fleeting German tourists who invade it during the summer season. This is a combination that is incorporated into the novel and, along with other features, produces its magnificent temperature. And among these other features just alluded to, the richness of language is certainly not the least, with an elegant prose full of flavor, and a richness of expression that guarantees its place among the best of Latin American literature.

That richness of imagination and of writing is quite rare: Latin American literature in general, and especially in Central America, is baroque, with a proclivity towards arborescent verbal abundance, whereas Alegría gives her story an essential kind of poetic expression, careful to avoid ever falling into that aberration known as poetic prose, or into verbal adornment. What she writes, on the contrary, teaches the great lesson of difficult simplicity, which we know is never really so simple but rather always demonstrates fullness and maturity of expression.

The "autobiographical" character of her story is more of style than of substance. By that I mean to say that she employs the cultural and geographical environment, the "wonder" of the place and the vicissitudes of its people, to produce a novel whose meaning and beauty are not based on the authenticity of the work, but rather on its capacity for infinite imagination, that is, for the multiplication of invention.

The earlier mention of Carroll is not entirely gratuitous if we also remember that after "Village of God and the Devil," Alegría published *Luisa in Realityland*, another fictional and "personal" book which is based in large part on autobiographical elements. It is also a self-referential book: it mentions the "Izalco massacre," a historical event which gave rise to her *Ashes of Izalco*, it recreates Luisa's early childhood in Santa Ana (El Salvador), it refers to her frustrated ambitions as a painter, it often mentions "Luisa" and Bud (Flakoll), it mentions their house in Deyá, and so forth. There are multiple references of this type throughout this deliberately fragmented book, even comments about her friends. For example, the chapter titled "Premature necrology" is based on a suspicious phenomenon known to the friends of "Mario" (although his full name is not mentioned, the reference is to Mario Benedetti, a friend of Alegría and a neighbor of hers and Flakoll's in Deyá): the many times that the international newspapers have published the news of the "death" of the writer, obligating him to inform them that he is still alive. In *Luisa in Realityland*, Alegría tells of how Benedetti was expelled from Peru after having left Argentina because of death threats from the Triple A, a paramilitary organization that opposes all leftist intellectuals.

Conclusions

In Alegría's writing at least two distinct projects are textual-ized. One entails the total liberation of the fantastic, which seems to be a desire for intimate aesthetic expression. The other project has to do with social commitment, which converts her texts into resistance literature by privileging her indignation before the arbitrariness of political power. In this second case what engenders the text is the personal social and political commitment rather than literariness. Literariness, as occurs with most testimonial literature, gives way to a social and representative Self, while the personal Self is relegated to another stratum of the narrative.

Nevertheless, both projects coincide: fantasy has a hold on reality here and there, through brief clues, or, to use an old Malraux image, to reveal a hidden presence, much like some desert plants allow us to know the course of underground rivers. At the same time, the texts that are closer to being "documentary" and objective are drawn with the expressive abilities of a consummate writer. In these texts there is a substitution of languages and their discursive strategies, but it never stops being writing.

This flexibility to switch from one project to another, or to maintain their currency like a juggler, is what some would call a contradiction. Others, like myself, would call it richness through complementariness. Instead of diluting what is public and private as a false antinomy, Alegría has enhanced every one of these categories by attributing a dose of the opposite element to each pole. What we have with this author is a unique example in contemporary Spanish American literature, so predisposed to extremes and exclusivity. Rather than pigeonholing herself into one particular project, Alegría has opted for a complex worldview that alternates and conjugates what is seemingly contradictory, and thereby makes those elements complements, as joy and sorrow, stone and smoke are part of one and the same reality.

WORKS CITED

Alegría, Claribel, and Darwin J. Flakoll. 1966. *Cenizas de Izalco.* Barcelona: Seix Barral.

———. 1989. *Ashes of Izalco.* Willimantic, Conn.: Curbstone Press.

———. 1983. *No me agarran viva: La mujer salvadoreña en lucha.* México: Ediciones Era.

———. 1987. *They Won't Take Me Alive.* Trans. Amanda Hopkinson. London: Women's Press.

———. 1984. *Para romper el silencio. Resistencia y lucha en las cárceles salvadoreñas.* México: Ediciones Era.

Alegría, Claribel. 1982. *Album familiar.* San José de Costa Rica: Editorial Universitaria Centroamericana.

———. 1991. "Family Album." Trans. Amanda Hopkinson. Willimantic, Conn.: Curbstone Press.

———. 1985. "Pueblo de Dios y de Mandinga." México: Edicones Era.

———. 1991. "Village of God and the Devil." In *Family Album.* Trans. Amanda Hopkinson. Willimantic, Conn.: Curbstone Press.

———. 1987. *Luisa en el país de la realidad.* México: Joan Boldó i Climent / Universidad Autónoma de Zacatecas.

————. 1987. *Luisa in Realityland.* Trans. Darwin J. Flakoll. Willimantic, Conn.: Curbstone Press.

Arenal, Electa. 1981. "Two Poets of the Sandinista Struggle." *Feminist Studies* 7/1 (spring): 19-27.

Beverley, John. 1987. "Anatomía del testimonio." In *Del Lazarillo al Sandinismo: Estudios sobre la función ideológica de la literatura española e hispanoamericana,* ed. John Beverley. Minneapolis: The Prisma Institute/I&L: 153-68.

Coronel Utrecho, José. 1989. *Líneas para un boceto de Claribel Alegría.* Managua: Editorial Nueva Nicaragua.

Forché, Carolyn. 1984. "Interview with Claribel Alegría." *Index on Censorship* 12/2 (1984): 11-13.

Hopkinson, Amanda. 1987. "Historical Introduction" and "Preface." *They Won't Take Me Alive.* London: Women's Press, 1-30.

Moore, Jr., Barrington. 1984. *Privacy: Studies in Social and Cultural History.* New York: M. E. Sharpe, Inc.

Moraña, Mabel. 1991. "Desde las entrañas del monstruo." *Brecha* 7/313 (29 de noviembre): 20-21.

Urrutia, Elena. 1988. "Letras del exilio latinoamericano." *La Jornada Libros* (Mexico) 193 (September 24): 8.

21

2

CLARIBEL ALEGRÍA'S RECOLLECTIONS OF THINGS TO COME

Arturo Arias

The 1960s witnessed the apparition of a new wave of Central American fiction which signified a fundamental break with the previous literature of the region. Among the outstanding initiators of this group were Lizandro Chávez Alfaro, Roque Dalton, and Alfonso Chase.[1] These new novelists experimented with discursive practices in fiction. However, they did not confuse formal experimentation with lack of social content.

For Central America, this attitude signified a rupture with the preceding period. The 1960s was a time of cultural revolution, and Claribel Alegría and Darwin Flakoll's *Ashes of Izalco* became the first of a series of novels to express this transformation in its literary form. This rupture was not a change of "themes." The contents were of a political nature. However, the new narrative made a significant break with traditional literary discourse.

Originally published in Spanish in 1966 as *Cenizas de Izalco*, *Ashes of Izalco* is a key work in trying to understand this transition in Central American narrative.[2] It not only experimented formally in order to create new symbolic codes and broke away from the old paradigms in order to tackle the task of redefining Salvadoran society from the perspective and viewpoint of the Matanza, it also generated a generic shift from poetry to narrative.[3] Other Central American poets such as Dalton or Manlio Argueta followed Alegría's example and plunged into the novel soon after *Ashes of Izalco*, contributing to the generation of a novelistic "mini-boom" within Central America in the 1970s.

This chapter examines the literary characteristics of *Ashes of Izalco* in order to explore how it opened up new directions for Central American narrative. It also analyzes how this transition in linguistic consciousness was linked to the changing role of Central American writers in the 1960s, as well as to the particular characteristics of Alegría's social origins and multicultural heritage.

The Exhaustion of Social Realism

Central American fiction has been motivated by political concerns from its very early origins. However, the novelistic tendencies prevailing from the 1930s to the 1950s—heavily influenced by the tenets of "social realism"—tried to place the novel "outside of language," in conceptual spaces normally reserved for philosophy, political theory, or the social sciences.

In other words, if we see the novel as a genre basically divided between those texts which center themselves around the representation of discursive practices and those which pretend to represent the world directly through the "transparency" of language, the "social realist" novel certainly belonged to the latter category.[4]

This style of narration corresponds to what German romantic critics (and especially Wolfflin) called a "linear style." This category was later adopted and expanded on by Bakhtin/Voloshinov.[5]

By the early 1950s, social realism was in decline throughout Latin America.[6] In Central America itself, despite the fact that it had peaked only in the late 1940s and was still very popular in the 1950s, it also began to be critiqued in fundamental ways by a new generation of writers.

This process began with the rediscovery of the value of the literary word and of narrative techniques. In Central America these characteristics had shined during the modernist period through the outstanding work of Rafael Arévalo Martínez (1884-1975), but were later buried by the "criollista" novel which preceded social realism. The new process was first addressed conceptually by the little-known Costa Rican writer Yolanda Oreamuno (1916-1956).

Oreamuno was the first writer who began to call for a change in the course of Central American literature. She led the search for new forms, the quest for a new language, the experimentation that

23

successfully penetrated and explored new modes of literary expression.[7] However, given the degree to which Oreamuno remained largely an unknown in Central America itself, it was the aesthetic search undertaken by Nobel Prize winner Miguel Angel Asturias (1899-1974) during the same years that served as a bridge between the old realism that came before him and the narrative form that began with *Ashes of Izalco.*

The Transition in Linguistic Consciousness

By the early 1960s, many young Central American writers were echoing Oreamuno's cry of twenty years before. At the same time, they were living a new age. The sixties represented both the Cuban revolution and the golden decade of Latin American narrative (*boom* literature). All of a sudden, it became plainly evident that one could be politically committed and write in new, creative ways. Not only that, it became equally evident that old ways of writing were just as obsolete as old ways of political thinking. It was an age for new, bold experiments, for discovering new ways of seeing the world.

No one knew this better than writers who had frequent contacts with the First World. It certainly had been no accident that all the boom writers (as well as their predecessors, Asturias, Borges and Carpentier) belonged in this category. Precisely because these writers stood with one foot on either side of the "great divide" between the First and Third worlds and were genuinely multilingual, they were able to undertake a new meditation on identity, the self and "otherness" steeped in the language of what we could now label "incipient postmodernism."

In Central America, only Asturias (1967 Nobel Prize winner) and Augusto Monterroso (1921-) were in this category. Nonetheless, even Asturias had embraced social realism when redirecting his literature towards politics; Monterroso's best work was still ahead of him.[8] However, at this very time a new generation of writers was coming to the fore which shared the basic characteristics of boom writers. First and foremost among them was Alegría. She was a Salvadoran citizen born in Nicaragua of the union of an anti-Somoza activist and a member of the Salvadoran oligarchy. She was educated in the United States and married to a U.S. expatriate who lived on the island of Majorca next door to Robert Graves and travelled frequently to Paris. Already a gifted poet of emerging international status by the early 1960s, it was only natural that she should initiate the generic transition from poetry to narrative and, in so doing, lead the transformation of Central American narrative.

Ashes of Izalco became, de facto, a parting of the waters, signalling the end of social realism. Since its appearance, the style and form in which a novel is written figures just as importantly as its contents for Central American fiction. In other words, it is not enough to write about "political themes." The work has to be aesthetically pleasing and innovative as well. By being conscious of the aesthetic quality of language as such—as opposed to its utilitarian "linear style" where language pretends to be nonexistent, transparent, or unseductive—the problem becomes one of narration, of finding voices which can effectively name the current reality.

The narrative transition initiated by *Ashes of Izalco* involved the substitution of "authoritarian discourse" by an "internally persuasive" one. That is to say, new fiction destroys the authoritarian discourse through the use of opposing connotations, contradictory images, and other technical resources with a special emphasis on a multiplicity of languages, voices, and ideologies which are inherent in the structure of the novel as a literary form. Indeed, this polyphony of belief systems, defined by language, is what defines the novel as such.[9] In the eyes of the novel, no language enjoys an absolute privilege. Shaped by a "Galilean linguistic consciousness," novels stage dialogues between and among languages.[10] Each language of heteroglossia views every other language, and each of them is in its turn viewed by the others.[11]

Alegría's work, then, implied the transition from a Ptolemaic to a Galilean linguistic consciousness in Central America. If the exponents of social realism, with their authoritarian discourse, were emblematic of the Ptolemaic linguistic consciousness, *Ashes of Izalco*, based on an intercultural dialogue, became the essence of the transition to a Galilean consciousness, and a new example of internally persuasive discourse.

New Voices, New Linguistic Interplays

The use of the internally persuasive discourse requires an active mode of reading on the part of the reader. The text does not offer predetermined explanations to help him or her. There is no omniscient narrator leading the reader by the nose. It is the reader who must produce the meaning of the text. Although more richly layered linguistically, meaning itself is less accessible precisely because the switch to an internally persuasive discourse usually implies a transition from the linear to the "pictorial style" as well.[12] In so doing, the novel also breaks from the traditional Aristotelian emphasis on plot, which had become the sine qua non of social realism.

In order to compare both styles, it suffices to read the very first paragraph of *Ashes of Izalco* in order to see how different it is from a traditional "realistic" novel:

> The luncheon dishes clash and rattle in the kitchen. María grumbles to herself in a steady monotone, and Dad, strangely shrunken now, defenselessly old, lies asleep in the darkened bedroom. I've taken off my sandals, and the chocolate brown tiles are cool against my feet. The whitewashed arches march around the patio: circus elephants linked tail to trunk, enclosing the blaring bougainvillea, the file of rosebushes, the central fountain where Alfredo and I used to splash and scream, the shaded jasmine, the papaya tree, the star pine with its ivy-choked trunk. (9)[13]

Shortly after that, we hear that Frank Wolff (whose last name we discover only at the end of chapter 2) mentioned in his diary the rumblings of the Izalco volcano when Carmen was seven years old (these descriptions will indeed appear in the diary at the end of the novel). But we still don't know who Frank is, nor that the narrator is Carmen, Isabel's daughter. We will find that out in the first chapter, but not right away. First, Carmen will visit the market in Santa Ana and mix her childhood memories with her reflections during the narrative present in which she is "telling" the story.

Her reflections are presented virtually as a stream-of-consciousness narrative—loaded with reported speeches—and mixed with free indirect discourse which always appears shot through with other voices:

> I should be writing letters, but there's plenty of time: I'll be here a month. Dad would be better off with us, but he doesn't want to leave his house, his town, his dead. He's too

old to make a change, and Paul would start resenting him before the week was out, would grow silent and irritable, would weave pockets of tension in the air with nervous fingers. I would have to absorb his sullen outbursts behind the closed bedroom door, while Dad sat in the living room, expecting it as his due to be waited on, entertained. Impossible! Besides, I tried last evening after dinner.

"If I leave Santa Ana," he said, "it will be for Nicaragua. If not, I'll just stay here." (12)[14]

As readers, we have to gradually build the story of Frank and Isabel in our own minds. We are not spoon-fed facts about the main characters, their setting and circumstances. Rather, they expose themselves to us, gradually and from within, through an introspective mode that reveals them as thinking and feeling people charged with subjectivity, and open to each other in a continuing dialogue, in a continual prying of each other's consciousness, yet revealed in their turn through the consciousness of Carmen. This novelistic process was utterly new and revolutionary in Central America with *Ashes of Izalco.*

In fact, Frank doesn't even speak for himself until his diary appears in chapter 5, and after many rumors, from his being a "communist" to his being a "harmless drunk," are circulated by other characters. Carmen herself will comment on the textual nature of these rumors in chapter 7: "Frank's candor, his brief enthusiasm to find his way back to his mountain paradise, gives him the wistful air of a lost child; irony adds the precocious cynicism of a child who had set aside his innocence reluctantly" (56).[15] In the process, the time sequences have also been broken. Whereas social realism traditionally narrates its stories chronologically and introduces us to the setting of the story in the first few paragraphs, *Ashes of Izalco,* like both European modernism and Latin American boom literature, breaks down the time flow and is not narrated in a linear manner.

The novel begins with a mature Carmen, living in Washington D.C. (a fact we will not know until the end of chapter 2), and married to Paul—the "Perfect Organization Man" (27), visiting Santa Ana again in order to attend Isabel's funeral. In the patriarchal house, Carmen remembers the patio where she played with her brother Alfredo as a child. On the day of the narrative present, the Izalco volcano appears about to erupt, which brings back memories of its eruption when she was seven. This, in turn, triggers memories of when her father lost the picture of Neto, Carmen's little brother, who died in 1931 when he was one year old.

From this point, Carmen's mind leaps backward to the day when, as a child, she was taken to the funeral of Margarita and saw a corpse for the first time, discovering that death was just "a deep sleep" (13). This scene foreshadows Isabel's own funeral at the end of the novel. Switching back to the narrative present, she remembers her mother as she used to dress for funerals. This leads to her first reflection on Frank's diary: "After reading Frank's diary I am confused, disoriented, as if I had never really known her at all. I need to order my memories, trace each feature and characteristic, rescue her from chaos and oblivion" (14-15). She begins then to rebuild her mother's life, and comes to understand that Frank knew her better than she herself: "Frank noticed Mother's quiet sadness; I have only become aware of it now" (16). Remembering that her mother never left Santa Ana but always dreamt of Paris and taught her French since she was a little girl, Carmen begins a meditation on Paris, understanding the different quarters of that city which were significant for her grandfather, for her father, and for her.

Finally, Carmen asks Maria Luisa if she remembers Frank Wolff, and her response is categorical: "How could I forget him? He was the communist who came here pretending he was writing a novel, the liar! He came on orders from Moscow. He and Martí were the ones who planned the whole thing . . ." (26).

In the first few paragraphs, then, we have been exposed virtually to the entire history of the Silva family (excluding Alfonso Rojas, whose own story will appear in another chapter), Santa Ana's ruling class, the salient traits of Carmen's life, and a long list of relatives and members of the family. All we still need to know is what (if anything) really happened between Frank and Isabel. However, this will be revealed by the development of Carmen's thought-process through discourse, rather than by complicating the plot in dramatic fashion. Maintaining the multivoiced "speech within speech" of Carmen throughout the entire length of the novel, her voice becomes an open-ended narrative which is juxtaposed to Frank's diary in order to wrestle with the essential theme: the Matanza of January 1932.

However, by becoming intertwined with the relationship of Frank and Isabel, the potential epic fresco which the Matanza theoretically could be becomes rather an intimate, personal drama. This underlines the novel's essential humanity, while making the Matanza more explosive precisely by reining in its epic possibilities. The novel portrays the Matanza through a subjective, intimate discourse in which it is lived from within the experience of one of the main characters, Frank, who drowns in self-pity and fear of losing Isabel in frequent bouts with alcohol. Meanwhile, the peasants are herded into the main plaza of the town of Izalco in order to be massacred.

> I drank carefully, keeping my eyes on the table, and gradually they [the peasants] lost their interest in me.
> Gingerly, unwillingly, as a man removing the bandage over a gangrenous wound and dreading what it may reveal, I forced myself to think back beyond your last words:
> "We can never see each other again, Frank." . . .
> I went over to say goodbye to the old lady and pressed one of my dwindling number of bills into her hand. Virgil had not been allowed to park Eduardo's car in the plaza itself, and we pushed through the crowd toward the corner where he had left it. The street mouth was blocked by soldiers.
> "Nobody leaves the plaza, a swarthy corporal informed us." (164-66)[16]

The Matanza is also lived through the emotions and personal viewpoint of Isabel, a member of the oligarchy who, by personal experience, has been forced to work through a kind of mental barrier into a position from which this experience can be viewed as validated and validating. Reflecting on Isabel's relationship with Frank, Carmen asks

> What was it Mother saw in Frank? Was she attracted by his worldliness, the aura of the successful author? Or did she feel, perhaps, an instinctive maternal impulse that went unfulfilled in her relationship with Dad? I'll have to start at the beginning. (45)

As such, the novel does not emphasize plot. We know the plot from the first two chapters. It emphasizes character development and, more specifically, the development and transformation of the characters' ideologies and view of the world, their own sense of self. And it does all of this through the use of reported speech, through the elaboration of a polyphony of voices which operates as a social (and aural) tapestry, dialogizing among themselves, and dialogizing with us as readers.[17]

Dialogical Subversion, Ideological Implications

Ashes of Izalco is equally pioneering in its attempt to establish an intercultural relationship by means of dialogism. In order to comment upon this aspect, I will start by making a reference to Bakhtin's own ideas on this subject. In "Response to a Question from *Novy Mir*," Bakhtin (1986, 7) states,

> There exists a very strong but one-sided and thus untrust-worthy, idea that in order to better understand a foreign culture, one must enter into it, forgetting one's own, and view the world through the eyes of this foreign culture. This idea, as I said, is one-sided. Of course, a certain entry as a living being into foreign culture, the possibility of seeing the world through its eyes, is a necessary part of the process of under-standing it; but if this were the only aspect of this understand-ing, it would merely be duplication and would not entail anything new or enriching.

Bakhtin's own argument points in the direction which is essential to dialogism: one has to be able to be outside of a culture in order to understand it. "In order to understand, it is immensely important for the person who understands to be *located outside* the object of his or her creative understanding" (7) because how we present ourselves outwardly can only be perceived by those located outside of us in space. This is so not only among individuals, but also among cultures. "It is only in the eyes of *another* culture that foreign culture reveals itself fully and profoundly" (7). The meaning of a particular culture—its own identity, its own symbolic compre-hension of itself—only becomes fully conscious to the degree to which one contrasts it with another whose notion of itself is different. The two cultures engage in a kind of dialogue, and this dialogical relationship overcomes the closeness and one-sidedness that an individual's own identity or symbolic understanding of self might possess.

> We raise new questions for a foreign culture, ones that it did not raise itself; we seek answers to our own questions in it; and the foreign culture responds to us by revealing to us its new aspects and new semantic depths. Without *one's own* questions one cannot creatively understand anything other or foreign (but, of course, the questions must be serious and sincere). Such a dialogic encounter of two cultures does not result in merging or mixing. Each retains its own unity and *open* totality, but they are mutually enriched. (7)

The dialogic process enables a culture to come to grips with meanings it possessed only nonconsciously, as a potential which had not been realized prior to engaging in this dialogic relationship. By addressing meanings through the contact with a foreign culture, they become fully realized.This process happens not only to one of the parties engaged in the dialogic relationship but to both, even if one does the questioning and the other the answering.

This procedure implies a breakdown of insularity. With insularity, there is no possibility of dialogue. With total relativism on the part of the observer or questioner, there is no dialogue either, because that too would imply a reducing to a single consciousness as it dissolves one or the other of the parties rather than establishing a dialogic encounter of the two.

We find such a procedure in the dialogic structure of *Ashes of Izalco*. It is a continuing dialogue between two cultures, Salvadoran and U.S., personalized in the relationship between Frank and Isabel (of which Carmen and Paul's is a pale echo). It is the insularity of both people (and, by extension, both cultures) which is being broken.

> "You and I are too much alike, Frank. I've asked myself: is it just fear of the unknown? Am I merely clinging to my house, my servants, the security that Alfonso offers? Could I face a new world at your side, knowing that both of us share the same doubts and indecisions? I couldn't answer the question. Perhaps I am a coward." (165)

The three main narrators (Frank, Carmen, and Isabel) are all displaced from within their own cultural orbit and are forced to confront themselves by confronting the other, to seek a synthesis out of their joint experience. The dialogue of Isabel and Frank implies an ongoing clash of disparate cultures, languages, symbolic traditions, and political systems, as evidenced when he implores her:

> You're made from a different mold than Santa Ana's. Your vitality, your thirst for a richer, fuller life, will turn against you if you choose to remain here. Have you glimpsed the interminable file of gray days and months and years stretching ahead, waiting to be filled with your self-abnegation, remorse, and the haunting thought that life might have been otherwise? (143)

Each character has to learn to live within the orbit of the other, and to seek a new syncretism out of the merging of their cultural referents. The "other" begins to operate inside each of them, making double others out of both of them, and placing them at the edge of their own respective cultures: between the conflict of North and South.

This dialogical process between characters which sheds light on self and other happens even between "gringos." In chapter 5, when we are introduced to Frank's diary (and, by extension, to Frank's voice and sense of self), he immediately begins confronting himself with Virgil, his childhood friend who has become a protestant missionary in Chalchuapa. Despite their common childhood and social background, Frank notices how Virgil has become alien to his way of being (36). He realizes that whereas he, himself, began to clamor for the world's attention, Virgil tried to erase himself. As such, they have become complete strangers to each other and have been "reduced to silence, punctuated by embarrassed snorts of laughter as each of us rummaged for something, anything, to say" (37).

Isabel also meditates about her sense of self and tells Carmen that even though she had lived all her life in Santa Ana, she felt only as if she were passing through, as if she did not really belong there at all. Her sisters and friends seemed from another country, and she was surprised not to find her bags packed and ready to leave when she entered her bedroom (53).

The essential cultural confrontation, however, takes place between Isabel and Frank. It will be emblematic of the ideological switch occurring in Central America, in which the U.S. comes to substitute Paris as the idealized mecca and utopian point of reference, as becomes clear in chapter 9 ("It's strange; Mother never talked to me much about Paul. . . ." "Mother liked Washington. . . ." "It might have been different in Paris . . .") (67).

One of the central aspects of the text is a meditation about the differences between El Salvador and the U.S. Thinking about herself and Paul, Carmen observes that "neither of us realized how difficult it is to build a bridge between two cultures, two backgrounds as different as ours. . . . What drove the wedge between us more than anything else was our different nationalities" (66). She mentions how they each would argue about the Latin American policy of the U.S. with the certainty that the other would eventually come around to the opposite viewpoint. Yet they only ended up hardening their own positions.

In the scene where Virgil wants to save the pigs, the children are making fun of him, calling him "Gringo! Gringo! Vaya al Chilpancingo!" (82). When he finally reaches them, he discovers they have hog cholera; they will have to be killed and the ground burnt with gasoline. For the locals, he is a representative of the devil trying to ruin the local butcher, and were it not for Frank's intervention, Virgil would be stoned to death.

However, the fundamental cultural clash takes place between Frank and Isabel; its essence is Frank's inability to understand why Isabel will never leave Alfonso for him, and her own inability to understand why Frank persists in his courtship and actually makes arrangements to flee with her. But, since Carmen discovers their relationship through Frank's diary, she becomes an indirect witness/voyeur and contributes actively to the meditation about cultural differences, interjecting her own meditations about her relationship with Paul.

In this context, given that the novel was published in 1966—at the peak of pro-Cuban and "Thirdworldist" (*tercermundista*) attitudes in Central America, when the slogan "Yankees go home" was still being chanted with full vigor and the world seemed to be unidimensional, black and white, with Cubans cast as the good guys and all gringos as the bad—it is fascinating to see the text stressing a U.S./Salvadoran dialogue. In it, Frank and Virgil are "gringos," but certainly not stereotypical ones. Whereas Paul (who does not appear actively in the narrative) is the stereotypical "Perfect Organization Man," Virgil chooses to die holding hands with the peasant man and child in the Izalco massacre (171-72), and Frank has been made to be "the communist . . . on orders from Moscow . . . who planned the whole thing," according to María Luisa (26), even if the reality is closer to the image of "a harmless drunk" as Alfredo describes him (29), or to that of an artist searching for his own inner soul.

In this process, the dialogical subversion implies the potential reader as well. It means to break the stereotypical attitudes about U.S. citizens and their involvement with the political affairs of Central America. Ideologically, it is a challenge within the text, and a challenge to the assumed ideological preconceptions of the potential reader.

This same attempt to break down existing stereotypes also manifests itself when confronting the image of the Salvadoran "oligarchy," known internationally as "the fourteen families." The Rojas family is unique because of don Alfonso, a Nicaraguan in exile who will contribute his entire life to the anti-Somoza struggle. However, he married into the Silva family, and its members are an integral part of the Santa Ana oligarchy. Nevertheless, through the Alfonso character, the stereotypical image of the oligarchs is broken down and given more depth, made more complex. Alfonso—the patriarch of the family—does the inconceivable by confronting the military: when Colonel Gutierrez mistreats a peasant, Alfonso challenges him for his lack of humanity (28). Isabel, his wife, worships French culture and sends her children to "Hector's school" where "all the other teachers are communists like that don Chico Luarca" and none of the children come "from good families" (31). Carmen, once an adult, becomes a poet, "an agnostic and Philistine," convinced that "science was the only worthwhile pursuit" (30). Meanwhile, Carmen's brother, Alfredo, will become, in his own words, "a harmless drunk" who will need the support of his mother more than Carmen does.

We have, then, a significant rupture from either the idyllic image of the oligarchy portrayed in the "criollista" novel, or else the equally idealized evil image that comes across in social realism. At the same time, the portrait in *Ashes of Izalco* is not a "whitewash" of oligarchical excesses. The contradictions which the social group represents are vividly portrayed, but once again, from within the

34

texture of interpersonal relationships, and by contrasting their behavior to the "American" behavior of Frank. The cultural dialogism enables the text to strip bare the provincialism and loneliness of the Rojas/Silvas without becoming proselytizing or confusing its own mission with that of a sociological tract.

The Changing Role of Central American Writers in the 1960s

During the late 1940s and 1950s, most "social realist" writers had been members of their own respective communist parties in Central America. As such, they began to play within their respective societies the role of universal intellectual in the Sartrean sense. The "universal" intellectual is the man or woman of wisdom who poses as judge and prophet and whose all-encompassing vision and profound knowledge grant him or her the authority to become a critic of his or her society and point the way towards a better world. Claiming that Sartre characterized the concept with Voltaire in mind, Foucault (1980, 124) states, "For a long time the 'left' intellectual spoke and was acknowledged to have the right of speaking in the capacity of master of truth and justice." Nonetheless, for most universal intellectuals—still caught in the notion which privileged reason over the body and the senses since the Enlightenment—literature was an ideological instrument rather than a genuine item in its own right.

The emergence of the Cuban revolution in 1959, however, and the apparition of guerrillas in Central America since 1961, created a divide between the "old Left" (procommunist and aligned with Moscow) and a "new Left" (pro-Guevarist, anti-Stalinist, and aligned with the romantic ideal of the Cuban revolution of the early 1960s as poetically expressed in the "Second Declaration of Havana"). It was a new generation of writers—younger, critical of the Soviet model—yet committed to the fight for social and economic transformations in their respective countries. This divide was not just political, but quickly became a cultural one as well. Sharing many of the values of the 1960s generation in the First World, this group not only made different political-ideological choices than the writers of the 1950s, they also chose to live differently, to deal differently with their own bodies, to insert themselves within the global framework of "counterculture." The 1960s was a time of cultural revolution, and *Ashes of Izalco* became the first of a series of novels to express this transformation in its literary form as well.

The switch of allegiances within the Left, as well as the questioning of the dogmatic approaches of the old neo-Stalinist communist parties, forced young, sensitive intellectuals to ask themselves basic questions. Writing became for some of them (such as Roque Dalton or Alegría herself, whose own social origins were closer to those of the exploiters than the exploited) a means of escaping from their class origins and redefining their own identity and allegiance within the newly emerging Central American revolutionary Left. This process implied, of course, a coming to terms with the U.S. in the context of the polarization of the 1960s. Whereas this was easy for some more traditionally middle-class intellectuals, it forced people such as Alegría (married to a U.S. leftist) and Dalton (son of a U.S. citizen) to confront that "otherness" which was constitutive of their being. This made them realize that it would be illegitimate to *speak for* another group, as was the leftist tradition of the 1950s. Instead, they reached different (though not necessarily contradictory) conclusions.

Dalton felt he could not speak for a group he did not genuinely represent and, thus, became a militant and political leader to the end of his life. This way, when he was genuinely "speaking for the Salvadoran people," he had become one with them; he had genuinely merged with their views, their interests, and was exercising his own leadership truly in their name.

Alegría also chose not to speak for another group. Though sharing most of Dalton's ideals, her option was rather to become a facilitator, to enable the oppressed Salvadoran social groups to speak for themselves. Like Dalton, she did not pretend to represent a group artificially. But—as a woman—she perceived the structures of domination in a stronger fashion, while simultaneously living from within a sphere of privilege. Her option then became not that of political leadership per se, but rather that of a search for a "popular" discourse. It was a long, drawn-out process that would take her all the way to *They Won't Take Me Alive* and many of her other compilations and contributions of the 1980s. But it began by a need to find, first of all, her own narrative voice. This emerged from confrontation with a dialogical relationship with the voice of her "other" (Darwin Flakoll) and by dealing with the reality of Salvadoran violence from the very start (the Matanza of 1932) as a pivotal point

36

for dealing with herself, given her own personal links to that sordid episode (her own family was a coffee-growing family from Santa Ana). In other words, Alegría searched within herself to define her own personal identity as a worldly personality, a Salvadoran, and a leftist. In this process of re-defining herself, she became articulated in the newly emerging social construct towards which El Salvador was gyrating by the middle 1960s.

Alegría's own growth was also an expression of the cultural element of the 1960s. This decade gave a new recognition to the legitimacy of artistic expression as such. Creativity was no longer just a vehicle for conceptual thinking as rationalism would have it. Clearly, poets—sensitized to language and its nuance—were better suited for recording discourses, voices, and creating them into a polyphonic melody, than were rationalist narrators with monophonic ears, more in tune with the trends of the 1950s than with the revolution in values of the 1960s. Thus, it is no accident that two poets (Alegría and Dalton) became the parents of the new Central American narrative.

Following the example of *Ashes of Izalco*, these novels were all written by writers who were sympathetic to the "New Left," or were militants of the "New Left," and who no longer felt the constraints of the 1950s against expressing themselves fully. In their aesthetic choices, they were also reacting against the "authoritarian discourse" of the pro-communist novels of the 1950s. But it was not just ideological. It was that the new decade brought about a new sensibility, a new way for Central Americans to think about themselves and new means of expressing this in the novel as the genre became fully legitimized by the boom and the literary experimentation which it implied.

Conclusions

New Central American fiction writers have opted for a style of writing in which the ideological challenge is to force readers to change their reading practices. Moving away from the passive consumption of realist discourse, the new fiction demands activity on the part of the reader. This is obtained through the constant displacement of language and its structures. That displacement forces the reader to transform his or her mental structures in the process of trying to make sense of the text.

The purpose of this writing is to make the reader conscious of language itself while conventional representations of reality are destroyed. This process echoes the destruction of Central American society, portrays its social chaos and the difficulty of apprehending the meaning of life itself when degraded by war and tragedy. What appears is the need to explore the fragmentation of society in order to try to make some sense of it and to be able to transform it.

Since the 1970s, this phenomenon has become the dominant trait of Central American fiction. However, this could happen only because of the publication of *Ashes of Izalco* in 1966. This text opened the way for a transition in narrative mode and led towards the creation of a new Central American novel.

The reason for the formal change is a political one. Alegría was deeply influenced by the personality and ideology of Salvadoran poet Dalton, as well as by those of Julio Cortázar, one of her closest friends. It was precisely because she felt secure in her convictions and well-respected by leading figures of the Latin American "New Left" that she could dare to break in *Ashes of Izalco* the stereotypes surrounding both U.S. citizens and members of the oligarchy. As such, her novel also dissolved the ideologically simplistic black-white stereotypical images which were characteristic of social realism.

NOTES

1. For a complete list and an analysis of their characteristics, see Arturo Arias, "Literary Production and Political Crisis in Central America," International Political Science Review 12/1 (1991): 15-28.

2. The original publication came out with Seix Barral, the famous editorial house in Barcelona, Spain, which was then publishing the Latin American boom writers. The fact that *Ashes of Izalco* became the first Central American novel to be edited by the prestigious Barcelona house at the peak of its fame was not insignificant for the writers who attempted to emulate. See note 13.

3. The Matanza was the assassination of anywhere between ten thousand and thirty thousand peasants in January of 1932. This action, carried out by the Salvadoran army under the direction of General Maximiliano Hernández Martínez, was the result of a peasant insurrection in which the latter manifested their discontent with the

economic conditions under which they were living. Among the dead was Farabundo Martí, a labor organizer, whose name is emblematic of the present-day Farabundo Martí National Liberation Front (FMLN). Salvadoran historians consider the Matanza as the beginning of the long, historical cycle which ended with the civil war of the 1980s.

4. In the social realism mode, texts pretend to ignore the existence of language and to convey the illusion of a direct link with reality. The most famous quote along these lines is the often-cited preface to Brazilian novelist Jorge Amado's *Cacau* (1955). He makes the following claim: "In this book I attempted to tell, with a minimum of literature and a maximum of honesty, the life of the workers of the cacao plantations of the south of Bahia. . . . It is not a pretty book, well assembled nor without repetitions. . . . On the other hand, I had no literary preoccupations whatsoever in putting these pages together" (my translation).

Nonetheless, they are linguistic discourses as well. As such, they imply particular ways of reading in order to convey their meaning. In fact, whether consciously or not, they end up determining their own reading by the use—and abuse—of what Mikhail Bakhtin calls an "authoritarian discourse," that is, by the use of a language that employs conventional and static symbols in order to convey a worldview. The realist text is organized to bestow identity upon the reader through the exclusion of the ambiguities and connotations of language. In other words, narrated action is transformed into represented action.

5. There is still some debate among scholars regarding the books signed "Valentin Voloshinov." Some claim Voloshinov—a disciple of Bakhtin—allowed his master to publish under his name. Others claim Voloshinov accepted censorship limitations imposed in the USSR and modified Bakhtin's manuscripts in accordance. Still others accept Voloshinov's authorship, though under the guidance and influence of Bakhtin. As a result, many scholars have opted for writing "Bakhtin/Voloshinov" whenever dealing with concepts which appeared in any of the books signed by the latter.

6. In this style, in which content is more important than rhetorical language-play, the referents ache to be free of their signifiers and strive for a direct representation as sense-data. According to Bakhtin/Voloshinov, the basic characteristics of linear style are "to

construct clear-cut, external contours for reported speech, whose own internal individuality is minimized . . . in which the author and his characters all speak exactly the same language . . ." (Voloshinov 1986, 120). The choice of linear style by social realist writers went beyond any genuinely "authoritarian" inclination on their part in the narrow ideological sense. This style was canonized, however, as the only acceptable one at the Congress of Soviet Writers in 1934. Subsequently theorized by Lukács, it essentially derived its character- istics from the nineteenth-century European novel. "Socialist realism" was considered a positive response to the "bourgeois decadence" of modernism. It was chosen because their literary aims were to educate the reader, to convey a thesis. Thus, social realist writers seek to make their ideological message as transparent as possible. This clarity is possible only through linear style.

7. In 1943 she wrote as follows (Oreamuno 1961, 28):

> Literarily, I confess that I am SICK AND TIRED, like that, in capital letters, of folklore. . . . The colorful tricks of this type or art are exhausted, the aesthetic pleasure that was produced before is now gone, the same scenes repeat themselves with numbing frequency, and the human emotion can no longer react before the inevitable tiredness of seeing what has already been seen before. It is necessary that we be done with such a disaster. . . .

Sergio Ramírez, vice-president of Nicaragua during the Sandinista government, wrote the following (1973, 52) about Oreamuno:

> In her prose work, chronicles, narrations, letters, novels, is revealed an intimate testimony of someone who struggles to free herself from the bindings of a paralyzed, static soci- ety. . . . All her personal anxiety is wonderfully liberated when she finds the techniques, that for her are a catharsis, of Proust, Joyce, Mann; and she is the first one who in the intellectually weak years of the 1940s finds those techniques and learns, in *Finnegans Wake*, in *Ulysses*, in *A la recherche du temps perdu*, the path toward her own liberation. . . . (my translation)

8. His "banana trilogy" was written during the 1950s. It represents, without question, the low point in his otherwise magnificent opera.

9. According to Bakhtin (1986, 336), the novel takes as its special concern the ways in which various languages of heteroglossia may enter into dialogue with each other and the kinds of complex interactions that these dialogues generate. ". . . The central problem for a stylistic of the novel may be formulated as the problem of *artistically representing language, the problem of representing the image of a language* (Bakhtin's emphasis).

10. A "Galilean linguistic consciousness" is one which denies the absolutism of a single and unitary language, refusing "to acknowledge its own language as the sole verbal and semantic center of the ideological world" (Bakhtin 1986, 366). Its opposite would be the "Ptolemaic linguistic consciousness," which has no sense of its own relativity but believes it is the "language of truth."

11. As a result, the fundamental impulse of the novel as a genre is to dialogize heteroglossia as intensely as possible. This creation of images of languages, however, is not an experience in abstraction where language spills out of control and out of responsibility, as with deconstructionism. On the contrary, it is a form of sociological probing, an exploring of values and beliefs:

> The image of such a language in a novel is the image assumed by a set of social beliefs, the image of a social ideologeme that has fused with its own discourse, with its own language. Therefore such an image is very far from being formalistic, and artistic play with such languages far from being formalistic play. In the novel formal markers of languages, manners and styles are symbols for sets of social beliefs. (Bakhten 1986, 357)

12. As Bakhtin says of "pictorial" style:

> language devises means for infiltrating reported speech with authorial retort and commentary in deft and subtle ways . . . the reported speech is individualized to a much greater degree—the tangibility of the various facets of an utterance may be subtly differentiated. This time the reception includes

41

not only the referential meaning of the utterance, the statement it makes, but also the linguistic peculiarities of its verbal implementation. (Voloshinov 1986, 120-21)

13. Claribel Alegría and Darwin Flakoll, *Ashes of Izalco*, (Wilimantic, Conn.: Curbstone Press, 1989). All further references will be to this edition. Even though Darwin Flakoll himself has translated the text, some of the salient touches which mark more clearly the differences between "linear" and "pictorial" style have been lost in translation. For example, in this very paragraph, the line "que rico estar descalza" has been translated as "I've taken off my sandals" instead of "how nice it feels to be barefooted." Thus, the active reflective element on the part of the narrator disappears, and instead we have a passive descriptive act, closer to the "linear" than to the "pictorial." The loss is also ideological. The active phrase is an ideologeme in the sense that it denotes a choice to be barefooted, underlining a link between Carmen and the poor, barefooted people of El Salvador. To wear shoes versus to be barefooted is a fundamental divide between rich and poor in Central America, and was especially so during the Matanza: after all, it was its perpetrator, General Maximiliano Hernández Martínez, who predicated that the poor people should go barefoot in order to absorb the effluvia from the earth. Growing up in Santa Ana in the 1930s, it is implicit that Carmen had to know and react to such information.

14. Again, these traits are more evident in the Spanish original. Phrases such as "lo conozco" and "lo más natural," which denote characterization and signify a particular worldview, have disappeared in the English translation. This latter translation sounds more descriptive and less "stream-of-consciousness." As such, stylistic analysis utilizing the English version becomes fuzzier than it would be in the original Spanish. Equally telling, the last line in Spanish says "If I leave Santa Ana," he told me . . . as opposed to "he said." The act of telling is more active than the passive "he said," and it denotes an interaction between the characters.

15. The original Spanish says, "En el candor *de su diario*, en el entusiasmo de su deseo por recobrar el paraíso perdido, *siento* a Frank como a un niño extraviado . . ." (69, my emphasis). This would translate as "In the candor *of his diary*, in his brief enthusiasm to find his way back to his lost paradise, *I feel* Frank as if he were a

lost child. . . ." Note the loss of dialogism, of the textual referent and of the active emotional affirmation of the female character in the extant English version.

16. In the Spanish version, the first line quoted here says "I drank carefully, keeping my eyes on the table. *Gradually, the peasants forgot my presence and went on talking in low voices, without changing the expressions in their faces* (198).

17. "Dialogizing" comes from Bakhtin's concept of "dialogism." As such, it is a special sort of interaction that cannot be equated with argument (dialogue). Whereas it does imply a relationship of every utterance to other utterances, it fundamentally points to the open-ended possibilities generated by all the discursive practices of a culture. It applies simultaneously to everyday speech, to popular culture, and to the literary and artistic tradition.

WORKS CITED

Alegría, Claribel, and Darwin Flakoll. 1989. *Ashes of Izalco.* Williman-
    tic, Conn.: Curbstone Press.
————. 1982. *Cenizas de Izalco.* San José: Editorial Universitaria
    Centroamericana.
Amado, Jorge. 1955. *Cacau.* Sao Paulo: Martins. Originally published
    1933.
Arias, Arturo. 1991. "Literary Production and Political Crisis in Central
    America." *International Political Science Review* 12.1: 15-28.
Bakhtin, M. M. 1986. *Speech Genres and Other Late Essays.* Trans.
    Vern W. McGee. Austin: University of Texas Press.
————. 1981. "Discourse in the Novel." In *The Dialogic Imagination.*
    Ed. and trans. Michael Holquist. Austin: University of Texas
    Press.
Foucault, Michel. 1980. "Truth and Power." In *Power/Knowledge:
    Selected Interviews and Other Writings.* Ed. Colin Gordon.
    New York: Pantheon.
Oreamuno, Yolanda. 1961. *A lo largo del corto camino.* San José:
    Editorial Costa Rica.

Ramírez, Sergio. 1973. "Introducción: La Narrativa Centroamericana."
    Antología del Cuento Centroamericano. Ed. Sergio Ramírez.
    San José: Editorial Universitaria Centroamericana.
Voloshinov, Valentin. 1986. *Marxism and the Philosophy of Lan-
    guage.* Trans. Ladislav Matejka and I. R. Titunik. Cambridge:
    Harvard University Press.

3

TESTIMONIO AND DIARIES AS NARRATIVES
OF SUCCESS OR FAILURE IN
*THEY WON'T TAKE ME ALIVE**

Ileana Rodríguez

I n Gayatri Spivak's introduction for *Selected Subaltern Studies* (Guha and Spivak 1988), one can find a number of ideas relevant to the study of the constitution of the subaltern as a revolutionary subject. Perhaps the most interesting are those which refer to questioning the concepts of success and failure in reference to the constitution of the subaltern. It could be that those two words are the loci of positivistic thought, readings of the "development" of the subaltern, but it could also be that their seductive nature is related to exactly the opposite, for success and failure are relativized when one uncovers their being as a mark of "cognitive failures." Success and failure are gnoseological concepts, and political concepts as well. They punctuate change as confrontation, something one wins or something one loses, or as transition, from one stage to another, whether we come to realize it or not. Success and failure are thus words framed within the great narratives of the modes of production.

There is a certain uneasiness, however, in the use of a terminology that makes us aware of the question of what terminology to use if we wish to trace the trajectory of the subaltern-woman-

---

* Translated by Robert Carr, assistant professor of English at George Mason University. This chapter is dedicated to Rodolfo, Fernando, Daniel and Daniel, Marta, Nubia, Isolda, and Pilar.

revolutionary on a graph, avoiding the reefs implicit in the idea of "development," implying in turn success and failure. There is no question that the terminology of "the moment(s) of change [needs to] be pluralized and plotted as confrontation rather than transition . . . and that such changes are signalled or marked by a functional change in sign systems" (Guha and Spivak 1988, 3). There is also no question that the terminology of change has corollaries for a theory of consciousness and culture which, as Spivak asserts, brings hegemonic historical thought to a crisis, and that this crisis branches towards a theory of reading.

For instance, in the case of Claribel Alegría and Darwin Flakoll's *They Won't Take Me Alive: The Salvadoran Woman in Struggle* (1987), the ideas of success and failure could be appended immediately to insurgent guerrilla movements and their current strategies. However, both texts could be read simply as a convergence of voices in a perpetual dialogue, as well as with the texts written by insurgent revolutionaries or with texts from previous insurgencies, where woman was decentered and kept on the margins of a social narrative which pretended to incorporate the popular masses. From this perspective, the text contributes to the study of subalternity, presenting us with a reading of woman as a revolutionary subaltern, central to the social text. Success means then, in this case, to secure the convergence of the plurality of voices, masculine and feminine, Salvadoran and North American.

They Won't Take Me Alive is a narrative of organization and of incorporation into the revolutionary struggle in which the gendered subject is constituted as a participant, as an equal (sameness) (McKinnon 1987, 33). Men and women have equal rights and equal politico-military responsibilities. From a gendered perspective the problem is that of the liberation of women. For in Alegría/ Flakoll's work, the problem of the liberation of women is confronted in the same terms as that of the liberation of men. The equation "national liberation equals collective liberation" presupposes "equal" representation of men and women within the term *collective*. However, the word *collective* is hollow; it has a built-in void wherein women are placed.

It has been well documented that the revolutionary leadership always asked women to wait and to postpone. For the sake of unity, they said, for their children's sake, for national security, not yet, please. Then, to say that "it was by means of the incorporation of

46

women into the revolutionary struggle . . . that woman was to liberate herself, acquiring her own proper and just dimension" (Alegría and Flakoll 1987, 74, my translation) was only partially true.* It is, in many ways, to constitute woman as man, by incorporating her into the male field of action, and it is to insert her into power as a man. And what about her femaleness?

Eugenia, the main protagonist of this testimonial, is always portrayed as asserting her feminine being—much to her sorrow. Javier, her *compañero*, tells us that "she was always very critical about all the little traits (notice the diminutive) of male chauvinism coming up in the separation of tasks for women and tasks for men" (74). Because Eugenia is critical of the gendered division of labor and gender roles, she is culturally mandated to prove herself as a man. In the process she disapproves of any "little" deference toward her by her companions in arms. For instance, she rejects any help in carrying a cache of arms and dismisses her companions when they want to alleviate her burden because her feet are bleeding. Equality, male and female, is defined here as identity (sameness) and is expressed in such phrases as, "what counts are the capacities" (83), or "she could not abandon the tasks because of her infant girl" (92)—phrases which interpellate women only. The underlying assumptions for this *recit* are, naturally, narratives of modes of production, for they acknowledge division of labor—masculine/feminine—as one of their main parameters.

Women's discussions and the discussions about women within revolutionary organizations of revolutionary societies, however, have sufficiently demonstrated that even if women's liberation equals national liberation, the participation and incorporation of women in the liberation of the people or country never proves a sufficient condition. It becomes imperative, then, to separate strands and break analogies such as "woman equals country equals sovereignty equals liberation."

Another important question this testimonial raises is related to the nature and logic of politico-military narratives. As in the case of the narratives of modes of production, of which the politico-military narratives are a subset, the encoding of both these narratives always prioritizes the parameters of class over any other. Consequently, they postulate themselves as narratives of progress and of transition,

---

* Subsequent notes are my own translation.

47

erasing the confrontations taking place in the intranational-domestic cultural spaces where the constitution of oppressive gender roles takes place. This type of teleological organization does not annul the questions of success and failure and, consequently, the positivistic patterns are always present.

What follows is that what is particular to the formation of women is flagrantly omitted, as it is in the other (male) narratives, where, again, men and women are evaluated on the basis of sameness. Eugenia will never permit her comrades to carry anything for her because that signifies not being equal, that is, not being like a man. The revolutionary sense of worth and of value is instituted in military training and in the military disposition to follow orders. Women and men are equal only to the degree that both are dedicated revolutionary combatants; that is, they excel in all organizational duties, in the execution of orders, in temerity and sacrifice, in military discipline, and in a full command of weaponry.

All the women under scrutiny in this text distinguish themselves in exactly the same manner, and all of them are characterized by their capacity to incorporate into their own feminine bodies all the adjectives put forth in Che Guevara's articles on the guerrilla for the guerrillero himself. I argue that the constitution of the revolutionary subject as male subject cannot but signify a sexuality, and that sexuality/textuality properly unveils itself as such in revolutionary legislatures, clearly denoting the bracketing of the question of gender as constituted here. The results bear two formidable consequences for the revolutionary state: first, the alienation of women, and second, the alienation of more than half the masses, for women makeup more than half of a country's population. In "Tirania-(patriarquia)" (Rodríguez, in progress), I explain the relation between the masses and women. The basic argument comes from the metaphorization of both as marginal.

Considering the appropriation of the narratives of empowerment by women, and trying to put aside the epistemes of positivism legislating success and failure, I want to suggest that the Alegría/Flakoll testimonial weaves together the dissimilar strands of military and romantic narrative protocols into a narrative of character formation, a kind of *bildungsroman.* The strands posit the convergence of man/woman in women and men as well as debate coupling, maternity, and love within the framework of revolutionary insurgencies and revolutionary organizations. The text addresses questions of maternity within the revolutionary processes or ideas that seem to postulate a role model of/for revolutionary maternity. Alegría and Flakoll also consider the formation of gender differences based on the incorporation of maternity to the revolutionary processes and the androgynous specular image of writing analyzed above. At stake, too, is a displacement from the representation of women/masses at the house and the plaza in *Ashes of Izalco* to the representation of oligarchy/revolutionary, plaza/bush, spontaneous insurgency in the mountain/urban guerrilla warfare in *They Won't Take Me Alive.*

In an initial methodological approach, I want to identify the adjectives that engender the feminine as revolutionary, occupying the place of the clandestine guerrilla. The same Christian series, "abnegation," "sacrifice," "heroism"—definitional terms taken from the patristic juxtaposed to the series of heroic romanticism—remain positioned within the revolutionary epistemologies. But in the case of women, selflessness and sacrifice also belong to matristics. They were and still are female attributes defining women—*stabat mater.*

Nevertheless, Eugenia is defined by a combination of adjectives, supporting my thesis of Eugenia's simultaneous representation as a woman/man. If we attend to posture, dress, and unconventional speech, we realize we are facing behavioral patterns classified within "the masculine." The list of adjectives adds to this image: (a) soft, agreeable, an attractive personality; (b) shy, nervous, silent; a worker in several social organizations—peasant organizations, cooperatives, human welfare organizations, women's groups; (c) brave, daring, politically skillful, a leader, an organizer with a strategist's mind, "She thought forwards, backwards, sideways, centerways" (54).

It is immediately apparent that the heroine is modeled on the image of the hero. But we never find her as heroic in masculine narratives. That is the reason for conceptualizing this writing as information retrieval. Alegría and Flakoll draw women out from "anonymity" and from the list of the "disappeared," nameless persons. That is why one of so many women serves as a representation of "the thousand girls, women and older Salvadoran women who continue facing the struggle without surrendering" (9). The informants are men and women, among them Marta and Ondina, Eugenia's sisters, María Elena Girón, her friend, and comandantes Ana María, Nadia Palacios, and Mercedes Letona. In narrating

Eugenia's life they narrate their own, and so the testimonial of one becomes a collective testimonial of the many.

In his article on Rigoberta Menchú, Robert Carr (1992) argues against this position. He posits that Rigoberta is not a transcendental signifier, that she can not represent all Indians. Dinesh D'Souza's argument (1991) is exactly the same as Carr's. However, the upshots of their arguments diametrically differ: Carr's is one of inclusion and D'Souza's one of exclusion. Alegría/Flakoll try to strike a balance in representing one woman through the voices of many. Thus the many become one and vice versa. Perhaps the problem is that both critics take extreme positions and, consequently, neither considers the possibilities and realities of popular and common front politics. And that is precisely the point of Alegría/Flakoll.

A commander-in-chief carrying out and issuing orders, Eugenia is a woman who not only merges masculine and feminine in her own persona but brings together two apparently antagonistic narrative strands. In the first chapter, military language frames the text. But it borrows from romantic language a vocabulary and a story invented by Alegría/Flakoll. The authors imagine how Eugenia was captured. Is it here, I wonder, where success and failure are located?

The authors "invent" because the book is written predominantly by using the testimonials of what is fundamentally a women's collective, and because the intention is to make these women visible, to give them voice, to place them in the theatre of history and to incorporate them into history through the incorporation of their actions and voice. But none of these women was a witness to Eugenia's capture. One of them accidentally heard about it on the radio. Thus, these authors invent a situation in which the decisive personality of the heroine is underscored. It is under her word, initiative, and strategic mind that we see the three members of the operative act swiftly. A woman, whose feminine intuition is used to detect danger, Eugenia can deliver arms from the city to the countryside. She can shout the final order, "Don't let them capture us alive!"

Within the logic of military narratives that opens and closes the text, a whole sentimental and emotional life is also being constructed. This sentimental life does not contradict the rules and logic of military life, but it does contrast with them. A narrative difference, the difference between the encoding of feelings and the encoding of orders, plots and assigns gender roles. Is it here, perhaps, that success or failure can be found?

If we now compare the first chapter with the last, we cannot help but compare the difference between love letters and military narratives. If in military actions the commandant falls (fails), in love letters she succeeds. Sentimental narratives are, therefore, in this text, narratives of success, framed by narratives of modes of production which, perhaps, ultimately, are all narratives of failure. At the beginning of the text, the type of story testimonials will tell cannot be predicted, and neither can the narrative mode, but both are insightful and reveal a strategy of inclusion. Thus both narratives succeed, although the political movements "fail." Small consolation for literature to succeed in place of politics.

It is in the interest of both writers and informants to stress the hardships of the struggle, the harshness of discipline, dedication, and commitment, which coexist with masculine/feminine tenderness, the famous tendresse, the development of couples and heterosexual love. The collective narrative of Alegría/Flakoll, to which Salvadoran men and women contribute, duplicates the structural dualities in which men and women, with the same strength, reinforce the sense of commitment and conviction put forth in *Ashes of Izalco*.

It is necessary to underline that this testimonial does not display the same contradictions other testimonials reveal. It does not ensnare women and the feminine within men and masculinity. However, the problems of the constitution of the social subject as a couple, and of "revolutionary" maternity return relentlessly.

I have been arguing that the writer's strategy is to show how a series of voices converge to render the presence of women in the historical stage of Salvadoran history unquestionable. This collective subject shows that both Eugenia and the informants are women very different from Woman as she has been portrayed in testimonials by men. Their actual presence in the struggle marks one such difference strongly. Their feminine debates on coupling, home, and maternity mark a second one. In fact, if this narrative has a shocking effect, it is located in the representation of a new "revolutionary" maternity. It leaves the idea of individual maternity behind and replaces it with a notion of collective maternity. Consequently, family is no longer defined by blood ties alone. Ideological bonds are now paramount.

For this new couple, love is predicated not only on sympathy and attraction but on sharing values. This is not a relationship that seizes women immediately but one that develops slowly. Love, marriage, coupling are instances of "revolutionary" life lived within a revolutionary frame and revolution, and the revolution is the fundamental and ultimate value. Javier and Eugenia know they were not going to be together all the time. After all, "marriage was going to constitute the beginning of her clandestine life" (63).

For this "brave new woman," for this woman who has proven herself in the military terrain, to extrapolate her courage, from the military to the formation of subjectivity as lover and as mother, is an arduous task. To discern and assimilate what is normal within abnormality must be exasperating. Heroic and profane characteristics do not mix. It is easier to accept Eugenia's heroic character alone, than to accept her as a normal human being who laughs, makes jokes, falls in love. It is odd to see her in full command of weapons and then fully displaying, through baby talk, her emotional vulnerability. The media discussion by Sally Quinn (1992) of the betrayal of the leadership based on a cleft between private and public does not hold here. Eugenia is not a two-faced character. Her man/woman nature, her rating as a third sex, voids her of any prior gender roles.

Conventional mores make it difficult for Eugenia to process her ideas on child rearing. I am sure the conception of revolutionary maternity will be rejected by women. Bringing up children as revolutionaries from an early age, enrolling them in revolutionary activities as informants will not find approval. Children growing up within a collective, confined to a party cell, explode bourgeois ideas of maternity. However, for those who reject monogamy and the nuclear family and bourgeois morality, this state is presented as both an alternative and a product of sheer necessity.

The parameters, structure, and strategies of the family as a social organization are targeted. The "new" behavior is mandated by regulations that mothers and fathers—mainly "revolutionary" mothers—must acknowledge. Freedom to have children means freedom to have them live on the edge of death and danger. It means to make their grandparents parent them again, for these children's parents live as if sentenced to death.

In this struggle between prior private and public categories, the military and the romantic narratives seek to strike a balance. For to accept one set of premises—military insurgency, for instance—is to accept the other: children on the edge of a nervous breakdown. "The boy or girl must live in a security house, under risks, the possible fall of their parents, etc." (68). Eugenia's ideas on maternity are that "our son would also be the son of the organization, a son of all the compañeros with whom we would share more closely the different moments of war" (68).

It is not without irony that in portraying this process of delivering the new, testimonials become narratives of success and not of failure. For they narrate the difficulties of a trying process: the difficulties of the moment in which transition as confrontation is being displayed; a moment in which weapons mediate between human beings as masses, and human beings as Army. From this perspective, patriotic narratives about women are always narratives of war. They are, consequently, situations of embattlement which jolt the foundation of social institutions—the family, child rearing, and maternity.

Under these circumstances, to ask about success and failure in the positivistic sense is almost meaningless, as it is to be concerned with strong positivistic ideas of improvement and progress. What is being represented is movement and confrontation. Improvement and development are locked in hope. Improvement, success, progress do not carry the same weight in revolutionary narratives. In fact the word used to signify "success" is *triumph*, which within revolutionary codes is a synonym of *apotheosis*, that is, a point of culmination and, therefore, of departure.

Alegría/Flakoll have come a long way in the history of their literary representation. If at the beginning of their joint writing career in *Ashes of Izalco* the contrasting terms for them were house and plaza, and a kind of "illicit" eroticism behind closed doors right at the center of the oligarchic hearth—the resting place of the patriarch, a benevolent tyrant—it later became a conflict of the nation-state. If earlier the tension was between eroticism and obedience, a dilemma of choosing one of two men, then in their contemporary narrative the tension is between the state and the state-armed opposition. In the diary and in the novel, Woman was the space where sensual attraction and security battled each other, and where self-determination was an impertinence. Is it perhaps in the nature of the narrative protocol of those two genres to confine women into the areas of sexuality, both in the form of sensuality and in the form of economic (moral) security? Is it in the codes of testimonial literature to trace different parameters, to uncover other circuits for Woman? In testimonials woman must break, it seems, with the inner parameters of home and walk towards the plaza, where she dies giving orders.

I want to propose that the phrase "don't let them take us alive," is, then, a metaphor for women as well as for the new man, written by an international couple as a new mode of coupling. In a certain manner, however, this new narrative does not abandon all the previous narrative strands. It wrestles with questions coming from the former oligarchic horizon, such as the concepts of home and coupling. Security and honor, however, are put on a different shelf. Analogy and simile between former and latter are no longer possible. In other words, the Salvadoran woman in struggle transforms the husband into a lover, into a transitory and temporal relation, clandestine not within the bounds of the oligarchic home but within the larger space of the state. Men and love, as character and plot of romantic narratives, become lover and love, lover because he unconditionally loves. The pressure inflicted on woman as wife in the prison house of monogamy is transferred from the family to the state and from the house to the nation. The power of the father/husband is reconstituted as the repressive state apparatus.

The masses at the plaza and the masses as combatants are juxtaposed in Eugenia's essence. Eugenia and the masses are in their vulnerability and death one and the same. In dying, Eugenia occupies their subject position. But the masses in *Ashes of Izalco* and the masses in *They Won't Take Me Alive* are not the masses either. In the former the masses are Indians; in the latter, they are the organized army of the people, a *National Liberation Front.* A word on how the cultural story of the subaltern subverts official accounts of history is relevant; Alegría/Flakoll's testimonial constructs Eugenia as a subaltern, enclosing her in ever narrower circuits, enveloping her in the web of political commitment, having her chased, as the Indians, in the public spaces of the State.

The oligarchic mansions have vanished. Lordly ethics are also gone. Very humble abodes and circumscriptions, the collective narrow spaces of the poor, have come to replace old stately houses, old gentlemanly visions and sensibilities. The problems and questions concerning the Salvadoran oligarchy have been pushed to the edge and emerge only as Army (positivistic success), displaying its brutish face (positivistic failure). As Ranjit Guha (1988) argues in his definition of the subaltern, the problems of the petty-bourgeoisie are compatible with the problems of the people. Hence, the politics of a common front. Although the informants on Eugenia's life insist that only the people can liberate themselves, Eugenia's problems are located side by side with the problems of the teacher, the seamstress, the petty street merchant.

Nevertheless, as in *Ashes of Izalco*, the narrative of the constitution of the subaltern gendered subject is woven postmortem. In *They Won't Take Me Alive*, Eugenia dies at the hands of the repressive state apparatus. The voices of friends and family reconstruct her for us. Eugenia, like the "little man" in the insurgent narratives of Sergio Ramírez, traverses the text swiftly. In her constitution, she weaves together the path of the convergence of the revolutionary popular organizations. The social and political histories of the popular organizations—Federación Estudiantil Centro Amercana (FECCAS), Asociacion Nacional de Estudiantes (ANDES), Frente Unificado Social (FUS), Farabundo Marti Liberación Nacional-Frente Democrático Revolucionario (FMLN-FDR), Bloque Populae Revolucionario (BPR)—and the personal, conjugal, maternal life of the protagonist are one and the same. This is the sign of the first triumph of women in the text, a sign of their empowerment. The same is not true in male texts. In male texts struggle is a male condition and does not concern itself with houses/home but with mountain, city, and *montaña*. In those testimonials, Woman is an image, a *figura*; in this one she is not invoked, she is not a parenthesis, a dash adjoining montaña and home/hearth, the resting place of male heroism, an expression, a script, but rather an unequivocal center.

These confluences are not evident if the reading follows the script of politico-military narratives, which nevertheless retain their own allure. Only if the reader considers immersing herself in the romantic love plot, the romanticism and eroticism of the love story, does the overlapping of the two worlds uncover its seams. The very sparse description of surroundings, the lack of lyricism and metaphors, the prioritization of action over reflection, are rhetorical devices forcing us to come to terms with the swift and accelerated pace of Eugenia crossing the stage, plotting Eugenia more visibly and immediately as an insurgent military woman. The construction of suspense could make the reader lose sight of the reflective character of the narrative that constitutes women as a subject. Reflection is the thread taking her from home to garrison, from paternal obedience to organizational obedience, first eclesia and subsequently politics.

Woman disengages herself from the family to engage herself with the state, and in so doing, she also defends her rights to a fulfilling coupling, to an emotional relationship, principles which signal her femininity. A string of equally weighted words are proof: the banana for the daughter, bullets and machine guns, a kotex for a friend, her diapers and clothing, menstruation.

In the convergence of these "little" details, the firm hand of a woman writer is evident, as much as the male hand is evidenced in keeping the borders between concepts of the masculine and the feminine moving always in close contact and dialogue with the concept "men" as maleness decentered. Javier, Eugenia's compañero, is naturally the sketch around which the underscored protagonists are modeled. But in this sketch one can note observations on sharing responsibilities, "little" home chores. And in revising macro topics, those of the master narratives defining the generational discussion at large—social classes, electoral struggle, popular prolonged war, oligarchies, the foco theory, mass politics, vanguards—the difficulties of the compañera, her disbelief in her own capacity for leadership, are also incorporated. Thus, in the same way geography plots the history of these little towns and hamlets into the national history of El Salvador for national and international consumption, the Christian education of middle-class women and their struggle with these two distinct ways of being a man and a woman emerge.

In the trajectory from *Ashes of Izalco* to *They Won't Take Me Alive* I present the idea that Eugenia was always future: "Eugenia was never static, was never the same. She was always developing. Eugenia was always future" (59). In the long road from novel to testimonials, the authors posit the collective production of textuality as sexuality. They trespass the borders of the seigniorial house of the oligarchy as well as the borders of the plaza of the oligarchy, the better to leave a printed register of a moment in the reflexive thinking of the heterosexual couple in reference to patriotic/erotic insurgencies. In the momentary but important seizure of the urban social spaces, and in decentering the importance of the house for coupling, we note the triumph of the collective narratives of Alegría, Salvadoran, and Flakoll, North American. In their collaborative writing life, there is proof of the possibilities inherent in erotic/patriotic international common fronts.

WORKS CITED

Alegría, Claribel, and Darwin J. Flakoll. 1987. *They Won't Take Me Alive*. Trans. Amanda Hopkinson. London: Women's Press.

Carr, Robert. 1992. "Re-presentando el testimonio: notas sobre el cruce divisorio Primer Mundo/Tercer Mundo." *Revista de crítica literaria latinoamericana* 28/36: 73-94.

Che Guevara, Ernesto. 1972. *La guerra de guerrillas*. La Habana: Ciencias Sociales.

———. *El diario del Che en Bolivia*. 1968. La Habana: Instituto del Libro.

D'Souza, Dinesh. 1991. "I, Rigoberta Menchu. A Modern Study in Cultural Hypocrisy." *The Federalist Paper* (October 21): 2, 7.

Guha, Ranjit. 1988. "On Some Aspects of the Historiography of Colonial India." In *Selected Subaltern Studies*, ed. Guha Ranjit and Gayatri Spivak, 37-44.

Guha, Ranjit, and Gayatri Spivak, eds. 1988. *Selected Subaltern Studies*. Oxford: Oxford University Press.

MacKinnon, Catherine. 1987. *Feminism Unmodified. Discourses on Life and Law*. Cambridge: Harvard University Press.

Quinn, Sally. 1992. "Who Killed Feminism? Hypocritical Movement Leaders Betray Their Own Cause." *The Washington Post* (January 19): C1.

Ramírez, Sergio. 1991. *Confesión de amor*. Managua.

PART TWO

FEMINIST REPRESENTATIONS

T he essays in this section engage in a feminist dialogic. Although
each writer recognizes Alegría's conflation of the personal and
political as key to her feminism, the reader will encounter a
community of views, a polyphonic chorus of voices which recognize
in Alegría's writing a political resistance not unlike that of the North
American writers Maxine Hong Kingston, Toni Morrison, and Alice
Walker, resistance which valorizes women's ways of knowing and
telling what they know.

The reader of this section will encounter many feminisms
within a diversity of points of view and methodologies. Some of
these feminist revisions (Boschetto-Sandoval, Riess, Crosby), in the
tradition of French feminist theory, conjoin feminism and poststructuralism in focusing on the construction of (re)presentation and
subjectivity, as well as discourse. Others (Sternbach, Treacy,
McGowan) focus on extratextual resonances and the intersection of
texts with social, historical, political, and archetypal contexts, in the
tradition of Anglo-American feminist criticism. Yet even as we make
these distinctions, we find them suspect, as most of these essays bear
witness to cross-cultural community through combining various
theoretical approaches.

It is now widely acknowledged that the aim of feminist
criticism is not solely to interpret text, but to change readers' notions
of community by raising their consciousness and challenging their
relationship to what they read. Alegría's work, through representing
the lives of narrators who use political repression as a catalyst for
redefining themselves, encourages in her readers the development
of a collective consciousness. If the feminist as "resisting reader" has

grown used to assuming an oppositional position to the dominant male-language text, Alegría's resistance to patriarchal paradigms encourages in the reader a feeling of recognition, of affirmation. As the essays suggest, Alegría's texts operate in the spirit of Bakhtinian heteroglossia, identifying again and again new modes of interrelationships in opposition to prescribed hierarchical relationships that demand conformity to established social (patriarchal) epistemologies.

In her essay on *Ashes of Izalco*, Sternbach engages the problematized mother-daughter relationship of the female protagonists Isabel and Carmen. She reveals how for Carmen, "the act of reading . . . becomes the mirror by which her own life is read, reflected and untangled," and how, for the reader, the mother-daughter story also becomes the story of El Salvador written during the simultaneous eruption of the volcano Izalco and the Matanza. Sternbach comments on the fact that, not atypically, the story of a woman is ensnared in a man's text, just as the story of El Salvador is "trapped within the now silenced collective memory of its people." As Sternbach acknowledges, the gradual awakening of both Isabel and her daughter Carmen to a feminist consciousness in *Ashes of Izalco* forms an "axis" for developing self-awareness in Alegría's female protagonists in subsequent texts.

In addressing Alegría's *They Won't Take Me Alive*, Treacy, like Sternbach, problematizes motherhood. In the *testimonio* of Eugenia, Treacy contends, the guerilla attains heroic stature through her transformation of such archetypal female qualities as maternal love, self-sacrifice, and family-centeredness into "sources for revolutionary change." Archetypal symbols of womanhood and motherhood are so compelling in times of war that they become models for "lasting social transformation."

The essays by Boschetto-Sandoval and McGowan both focus on Alegría's hybrid prose/verse autobiographical novel *Luisa in Realityland*. Boschetto-Sandoval's essay examines the polyphonic and "quasi-testimonial" form of *Luisa* as feminist "reading lesson." Boschetto-Sandoval elucidates the manner in which the text invites us as readers to recognize textual practices and relationships that reflect the conjunction of feminist theory with praxis: relationships that not only "extend (our) community" but must also respond to changeable realities. McGowan addresses the redemptive power of *Luisa*, locating in it qualities of the female *Kunstlerroman*, and examining the extent to which Alegría, in constructing Luisa's subjectivity, is "writing a woman's life."

Riess's discussion of Latin American feminism in *Despierta, mi bien, despierta* (Awake, my love, awake) focuses on the dialogic relationships in the text between oral and written epistemologies and between the discourse of the social hierarchy and the protagonist Lorena's developing discourse. Like Boschetto-Sandoval, Riess emphasizes the role of the reader, who gains insight by engaging in the examination of discourse on both intratextual and extratextual levels.

Finally, Crosby reminds us that, like many of Alegría's protagonists, Ximena in "Family Album" is also struggling with a redefinition of self. Crosby traces the ways Alegría constructs Ximena's subjectivity "through her gender, class, ethnicity, family relationships, and access to language." As Alegría's texts through language, category, and theme fracture the paradigms of hegemonic discourse, so do the texts of the writers in this section, whose central concern is the how and why of the struggle for subjectivity of Alegría's female protagonists.

Claribel Alegría with her husband Darwin J. Flakoll, 1972.
(Courtesy Claribel Alegría.)

Claribel Alegría with the author Julio Cortázar, 1982.
(Courtesy Claribel Alegría.)

4

ENGENDERING THE FUTURE: *ASHES OF IZALCO* AND THE MAKING OF A WRITER

Nancy Saporta Sternbach

In her early novel, *Ashes of Izalco*, cowritten with her husband, Darwin Flakoll, Claribel Alegría develops the eclectic array of talents, anticipates all the genres she will later cultivate, and exhibits all the literary elements in this text that will appear in her future works. That is to say that the thematic, stylistic, generic, as well as structural concerns that she employs as a young writer here remain with her throughout her literary career. In such a reading, then, *Ashes of Izalco* is an early manifestation of the committed feminist and political poet who also lends her pen to fiction and testimony, and who metaphorically employs the tactic of a woman imprisoned in a man's text.[1] Thus, the imprisonment of women, their words and stories, parallels the political drama of Alegría's subtext, a country under siege by its own leaders.

In her own words, here is how the novel developed:

> *Cenizas* fue finalista del concurso Bibioteca Breve de Seix Barral en 1964 y se publicó por primera vez en España en 1967. Diez años más tarde, el dictador Molina de El Salvador, que ya se iba del poder, quiso quedar como un verdadero demócrata y autorizó al Ministerio de Educación para que publicara los libros de autores salvadoreños que a ellos les pareciera. Entre los asesores había dos muchachos de izquierda y decidieron publicar *Cenizas*. Como era libro publicado por el Ministerio, el Ministro ni siquiera lo leyó

pero sí consintió en que fuera obligatorio en secundaria.
Todos los estudiantes de último año tenían que leerlo y
comentarlo. . . . El libro lleva ya como quince ediciones en
El Salvador y realmente casi todos los salvadoreños que saben
leer lo han leído.

Un muchacho, a quien mi marido y yo entrevistamos el
año pasado para un libro que publicamos sobre la represión
en las cárceles salvadoreñas nos contaba que nuestro libro era
de los *poquísimos* que entraban a la cárcel y todos lo leían y
comentaban. (Alegría 1985)

(*Ashes* was a finalist in the Biblioteca Breve competition
sponsored by Seix Barral in 1964 and was first published in
Spain in 1967. Ten years later, the Salvadoran dictator Molina,
who was stepping down, wanted to be remembered as truly
democratic so he authorized the Ministry of Education to
publish the books by Salvadoran authors that they thought
most appropriate. Among the evaluators were two young
leftists and they published *Ashes*. Since it was a book
published by the Ministry, they never even bothered to read
it, but they did agree to make it a requirement in secondary
school. Every senior had to read it and comment on it. . . .
The book now has about 15 editions in El Salvador and really
any Salvadoran who knows how to read has read it.

Then, last year we learned from someone who my
husband and I interviewed for a book about the repression in
Salvadoran jails, that our book was among the *very few* that
entered the jail and that everyone read it and commented on
it.)

As Alegría makes evident in this 1985 declaration, even twenty years
earlier the political motifs that characterize contemporary Salvadoran
life were already visible. In the text, that politicization alternates and
intertwines the narration among three brewing stories: the eruption
of the volcano Izalco; the 1932 Matanza, a political event that had
traumatized the young Alegría; and the now-disclosed story of the
love affair between the protagonist's mother and the North American,
Frank. The trauma of the massacre is actualized in literary terms as
the narrator attempts a resolution to the conflicts represented in her
personal memory as well as in the collective memory of the country,

both of which visit her like angry ghosts. This meeting point and playing field for all these issues erupts in the problematized mother-daughter relationship.

The bourgeois Salvadoran protagonist, Carmen, married to a North American and resident of Washington, D.C., returns to her native country for her mother's funeral. By means of a literary object, a diary containing several letters written by Frank, the narrator is able to untangle a little-known past, both of her mother and her country. Likewise, the reading of this diary, which is her only inheritance from her mother, serves as the structural axis of the novel, since the reading itself is what triggers the unveiling, unknotting, recuperation, and recovery of her mother's story and her country's story. The act of reading, then, becomes the mirror by which her own life is read, reflected, and untangled. By the same token, through the simultaneity of the three events, Carmen's story and her mother's story also become the story of El Salvador.

Thus we encounter the first of Alegría's feminist motifs in the novel, ideas which will continue and crystallize in all her future work. In 1964 it was revolutionary enough just to write about the Matanza, but to claim that women count enough so that their stories really are the stories of their countries allows us to examine women's roles in the formation of national states. Likewise, in those years of the "feminine mystique," women's discontent with what was considered to be a good life was only beginning to be articulated. By placing women's discontent in both the U.S. and Salvadoran context, through Carmen and her mother, Isabel, the narrator not only universalizes the problem, but allows it to cut through class boundaries as well.

Equally important is the fact that the diary, the text we read, is already framed within the text of the original novel. Thus the narrator, a woman, shows us that the only way to truly learn a country's history is through its family documents, those often-considered "feminine" objects almost always left in a woman's safekeeping, almost always considered too trivial for the "true" business of the country. The mother's reasons for leaving the diary to her daughter are not actually apparent or obvious, so that even though the diary forms a structural axis of the novel, it also permits the narrator to question her mother's motives, to understand her mother outside the maternal role, and more importantly to give birth to a new model: woman as reader and, therefore, interpreter and inventor of her own reality. That is to say that the mother's legacy of the written word permits the daughter first to question who she is and then to rewrite herself in her own image and according to her own ideas. At first, she wonders

> Por qué me dejó mamá este diario, este cuaderno amarillo, escrito de prisa, tachos, con la tinta desteñida, después de treinta años? . . . ¿Qué la impulsó, después de haber guardado el secreto todos estos años, a entregármela así, sin palabras, sin explicaciones, como un golpe repentino en la cara a través de la tumba? (Alegría and Flakoll 1966, 123)

> Why did she leave me this diary, this yellowing notebook with its hasty, inked scrawlings now faded after thirty years? . . . worn with much handling and rereading. What moved her, after holding the secret all these years, to pass this to me wordlessly, with no explanation, like a sudden slap in the face from the other side of the grave?) (Alegría and Flakoll 1989, 121[2]

Indeed, the reader, too, questions why the mother would leave the diary for her daughter. After all, it was not even her own diary, but that of a North American white male whose initial contact with the country is to exoticize it. Here is where Alegría's future metaphors begin, for we learn that Isabel (and her story) are trapped within Frank's story. We learn that El Salvador's story is trapped within the now silenced collective memory of its people. As we see here, sometimes it is the outsider who is able to initiate and to trigger the process of memory.

When questioned about how she, the writer, was able to *un*silence the story of the Matanza, Alegría tells us that she found three newspaper clippings hidden in her father's library that enabled her to reconstruct the event.[3] Until then, Alegría claims, there was absolutely no documentation about it thanks to the round of dictators whose efforts produced a national amnesia. Therefore, in much the same way that her father's newspaper clippings help to produce the novel for the author, so, too, do the existence and survival of family texts such as Frank's diary help to reconstruct history, shake memories, and ultimately recreate national episodes that had been erased. Thus Frank's diary serves two purposes in the text, for it tells two secret stories: one is the transgression of a married woman and the other is the recuperation of national history. Wolff, both in his role as sole witness to the simultaneous eruption of the volcano Izalco and the rising of the peasants and as the protagonist in the mother's secret love affair, becomes a privileged narrator who shares his knowledge with the reader. Yet the confluence of all this information reaches an ardent crescendo at the moment that Frank understands that he has also created a fiction of his own life and its possibilities. It is here that the narrator, as reader, also feels the need to examine her own life. Frank's epiphany also motivates the narrator to question her comfort and privilege.

In the town of Santa Ana, the site of many events in Alegría's fiction and poetry and therefore both a real and fictitious place, everything seems normal if we observe it only on the most superficial level, as in her poem "Todo es normal en nuestro patio" (Everything is normal in our patio). However, one of Alegría's trademarks has become the representation of that space just underneath the surface where life is more problematic and complex. In Alegría's text volcanic metaphors inform her readers of another revolution being prepared: that of a woman who begins to take the reins to control her own freedom and destiny. This is why the silences that characterize the relationships within the family are not indicators of having nothing to say, but rather eloquent pauses that signal the force and strength of the bourgeois way of life in the town, including "la hora de los chismes" (79) (gossip hour), a pastime simultaneouly trivialized for its bourgeois monotony and significant for the information it imparts about the town's inhabitants. Thus the silence that revolves around the relationship between Isabel, the mother, and Frank, the journal writer, serves as a kind of bridge between social, cultural, and political relations of the country on the one hand, and the private and intimate life of the daughter on the other. The act of reading the diary, then, engages the protagonist, Carmen, and challenges her to embark upon a path of self-knowledge. Ironically, it was the same path that had led her mother to become such a dreamer. It was the monotony of the town, the limitation of movement imposed on women that had turned the mother inward, to become a "ratón de biblioteca" (112) (bookworm). That inner life, so often women's salvation, had led the mother to a world of exotic sophistication, but a fantasy world all the same. When in real life, a real and true escape becomes available to her, she is so convinced that she cannot do it that she lets it go by. All her suppressed and repressed dreams then become the daughter's inheritance.

Throughout the text, the reader encounters the classic theme of a mother wishing a better life for her daughter, of being able to provide for her what she herself could not have. The daughter too is a woman nourished by reading, and not only of the diary. As a child, Carmen's mother read Santa Teresa's poems to her (Alegría and Flakoll 1989, 30), and her father recited verses from Rubén Darío, as if in preparation for her future vocation: to become a poet (Alegría and Flakoll 1989, 29). Both women become faithful readers of Frank's diary. Perhaps because we cannot know the mother's reaction to it, the daughter's interpretation is all the more provocative. What we do learn is how much value Isabel placed on it: "Las páginas están gastadas de tanto manosearlas, de tanto ser releídas (123) (The pages are dog-eared, worn from so much handling and rereading) (121).

When Frank arrives in Santa Ana, escaping a life he had invented and rejected, he seems to do everything to contradict the significance of his name. He is anything but honest when he introduces himself to the town as a novelist of Mayan stories. His presence in El Salvador permits him to create a story other than his own, a history based on success, rather than the real one drowned in alcoholism and failure. The diary, on yet another level, permits him to create a text, a fiction, that at the same time helps another person, the narrator, to untangle her own fiction and to separate it from the real and authentic. Frank's fictionalizing goes beyond his own life; he also converts the lush landscape of El Salvador in general, and of Santa Ana in particular, to a paradise on Earth. For him, they become the garden of Eden. He writes, "La vegetación exuberante y verde que se veía desde el tren, los conos volcánicos en el horizonte prometían un paraíso tropical" (65) (The lush green vegetation visible from the train window, the volcanic cones on the horizon, promised an exotic tropical paradise) (63).

The chronological time of the writing of the novel corresponds to the years of the incipient Peace Corps, and there is much in the attitude of the three North American men in the text that recalls the objectification of another culture by the United States. In Frank's case, for example, his initial exoticized exuberance for the country permits him to equate it with a tropical Garden of Eden;

later, once the romance with the country and the woman have ended, he manages to convert this paradise into his personal hell, a world turned upside-down. The paradise had never existed, he concludes, except in his own imagination.

As a result of reading the diary, the narrator/protagonist also begins to fantasize her own story. For this reason, the novel is written on two time levels: Frank's life in 1931 and Carmen's in 1962. Each time she reads Frank's words from thirty years earlier, the narrator identifies with his search: "niño extraviado . . . irónico e introvertido que perdió de mala gana su inocencia. Ya la perdí también" (57) (a lost child; irony adds the precocious cynicism of a child who had set aside his innocence reluctantly) (56). The original Spanish also includes a final comment from Carmen central to my point here and missing from the English version of the text: "I lost mine too." For him, that loss consisted in arriving in Santa Ana, earthly paradise, for her, just the opposite, leaving Santa Ana, earthly hell. What connects each of them to his or her search is Isabel, Frank's lover and Carmen's mother, who beckons the former while abetting the latter in her escape:

> Cómo pudo aguantar mamá? Todo está igual que antes y peor. Todo ha ido en declive; no pasa nada en Santa Ana. Los días, los meses, los años no significan nada, nada. . . . Nada en qué ocupar las horas. . . . Un mundito ciego sobre otro mundo estrecho y más munditos sofocantes abajo: los siete círculos devastadores de Santa Ana en la quietud de su infierno. (72)

> How could Mother stand it? Everything is the same as it always was. Worse. Everything is sliding away, wearing out; nothing ever happens. Days, months, years don't mean a thing; there still isn't a single bookstore, theatre, or restaurant. Nothing to do but drink, if you're a man, or gossip and complain about servants if you're a woman. One little blind world on top of other narrow, choked worlds below: the seven, self-destroying circles of Santa Ana forming a motion-less inferno. (70)

Yet Santa Ana is not only a hell for Frank and Carmen. With the eruption of Izalco and the peasant uprising they, too, experience its hellishness on another level. Although Frank's initial encounter with the town is with the ingenuousness of any gringo in love with the tropics, at the novel's end, he too understands its hellish or diabolical underside. Finally, he sees that Satan's mark is stronger than his love for Isabel. The figurative hell of Santa Ana becomes a real one with the eruption of the volcano. Finally, Frank sees the town as Isabel did and Carmen will, that is, as the "center of hell" (Alegría and Flakoll 1966, 155):

> No es sólo que Santa Ana sea un pequeño rincón del infierno; se trata de algo más importante, del que de que sus fundadores trajeron con ellos la semilla de miedos inmemoriales, de prejuicios endémicos que se trasmiten por la sangre, que se absorben con la leche materna. (147)

> It is not merely that Santa Ana is a small, undeveloped corner of Hell, but even more important is the fact that its settlers brought to it the seeds of immemorial fears and prejudices — the kind that seem to be transmitted through the blood, absorbed along with mother's milk. (145)

Like other works by Alegría, this novel, too, can be read as a political mediation. As Central Americans, Carmen and her mother represent or symbolize the Central America that struggles for its freedom and autonomy, while the three North American male characters, Paul (Carmen's husband), Virgil (the evangelistic precursor), and Frank can be read as a representation of the political, cultural, military and even religious presence that the United States has exercised in the region. Each presence wields a kind of power over the region that mirrors the way in which differing North Americans have approached their relationship with Central America. The Carmen-Paul dynamic borders on the military:

> Cuando nos vamos de vacaciones o hacemos cualquier cosa fuera de nuestra rutina, Paul insiste en planearla como si tratase de una operación militar . . . no hay nada espontáneo . . . estoy casada con el *"perfect organization man."* ¿y qué remedio hay para eso? (27)

When we go on vacation or do anything outside our normal
routine, Paul plans it like a military operation. He enjoys that
more than doing the thing itself. . . . I'm married to the
Perfect Organization Man. And what remedy is there for that?
(27)

Frank, on the other hand, is likened to an early hippy on the
gringo trail, the route that so many would take during the sixties and
seventies in search of the exotic, in order to escape Nixon's politics,
in order to "find" themselves anywhere but at home. Nevertheless,
despite what may have been his good intention, his earlier foray into
the Sierras of California in search of gold likens him to a conquista-
dor, and he never really loses that aspect of his character either. His
relationship with Isabel, his assumption that he could offer her a
better life, his unquestioning position of supposed superiority, all
speak to the kind of presence that North Americans have sustained
in the region, and which Alegría and Flakoll have later documented
in their historical and testimonial work. Yet at the same time, Alegría
and Flakoll tacitly suggest that Frank may have some redeeming
qualities and that alliances are possible between Central Americans
and North Americans, an idea that underpins much of their later
collaborative work.

Virgil is another story altogether. With him the authors
envision a future of Central America dominated by monolingual
English-dominant evangelist veterinarians who have more time for
animals than for people. With chilling precision they point to the
connection between the idealistic wanderer (Frank) and the religious
interloper. While Frank is busy investigating Mayan ruins, thus
confirming the pre-Hispanic past of the region, Virgil's actions uproot
their present by stripping them of their own religion, so inextricably
linked to their Mayan past. It is, however, Frank's role as lover that
truly intervenes in the text, for if we turn the roles around, we see
that Frank becomes the catalyst by which Isabel, and then Carmen,
can discover their sexuality.

By means of their sexual autonomy, these women serve as
precursors to Alegría's later works where a woman's political and
feminist consciousness coincide. Indeed, it is the confluence of these
two ways of thought in her women protagonists that has characterized almost all of Alegría's subsequent texts. These women,
protagonists also of *Album familiar* (Family album) and *Despierta,*

mi bien, despierta (Awake, my love, awake), who have chosen and had the privilege of choosing a comfortable life of the well-to-do class outside their Central American nations, do not represent a political exile, but rather feel complacent with their washing machines and other technological advances available only to the elite of their country. In Alegría's narratives, she often interjects an abrupt change in their lives, whether it is a return to their native country, a visit from a politically active cousin, or the love affair with a revolutionary that literally shakes the ground the woman walks upon. For this reason, the metaphor of the erupting volcano is so often present in these works, whether fiction or poetry. For that reason, *Ashes of Izalco* is so representative of what would come later. In this case, it is often the political awakening of the bourgeois woman as she establishes herself as a woman and a citizen of Central America. What is clear is that in her strategy, Alegría is attempting to dismantle the values of the dominant class and oligarchy, thus showing that the revolution must be the result of the change of consciousness of all social classes. Nor is it insignificant that Alegría positions social and political change in the hands of women. In so doing, as she suggested earlier in *Ashes of Izalco*, she not only accords women their full role as citizens, but at the same time indicates that any revolution worthy of that name must also include a reorganization in the social construction of gender.

Carmen's self-conscious questioning of her position, as well as her political awareness, Isabel's sexual awakening, and their gradual awareness of a feminist consciousness form the axis of Alegría's work after this novel as well. Most of her female protagonists will share this preoccupation with a woman's situation and gradually use their feminist awareness as the optic by which they view all social and political history. Of course this leads to their questioning of the very circumstances of their personal lives, thereby destabilizing the apparently neat and ordered relationships that characterize their marriages.

To contrast further the effect of the change, Alegría often situates these women in a fog that we might call "before the volcano." None of them has been prepared for the explosion or confrontation that the change ultimately requires, for in all cases it is precisely that situation which makes them take a stand. For example, realizing the revolutionary struggle of their people helps them to recognize their own previous ignorance as well as to realize their own role in the struggle. For this reason, perhaps, the class struggle in Alegría's works often takes place within the confines of the family. The protagonist's new awareness often finds itself in direct conflict with her father, brother, or husband, as in *Despierta, mi bien, despierta*. For this reason, the protagonist understands that her liberation as a woman is inextricably linked to the liberation of her country. By freeing herself of her sexist husband, for example, she becomes aware of his role as a butcher in the murder of innocent people, a revelation that alienates her from him and his values at the same time that it leads her closer to the liberation struggle. The fact that this awakening of the protagonist in almost all of Alegría's work is framed by another story—a love story, past or present; the appearance of ghosts; the magical quality of life—also conflates the personal with the political, one of Alegría's trademarks.

In *Ashes of Izalco*, the presence of the diary, along with its political and symbolic importance, anticipates the use that Alegría will later make of the written word as a woman's testament. In the complicated relationship between Luisa and the gypsy in *Luisa en el país de la realidad* (Luisa in Realityland), the latter, by fomenting the literary and creative talents of the young Luisa, also inspires her to take note of the written word by dictating love poems to her "en un cuaderno que era especial para eso" (22) (in a special notebook she kept by her bedside [17].) These two techniques, to take note of the words of another woman through her conversation and to tell stories through the appearance of familiar objects such as diaries and photograph albums, have begun to take on a great symbolic importance in Alegría's works. More importantly, however, they prefigure the same technique that Alegría and Flakoll will use in testimonial literature such as *No me agarran viva* (*They won't take me alive*) and *Para romper el silencio* (*To break the silence*). These last works show how the objects themselves begin to act as if they had their own life, thereby enacting a metamorphosis through circumstances. When, for example, the face of her activist cousin becomes erased from the album of family photos in *Album familiar*, Lorena, the protagonist, not only knows that he has fallen, but also that now it is her responsibility to replace him in the struggle against the Somoza regime.

Structurally, the novel *Ashes of Izalco* also prefigures the way in which Alegría, whether writing solely or with Flakoll, makes productive use of silences, converts them into metaphors, and

71

recreates them so that they signify a world of myths, women's untold tales and political history. In the novel, the reader must be prepared to style her or his own story from the fragments, for the writers continually interrupt one story with another, allow one layer or sediment of it to flow into another, and disconnect rather than join all the pieces. But what could be more effective in the telling of El Salvador's history than this device? If one of the purposes of testimonial literature is to break silences, Alegría's own prose anticipates broken fragments and silences in *Ashes* that will later be used metaphorically in *No me agarran viva*. Similarly, the polyvocal narrator of *Ashes* anticipates the rebuilding and reconstructing of the story in the testimonial text, where the authors first tell us the story of the protagonist's death and then go on to reconstuct her life based on the stories that others tell about her. In the same manner that this technique was so effective in retelling the story in *Ashes*, here, too, it serves to rebuild a nation's history by disclosing its secrets. In each case, it is as if Alegría (either alone or in her collaboration with Flakoll) begins with what appears to be a straightforward story and then unwraps it layer by layer to reveal a deeper truth, one that allows multiple interpretations and lends itself to multiple readings.

In the twenty years that separate *Ashes of Izalco* from *Luisa in Realityland*, with the important publication of *Sobrevivo* (which includes her famous poem "Flores del volcán" [Flowers from the volcano] right in the chronological middle), Alegría has shown that not only has she learned to live with her dead, but her personal evolution now includes knowing how to celebrate them. While the early works can tend to be on the sad, hermetic, or pessimistic side, imbued with trauma and horror, the more recent ones confirm the fact that literature, that so-called esoteric and elite form of communication, was actually responsible for helping the writer shake away her dead from her own being. I do not merely mean to imply that Alegría's dead have learned how to console her, or that she has learned to take consolation from them. Rather, what all Alegría's works signify is that the struggle of her dead will not have been in vain, they will not have sacrificed themselves gratuitously, if the indignation is public and international, if the world knows of the atrocities committed in that small corner of the world known as El Salvador, the place Frank calls "minúsculo y absurdo" (41), an "absurd little country" (39). For this reason, perhaps in Alegría's prose and poetry she continues to name her dead. By so doing she keeps them alive. By pronouncing their names, the dead of El Salvador live beyond their physical bodies. In this process, Alegría not only converts the voices of the dead into living texts, but also points the way to a new vision of the future where women's voices *are* the voices of their countries. Indeed she has envisioned a future where there is equality among classes and races as well as between genders.

NOTES

1. I am grateful to my student, Christa Mariner, for her paper on the novel which led to this insight.

2. In the remainder of the text, Spanish quotations refer to the Spanish edition (1966) and English quotations refer to the English translation (1989).

3. Interview with Claribel Alegría, April 1986.

WORKS CITED

Alegría, Claribel. 1984. *Album familiar.* 2nd ed. San José, Costa Rica: Editorial Universitaria Centroamericana (UCA).
———. 1985. Correspondence with the author. 13 November.
———. 1986. *Despierta, mi bien, despierta.* San Salvador: UCA (Universidad Centroamericana) Editores.
———. 1977. "El detén." Barcelona: Editorial Lumen.
———. 1982. *Flowers from the Volcano/ Flores del volcán.* Pittsburgh: University of Pittsburgh Press.
———. 1987a. *Luisa en el país de la realidad.* México: Joan Boldó i Climent, Editores. Universidad Autónoma de Zacatecas.
———. 1987b. *Luisa in Realityland.* Trans. Darwin Flakoll. Willimantic, Conn.: Curbstone Press.
———. 1978. *Sobrevivo.* La Habana: Casa de las Américas.
Alegría, Claribel, and Darwin J. Flakoll. 1989. *Ashes of Izalco.* Trans. Darwin J. Flakoll. Willimantic, Conn.: Curbstone Press.
———. 1966. *Cenizas de Izalco.* Barcelona: Seix Barral.

————. 1983. *Nicaragua: La revolución sandinista*. México: Ediciones Era.

————. 1983. *No me agarran viva: La mujer salvadoreña en lucha*. México: Ediciones Era.

————. 1984. *Para romper el silencio: Resistencia y lucha en las cárceles salvadoreñas*. México: Ediciones Era.

————. 1987. *They Won't Take Me Alive*. Trans. Amanda Hopkinson. London: Women's Press.

5

CREATION OF THE WOMAN WARRIOR:
CLARIBEL ALEGRÍA'S *THEY WON'T
TAKE ME ALIVE*

Mary Jane Treacy

F or over thirty years Latin American revolutionaries have turned to guerrilla warfare to transform their societies. Although recent changes in world politics as well as openings in Latin American political systems have reduced the number of active guerrilla groups, the revolutionary culture these fighters inspired remains to bear witness to their ideals of social justice and desire to create a new world. From the famous face of Che Guevara and the silhouette of Sandino which beckon from posters to the protest songs and literature that recall the confrontations of the 1960s and 1970s, Latin American popular and high culture is reworking the image of its heroes, its history of violent social conflict, and the legacy of revolution for all the people of the region.

One genre that has emerged since 1970 is the testimonial narrative, a retelling of events by a participant or witness to them. As John Beverley and Mark Zimmerman (1990, 173) point out, these are not just any events, but rather those that comprise "a story that needs to be told—involving a problem of repression, poverty, subalternity, exploitation, or simply struggle for survival, which is implicated in the act of narration itself." *Testimonio* is part of a literature of resistance that attempts to "speak the truth" and stand in opposition to the falsified accounts presented by hegemonic, often counterrevolutionary, culture. Not surprisingly, several real life guerrilleros have taken up the pen to describe their experiences fighting government troops. Going beyond Guevara's field notes in *Reminiscences of the Cuban Revolutionary War* and his Bolivian diaries, the Nicaraguan Omar Cabezas (1982) and the Guatemalan Mario Payeras (1985) reveal what has been hidden away from public view: what life is like in the remote mountains or jungle, how men cope with physical hardships, how they adjust to dependence upon one another, sexual deprivation and hunger, anger and isolation, and killing the enemy. These guerrillero writers, as well as journalists who join guerrilla groups in order to write about their experiences later, attempt to reveal the humanity of the dedicated fighters who are shown with all their flaws as they slog through days of very unheroic marches and battles with nature.[1] The triumphs here are most often small and personal rather than epic tales of military triumph.

In spite of the fact that women have been joining guerrilla groups in increasing numbers since the 1960s—current estimates suggest that women made up at least 30 percent of the Salvadoran Frente Farabundo Martí para la Liberación Nacional (FMLN) and perhaps as high a percentage are involved in Peru's Shining Path—*guerrilleras* have not written autobiographical accounts of their training, fighting, or daily life in urban or rural guerrilla camps.[2] Until these women have the interest, time, and safety to speak their own truths, we have to rely on others to tell their stories. To date the majority of these "storytellers" have been either Latin American leftist men who extoll the guerrillera's self-sacrifice or foreign progressive women who emphasize the guerrillera's dedicated struggle against a corrupt state and sexist culture.

Latin American revolutionary culture has cultivated a potent image of the woman warrior since the 1960s, perhaps beginning with the idealization of "Tania," the German-Argentine Tamara Bunke who accompanied Guevara to Bolivia and died there with him, creating a symbol of a new woman who would combine traditional feminine beauty with the masculine power endowed by her gun.[3] As Daniel Viglietti demonstrates in his song dedicated to the Tupamara of Uruguay, the guerrillera is loved for her rebellion against restrictive sex roles, but she is celebrated only insofar as she remains a symbol, asks nothing for herself, and places her newly won freedoms at the service of the *patria* (fatherland).

La muchacha de mirada clara
cabello corto
la que salió en los diarios
no sé su nombre, no sé su nombre
Pero la nombro: primavera.

Estudiante que faltaba a clase
yo la recuerdo,
la que dijo la radio
dijo su sombra, dijo su sombra
Pero la veo: compañera.

Caminante que borra sus pasos
yo no la olvido
la que no dijo nada,
dijo mi patria, dijo mi patria. . .
Pero yo digo, guerrillera.

La que sabe todas las esquinas
parques y plazas
la que la gente quiere
aunque no digan, aunque no digan . . .
Pero yo digo, mujer entera.

Pero la nombro: Primavera
Pero la veo: Compañera
Pero yo digo: Mujer entera
Pero yo grito: Guerrillera.[4]

(The girl with the clear gaze
Short hair
Who was in the papers
I don't know her name, I don't know her name
But I call her Springtime.

The student who cut class
I remember her
The one the radio mentioned
Talked of her shadow, talked of her shadow
But I see her: Compañera.

77

Traveler who erases her steps
I don't forget her
The one who said nothing
said my country (fatherland), said my country . . .
But I say: guerrilla fighter.

The one who knows all the street corners
The parks and the plazas
The one the people love
Even though they don't say so, don't say so
But I say: real woman.

But I call her: Springtime
But I see her: Compañera
But I say: Real Woman
But I shout: Guerrilla Fighter.)   [translation mine]

Some ten years later, the Nicaraguan songwriter Carlos Mejía
Godoy repeats the same praise of the guerrillera's springlike
sensuality and her willingness to shift loyalty from one man to the
greater, masculine nation state.

Lovely girl of the FSLN
with your boots and pants of drill
machine gun in hand
your long flowing hair
that grew in the month of April.

You left your lover
to begin another relation
for your true love
is not he but another
it's the love of an entire nation.[5]

Women sympathizers of revolutionary causes are less likely to
imagine nameless, faceless beauties whose association with fertility
adds a sort of mystic hope to a political movement than to talk with
real women in the guerrilla and publish their interviews in magazines
and books.[6] Thanks to these texts, we learn that the guerrilleras are
proud of developing their physical strength, are confident leaders of

men and women, and are quick to address any sexism that emerges in their units. We see that they have skills and ambition to continue working after the revolution, they have or plan to have heterosexual relationships based on equality and shared responsibilities in the family, and they want to have children or to be reunited with the children they already have. Indeed, since some or all of these elements are present in every dialogue with a guerrillera, they appear to be formal features of an almost generic counterhegemonic female life story. That is, they reveal less about the guerrillera herself than about the story she is expected to tell or the story her listeners make sure to hear. Because most of the interviews with guerrilleras are so short, there are few other comments to elaborate, contradict, or problematize the expected story. As a result, guerrilleras from different countries and engaged in quite different struggles seem to blend together into one collective voice.

Claribel Alegría, writing with Darwin Flakoll, was the first Latin American woman to dedicate a full-length book to the exploration of one guerrillera's life. Their *No me agarran viva: La mujer salvadoreña en lucha* (1983) (*They Won't Take Me Alive* [1987]) is both a biography of Ana María Castillo Rivas, also known as Eugenia (1950-1981), and a testimonio by friends and family that charts the young woman's transformation from a middle-class religious girl to committed revolutionary. Like the more common autobiographical testimonio, this biographical collage of testimonios has a specific political purpose: to create a guerrillera who is exceptional enough to be a modern hero and common enough to represent all women involved in political resistance.[7] As Alegría makes clear in her prologue, she intends to give us a Eugenia who is both "modelo ejemplar" (an example) and "caso típico y no excepcional de tantas mujeres salvadoreñas que han dedicado sus esfuerzos, e incluso sus vidas, a la lucha por la liberación de su pueblo" (1983, 9) (a typical and not exceptional case of so many Salvadoran women who have dedicated their efforts, even their lives, to the struggle for the liberation of their people), that is, a woman the reader can both admire and hope to emulate.[8]

It soon becomes clear that, like the songwriters who idealize an abstract woman warrior, Alegría is about the business of creating myth. As collector of testimonios and biographer, Alegría provides little more than an overview of Ana María's life and includes no photographs which could make the guerrillera's existence distinguishable from that of many others. And while the political nature of testimonial narrative does preclude, as Beverley and Zimmerman (1990) point out, celebration of an individual bourgeois hero in favor of a representative of a social movement, Alegría tells far less about Ana María than that which is revealed in the more famous testimonios of Domitila Barrios de Chungara and Rigoberta Menchú. Whereas in these latter texts the narrator/protagonist claims singularity within the collective as she tells of her formative experiences, Ana María unfortunately cannot speak for herself, and her friends, perhaps thrown into the role of eulogizing the dead woman, seem reluctant to deviate from the generic guerrillera life story. Therefore Ana María's story belongs to any and almost every woman who follows the guerrilla path toward revolution.

If guerrillera life stories seem the same, it is because they contain the stories and symbols these rebel women use to make sense of the revolution and their place in it. French specialist in oral history Marie-Francoise Chanfrault-Duchet (1991, 81) suggests that every life story contains identifiable narrative models taken from literary forms that have been disseminated throughout a particular society by means of literature, oral tradition, television, and other forms of popular entertainment. Moreover, these narrative models provide myths or culturally specific archetypes that "allow speakers to communicate—in social terms—the meaning they want to give to their experience." In the case of *They Won't Take Me Alive*, it is Alegría and her interlocutors rather than Ana María who establish the narrative models to explain the guerrillera's life. However, since the models and the myths they offer emerge from a culture and represent a semiological system that culture has developed to understand the world, it may be that Ana María herself would concur. Surely her husband Javier, who asked Alegría to write this biography of his dead wife, appears to have been pleased with this veiled—almost impersonal—story of her life.

Chanfrault-Duchet explains that women's life stories tend to be organized around two interconnected axes: one referring to collective history, the other to the individual's history. So too Alegría presents two intertwined narratives of Ana María's life: one focusing on her emergence into the public sphere as a revolutionary and participant in a heroic battle for social justice and the other marking her personal development into an example of "abnegación" (abnegation) and "sacrificio" (sacrifice) (1983, 9).[9]

80

Alegría makes use of an epic model to present Ana María as heroine. Like so many male warriors before her, Ana María is called upon to leave home, to do battle against the forces of evil, and to contribute to the well-being of society through her deeds and example. The story of her life tells us that she was born into a progressive bourgeois family of anti-Somocista dissidents living in El Salvador. Her childhood appears to have been quite ordinary, except that her father was both extremely religious and devoted to social justice. We are told two things about him: that he took his family to mass in the shantytowns so that the children would be aware of the poverty in their midst, and that he saved a drowning child, then immediately suffered a heart attack and died, sacrificing his life for another in need. Thus Ana María can be seen to have been educated in the spirit of love and dedication to others, while her own work in Catholic youth groups taught her discipline and teamwork. She hears the standard call to heroic adventure while at the university. There she meets Marxist-Leninist revolutionaries, politicizes her moral commitment to the poor through class analysis, and immediately recognizes the need for armed struggle. Since for all heroes, this call into the public sphere demands a leaving "home," so too Ana María must leave her family's house to go underground and begin her political education. Yet there is more here, for young Ana María has had to sever permanently her ties to family and to a feminine domestic sphere—what Alegría calls "el seno del hogar" (the heart of the home) (1983, 34)—due to conflict with her mother over her political activity.[10] She is left to align herself with the revolution, an act that is consecrated by her acceptance of a nom de guerre that erases any connection to her origins or to her new husband. Ana María becomes simply Eugenia.

Unlike traditional heroines who sally forth to change the world, Eugenia is a woman educated in a traditional society that expects women to be nurturing, maternal, domestic rather than martial. To be sure, Alegría celebrates Eugenia's rebellion against the state and the ruling classes: she renounces bourgeois materialism, organizes peasants, engages in guerrilla activities. However, this behavior has a transgressive potential that threatens not only the oppressors of the people but also the gender arrangements of the people themselves. Women break out of masculine protection and live on their own; wives demand that their husbands take second place to the revolution; mothers make bombs and learn to shoot guns; mothers leave their children. Women fight. Women kill. The guerrillera, who most often says nothing about sexual politics, in practice challenges firmly held beliefs in an inherently passive or maternal female nature just as she uses political commitments to transcend male domination and the limits of traditional family life.

Alegría attempts to resolve the tensions of sexual difference implicit in the hybrid nature of the woman warrior by emphasizing a specifically female heroism: that is, she has the guerrillera transform self-sacrifice, maternal love, and dedication to family into sources for revolutionary change. She gives to the reader women who identify more as mothers than as fighters. Ana Guadalupe Martínez (a famous leader who wrote *The Secret Jails of El Salvador* [Las cárceles clandestinas de El Salvador] based on her prison experiences) reveals in *They Won't Take Me Alive* that women commanders like herself want large families of eight or more children, and goes on to state her belief that all women want children: "[y]o creo que todas las mujeres aspiramos a tener hijos y bastantes" (1983, 100) (I believe that all of us women want to have children, and plenty of them [109]).[11] For these women, motherhood is a revolutionary act that supports their opposition to the government.[12] Nadia explains that social conditions in El Salvador are so bad that a mother is faced with the obligation to take part in a liberation struggle in order to have the moral authority to raise her own child and to create a good society for all children.

> En condiciones de guerra y en el sistema que vive nuestro país, yo como madre no puedo velar sólo por un niño, hay millones de niños en el país. Incluso, pienso yo que ante mi propio hijo no tendría solvencia moral para educarlo, si no participo directamente en la liberación de mi pueblo. Sería una hipócrita que está colaborando con el estado de cosas del país. (99)

> Under the war conditions and system imposed on our country, I don't feel my concern as a mother is restricted simply to one child, there are millions of children in the country. I even believe that I wouldn't have the moral qualifications to educate my son with, if I weren't directly taking part in my people's liberation. It's an act of hypocrisy to collaborate in the way things are in this country. (108)

Given this emphasis on a "feminine" heroism, Alegría does not show Eugenia roaming and fighting battles, conquering territories, or other activities usually associated with the male hero. Indeed, she does not describe Eugenia's military training and permits few vague references to her participation in violent deeds: "Ya ella había tenido muchas prácticas en acciones militares pequeñas . . ., sobre todo en propaganda armada. También tenía alguna preparación básica en lo militar" (123) (She'd already had considerable experience of small military actions . . ., especially within the 'armed propaganda' campaign. She had also received a basic military training [128]). Instead, Alegría presents a guerrillera who adores her husband and infant daughter, Ana Patricia. The image of Eugenia as the guerrillera wife and mother is highlighted by the incorporation of Eugenia's letters to Javier—the only time she actually speaks for herself in the text—in which she tells of her love, gives childcare tips, and expresses her fears and frustrations about the political difficulties of the moment. She is the ideal compañera who leaves little bags of peanuts around the safe house for Javier to find later, who is overwhelmed with love for her daughter, and who can place both to one side to get all her revolutionary work done: "[n]unca la niña se convirtió en un obstáculo para las tareas revolucionarias ni éstas fueron un obstáculo en la educación de la niña" (107) (the child was never turned into an obstacle to her revolutionary commitments, nor were these allowed to hinder our daughter's education [114]). Moreover, according to Javier, she is a good homemaker as well:

> Ella era una fanática del orden. Por muchas tareas que tuviera, siempre sacaba tiempo para antes de salir barrer, arreglar la cama, "ponerme" a mí a trabajar en eso. (108)

> She was fanatically tidy. However many jobs she had on, she always took the time before leaving to sweep up, make the bed, getting me to do my share. (116)

The idealization of Eugenia as a warrior/housewife brings the guerrillera back into the feminine domain where she is less likely to challenge conservative notions about women's nature or to disturb the reader as an example of the monstrous woman warrior. Alegría comforts her reader with the thought that if Eugenia does fight and kill, at least she remains a "real woman" dedicated to home and family.[13]

Alegría and her informants admire Eugenia more for her character than for any particularly heroic accomplishment. They tell anecdotes intended to illustrate her ideological purity, her dedication and hard work, her simplicity and humility, and especially her willingness to sacrifice. Moreover, she is portrayed as sickly and weak, conditions that she overcomes with self-discipline.

> La compañera era débil físicamente, constantemente estaba con asma, agripada, con alergías, era muy sensible pues. Ni el dolor que le causaban sus sentimientos, ni el dolor físico quebraron jamás la moral de Eugenia. Eso era lo que nos impresionaba. Jamás, jamás se quebró. (56-57)

> Eugenia was physically weak, she always had asthma, and suffered from colds and allergies, in other words she was highly susceptible. Neither physical pain nor that caused by emotional difficulties ever sapped Eugenia's spirit. That's what impressed us. She never gave in. There's not a single instance one can point to and say, that's where Eugenia slipped up or got stuck. Eugenia was always in the vanguard.) (74)

These kinds of recollections converge to form a hagiographic narrative model that is intertwined with the more obvious epic theme. Present from the first pages of *They Won't Take Me Alive*, where Alegría gives a fictionalizied account of Eugenia's death in an ambush by government agents, this narrative develops a Eugenia whose adult life is a process of purification leading to her martyrdom for the revolution and her current presentation as a manner of secular saint.

Alegría makes use here of a hagiographic or martyr narrative, which is very common in Latin American revolutionary rhetoric. From the time that Guevara posited his idea of a new man, guerrilleros have been almost as much concerned with moral development as with military triumphs against the enemy. The guerrilla is supposed to be, after all, the vanguard charged with leading the people in the creation of a new way of being. But the guerrilla fighters themselves have all the imperfections of their corrupt and unjust societies. Thus sacrifice becomes a means to purge their old selves of bourgeois egotism, arrogance, and ambition in order to become the humble, loving new men who will have the moral authority to build a new world. As Cabezas (1982, 1986) reveals, the hardships he encountered in the Nicaraguan mountains made him a better man and better revolutionary:

> Allí aprendimos a ser humildes porque vos solo no valés ni mierda ahí adentro, aprendés a ser sencillo, aprendés a valorar los principios, aprendés a apreciar los valores estrictamente humanos que allí van saliendo a fuerza, y poquito a poco se van muriendo todas las lacras, por eso decimos que la génesis del hombre nuevo está en el FSLN. (48)

> (We learned to be humble, because you alone are not worth shit up there. You learn to be simple; you learn to value principles. You learn to appreciate the strictly human values that of necessity emerge in that enviornment. And little by little all our faults faded out. That was why we said that the genesis of new man was in the FSLN.) (86-87)

Guerrilleros are expected not only to leave behind their old way of life, but also to offer their lives for the revolution. This is seen as a kind of martyrdom, a death that is not an end in itself, but one that inspires others to act. Thus, death for the revolutionary leads to a rebirth in others and a rekindling of fervor to fight.[14]

Alegría shapes Eugenia's life story to show that the young woman was particularly well suited for her role as ideal guerrillera and martyr. Her Catholic upbringing (Juventud de Estudiantes Cristianos and missionary work in Guatemala, later Universidad Católica and Acción Católica Universitaria) seems to have prepared her to value poverty, humility, and self-sacrifice. Then she entered a wing of the Salvadoran guerrilla (Fuerzas Populares de Liberación "Farabundo Martí," or FPL) that conceptualized revolutionary commitment in terms of religious experience: members were to leave behind "normal life" and their "old selves" in order to enter a new life of service and obedience.[15] According to founder and leader Salvador Cayetano Carpio, this included continual sacrifice of personal comforts and desires. In addition to this total commitment (*entrega*), the FPL also demanded that its members be ready to die for its principles. To join, Eugenia vowed (1) to be loyal always to the poor and the humble, (2) to defend the working class with her life and the lives of her loved ones, and (3) to be faithful to the FPL and to honor the cry of "Revolution or death."

Alegría suggests that Eugenia had little trouble adapting to guerrilla life and the sacrifices it was to require of her. Her politicization at the university was rapid, she adjusted easily to work in the countryside with peasants, she had an exemplary proletarianization, and she was not afraid of dying. "Eugenia se enfrenta, sin titubear, a la muerte" (106) (Eugenia confronted death without wavering [114]).[16] Indeed *They Won't Take Me Alive* and its vivid account of Eugenia's last hours emphasize that Eugenia is dead, she has died just as she wished, and that her "good" death for the revolution is a martyrdom. Thus Alegría suggests, in agreement with Javier, that Eugenia's death was the culmination of a life of sacrifice and that her death should be celebrated rather than mourned.

> Yo considero que Eugenia muere plena. Plenamente feliz. Su muerte no es sino coronar con heroísmo una vida profundamente entregada, sin ninguna reserva. (146)

> I think Eugenia died in this fullness. Fully happy. Death merely bestows the crown of heroism upon her profoundly committed life, without reservations. (145)

In her prologue, Alegría states that sacrifice and abnegation are the two virtues which characterize Eugenia, and she even suggests that these qualities make the young guerrillera a heroine. Later Alegría dedicates her work to all the "héroes y mártires reconocidas de la revolución salvadoreña" (9) (acknowledged women heroes and martyrs of the Salvadoran revolution [translation mine]), again equating female heroism with sacrifice and death.[17] Although these virtues could be applied to judge guerrilleros as well as guerrilleras, Alegría does not question how the revolutionary veneration of sacrifice may affect women nor how it has shaped her account of Eugenia's life.

Male revolutionaries who tell their life stories speak for themselves and establish their own subjectivities for the reader. They not only have a sense of their own identity, they also freely express their idiosyncrasies, personal responses to life events, strengths and flaws. Some, like Guevara, whose deathbed photograph has placed him firmly in the ranks of revolutionary martyrs, revel in fame and notoriety during their lives. Others, according to Cabezas (1982) and Payeras (1985), struggle to overcome their individualism. All these men start from a social position of some privilege—be it as bourgeois, knowledgeable doctor or university student, or simply as humble peasant who has learned to survive in a harsh environment—and then sacrifice this privilege, along with personal comfort, for the greater revolution. Indeed, the guerrilleros' narratives suggest that the "new man" is one who has even forfeited male privilege to take on domestic chores, sensitivity, sacrifice of self, and love of others.

Latin American women, however, do not come to the guerrilla from the same privileged social position as do their male counterparts. While each Latin American society and class within that society has its own particular roles for women, it is generally true that women are expected to put aside private aspirations in order to find happiness in caring for others. As Evelyn P. Stevens (1973, 94) finds, the ideal Latin American woman has a "semidivinity, moral superiority, and spiritual strength. This spiritual strength engenders abnegation, that is, an infinite capacity for humility and sacrifice." While guerrilleras challenge notions of female physical weakness and subservience, they also seem to support the traditional view that women are by nature more spiritual and giving than men. As comandante Nadia of the FPL explains,

> Donde hay mujeres el trabajo es más alegre y hay más comprensión. Eso los mismos compañeros lo ven, a tal grado, que ellos piden que haya mujeres en la mayoría de organismos porque, quiera que no, es un elemento positivo de comprensión, de ternura, que los varones no lo tienen, no es parte de sus características. (82)

> Where there are women there is more understanding and the work seems more cheerful. This is something even our male comrades can see, to such an extent that they themselves ask that there should be women in the majority of the cells because, whether one likes it or not, they contribute a positive element of understanding and compassion lacking

among men who feel such things do not conform to their self image. (94)[18]

It would seem that the guerrillera does not have to use sacrifice to purge herself of bourgeois self-centeredness. To the contrary, traditional and bourgeois societies have encouraged her to devote herself to others as well as to practice abnegation and sacrifice, and she brings these values to the revolution, using them, if not to change the men, then at least to mitigate some of their more divisive characteristics.

Alegría views Eugenia's sacrifices as unequivocally positive, her abnegation and even her death as the stuff of heroism. There are no flaws in Eugenia: no bad moods, no anger, no days of exhaustion, no emotions other than those of devoted wife and mother. There are also almost no distinguishing idiosyncracies: no tics, no favorite pleasures, no pet peeves.[19] Unlike both the male guerrilleros and the female subjects of first-person testimonios, Alegría's Eugenia does not forge an identity within the collective; she never achieves an identity at all. To be sure, she gave up a bourgeois identity when she joined the guerrilla and left Ana María behind her. Once in the guerrilla, she gained a political identity as a member of the FPL and a female identity as mother of Ana Patricia, but Eugenia the woman disappears into the role of female hero martyr.[20] The narrative models join to convert the guerrillera into a symbol from which she never escapes.

The reader who approaches *They Won't Take Me Alive* as testimonio may be looking for a story about a political struggle, about women in the guerrilla, or about one woman's experiences in the struggle. The reader may also want a sense of solidarity with the Salvadoran struggle and may hope to use the life story in order to raise his or her consciousness.[21] *They Won't Take Me Alive* certainly fulfills the function of didactic tool, as it presents both a guerrilla sanitized of the internal violence for which it has been famous and an idealized Eugenia held up as an example of abnegation and sacrifice for the reader to follow. The lesson may well politicize and inspire revolutionary fervor, but it does so at the risk of reinforcing those values which have functioned as the ideological underpinnings of women's subordination. This is a tricky issue. Has Alegría reproduced traditional ideas of women's nature and social role here, veiling a reactionary stance on gender with a revolutionary politics?

Or has she, in the words of Jean Franco (1988, 513), attempted to "resemanticize" the term *woman*, putting previously conservative interpretations of womanhood to revolutionary uses?

To approach these unanswerable questions, it is perhaps useful to think of *They Won't Take Me Alive* less as a testimonio that is to present the complex human being who was Ana María (Eugenia) than as a prose poem that expresses Alegría's attempts to make sense of the vast destruction of El Salvador and its people. Barbara Harlow (1987, 8) points out that, unlike revolutionary narratives,

> poetry and poems of organized resistance movements struggle to preserve and even to redefine for the given historical moment the *cultural images* which underwrite collective action, military as well as ideological, of a people seeking to liberate themselves from the forces of oppression. (emphasis mine)

Viewed as a poetic text, the biography merely provides a structure for presenting clusters of images or, in Chanfrault-Duchet's terms, "culturally specific archetypes" that transform death into life (1991). Eugenia becomes the key to many well-known female archetypes: the mother who brings forth new life, nurturer/educator who creates the new men and women of the future, and the dead who returns to inspire the living.

Sternbach (1991, 94) recalls that Alegría once called herself a "cemetery," a poet who writes of and for all the dead throughout Latin America. Death, violent death, and the threat of death pervade *They Won't Take Me Alive.* Eugenia's role, as representative of the guerrilla and specifically the female guerrillera, is to defeat the many agents of death, even death itself. Obviously the foremost enemy is the Salvadoran government, which was killing its people slowly by injustice and directly through the actions of its army and death squads. Although the guerrilla also employs violence to fight the government, Alegría does not question its use of force. However, she does imply that revolutionary counterviolence is not sufficient to overcome the destruction of the Salvadoran people. This she sees as the task of the guerrillera, a woman with the correct politics who is able to bring forth new life and nuture those who are already living. For this reason so many of the rebel women interviewed speak only of children: Mélida Anaya Montes has never married, but sees all the young revolutionaries as her own children; Martínez plans on having children and adopting many of her country's orphans so that her house is full of children; Eugenia desires a child of her own.

A central moment occurs when Eugenia's future as a mother is in jeopardy. Alegría makes clear that the FPL, unlike the government, supports the family and cherishes its children; she tells us that the guerrilla movement keeps couples together as much as possible and encourages communal child-care. However, guerrilla life is difficult. First Javier is imprisoned and the couple is separated for long periods of time. Then, once pregnant, Eugenia finds that she is in constant danger of miscarriage just as the guerrilla needs more of her time and effort. She has to make the decision to keep working and endanger the pregnancy or to rest and take care of herself. Being Eugenia, she sacrifices her health for the guerrilla. Yet, also being a symbol of rebirth, Eugenia is not willing to face the possible death of her child without bringing some good out of so great a potential loss. According to Javier,

> La opción la hacemos prácticamente convencidos de que ella no iba a abortar, pero si eso llegara a suceder como consecuencia del cumplimiento del deber revolucionario, sería un nuevo dolor que nosotros concebíamos como un golpe del enemigo, un dolor que profundizaba por un lado el amor a nuestro pueblo y por el otro, el profundo odio de clase. (92)

> The decision we'd gone for spelt out that she probably wouldn't miscarry, but that if it resulted from our fulfilment of revolutionary duty, it would be a fresh point to concede the enemy, a pain that on the one hand would be deepened by our love for our people and, on the other hand, class hatred. (102)[22]

Eugenia does have her child and takes advantage of the many painful absences from little Ana Patricia to teach the girl that she has many mothers and aunts within the organization; that is, she begins to forge a "new child," one who is less emotionally dependent upon her parents and therefore better integrated into the collective spirit of the revolution. When Eugenia can be with her daughter, the daily activities that an infant requires—all made much more stressful when mother is a guerrilla in a safe house and every foray into the streets for a doctor or toy brings life-threatening danger—demand subordinating the self for the well-being of the child. This is not the male sacrifice to purge imperfections, but rather a way of being that epitomizes Guevara's statement that the true revolutionary is one who is forged in love.[23] Motherhood then is a practice that brings about revolutionary change and, because it fosters life, perhaps can even be considered the model for lasting social transformation.

If Alegría constructs her biography around the images of woman=motherhood=affirmation of life, it is because she sees these traditionally female forces as the only ones capable of overcoming death and destruction. She minimizes Eugenia's life as a woman and as a warrior in order to create the symbol of mother and martyr, a being who dies but whose legacy lives on directly in her daughter and, through this poetic biography, in us, the readers. Alegría does not challenge the symbols and images associated with women, but she does show how compelling they are in times of war.

NOTES

1. Journalists whose books are readily available include Iosu Perales (*Chalatenango: Un viaje por la guerrilla salvadoreña* [Madrid: Editorial Revolución, 1986]), Wendy Shaull (*Tortillas, Beans and M-16s: A Year with the Guerrillas in El Salvador* [London: Pluto Press, 1990]), and Nicolas Andersen (*Guatemala, escuela revolucionaria de nuevos hombres* [México: Editorial Nuestro Tiempo, 1982]).

2. A former Uruguayan guerrillera in exile in Paris did publish her conversation with other Tupamaras about being women within the guerrilla movement. See Ana María Araujo, *Tupamaras: Des Femmes de L'Uruguay* (Paris: Des Femmes, 1980).

3. See *Tania: La guerrillera inolvidable* (La Habana: Instituto del Libro, 1970).

4. Cited in Araujo, *Tupamaras*, 119-20.

5. Cited in Margaret Randall, *Sandino's Daughters: Testimonies of*

Nicaraguan Women in Struggle (Vancouver: New Star Books, 1981), 129.

6. In addition to the book cited above, Maraget Randall has also written a life story with her subject in *Doris Tijerino: Inside the Nicaraguan Revolution* (Vancouver: New Star Books, 1978). Other collections of interviews include Pilar Arias, *Nicaragua: Revolución. Relatos de combatientes del frente sandinista* (Mexico: Siglo XXI, 1980); Denis Lynn Daly Heyck, *Life Stories of the Nicaraguan Revolution* (New York: Routledge, 1990); Paz Espejo, *Mujeres de Nicaragua: Des Femmes du Nicaragua* (Paris: Editions des femmes, 1980); and Brenda Carter, Kevan Insko, David Loeh and Marlene Tobias, eds., *A Dream Compels Us: Voices of Salvadoran Women* (San Francisco: New Americas Press, 1989).

7. I am distinguishing here between testimonio with a first-person narrator and *They Won't Take Me Alive*, in which Eugenia can be only the object of discussion. I do not mean to imply that the testimonio with a first-person narrator is necessarily autobiographical. Indeed, the author Doris Sommer has clearly pointed out the danger of subsuming a counterhegemonic genre into a First World paradigm: one neglects to see the collective subject of testimonio. See Doris Sommer, "'Not Just a Personal Story.'"

8. Amanda Hopkinson does not include Alegría's Prologue in her translation.

9. These words are taken from Alegría's Prologue and are not found in the English edition. The quote is: "Eugenia, modelo ejemplar de abnegación, sacrificio y heroísmo revolucionario, es un caso típico y no excepcional de tantas mujeres salvadoreñas . . ." (Eugenia, a perfect example of abnegation, sacrifice, and revolutionary heroism, is a a typical rather than exceptional representative of so many Salvadoran women . . .) (translation mine).

10. Translated in the English edition as simply "back at home," the original Spanish makes clear that the home is a female space. Literally, "el seno" means "breast," and here it is used to mean "the heart" of the home.

11. In the remainder of the text Spanish quotations refer to the Spanish (1983) edition and English quotations refer to the English (1987) translation.

12. As Jean Franco has pointed out, recent military governments have invaded the traditional female territory of the home, and in the face of masculine violence, the mother's or women's sphere often seems utopian. She and other critics have shown how women's understanding of their roles as mothers has led them to social rebellion. Franco speaks of the Mothers of the Plaza de Mayo (Argentina) in "Beyond Ethnocentrism." Marjorie Agosín has also written on the Mothers as well as on Chilean women who use domestic embroidery to make political *arpilleras* [see p. 193, n. 5]. See her *Scraps of Life: Chilean Arpilleras* (Trenton: The Red Sea Press, 1987) and *The Mothers of the Plaza de Mayo* (Trenton: The Red Sea Press, 1990).

13. This ambivalence over the figure of the warrior woman can be seen in the choice of cover art for both the Spanish and English editions. The Spanish text has a photo of a guerrillera holding what looks to be rifle in almost an aiming position. She is possibly aggressive, but not necessarily so. Moreover, the photo is mostly blackened out, so the woman's features or expression cannot be determined. The cover of the English edition is a colorful scene from a guerrilla camp. The background has blue sky, green mountains, a pink building and one guerrillero putting a kerchief on another man. In the forground is the guerrillera—like the men dressed in cheerful colors even though they are clearly getting ready for military action—holding an automatic rifle up in the air as if checking to see if all its parts are in place. A large-leafed bush is to her right. The drawing suggests a woman who is thoughtful but not aggressive; her baseball-style cap and bright yellow jersey make her seem more like a young child than a soldier.

14. Some Salvadoran guerrilla lore seems to court death more than affirm life. Martínez (1980, 185) includes a song that was popular among political prisoners in jail. Called "The Party," it celebrates sacrifice and death. "If you don't come to give/ your heart/your life/don't bother entering here/because entering is the first step in leaving. . . . This place is only for sacrifice."

15. The FPL, like religious organizations, brings potential members in on a trial basis as "aspirantes" under the wing of a "responsable" who guides their political, moral, and ideological development. In due time, they take vows to the organization in a formal ceremony.

16. A new guerrillero is expected to undergo a spiritual transformation to become one with the peasants. Javier describes the process in baptismal-like language: it is a "sumergirse en la vida de ellos y surgir con ellos a una nueva alternativa" (46) (submerging herself in their lives, in order to rise with them in pursuit of a new alternative [60]).

17. Again, this prologue is not in the English edition.

18. There is a key difference between the original Spanish and English translation. Nadia says that understanding and tenderness are not "characteristics" of men, implying that these qualities are not in men's nature. The English has shifted this notion to a question of image, implying that men have but cannot publically demonstrate these qualities.

19. One of the few distinguishing traits that Alegría mentions is that Eugenia always sang out of tune.

20. Many scholars point out the difference between the bourgeois hero or autobiographical voice and the narrator/protagonist of a testimonio. I am using here Doris Sommer's (1988) explanation that the testimonial narrator indeed has an indentity, but it grows out of the collective rather than standing in oppositon to the social group. My point is that Eugenia never achieves an individuality within the collective.

21. George Yúdice states convincingly that testimonio does not stress the representation of a subjectivity, but rather a consciousness-raising praxis ("la praxis conscientizadora"). See his "Testimonio y concientización," in *La voz del otro: testimonio, subalternidad y verdad narrativa*, ed. John Beverley and Hugo Achugar (Lima: Latinoamericana Editores, 1992).

22. The original Spanish refers to a possible miscarriage if Eugenia works too hard (that is, fulfills all her revolutionary duties); the English translation suggests that Javier's work could influence

Eugenia's state of health and is an incorrect expansion of biological motherhood to include male parenting.

23. Ernesto Che Guevara. "Socialism and Man in Cuba," in *Che Guevara On Revolution.* (Coral Gables: University of Miami Press, 1969), 126-43.

WORKS CITED

Alegría, Claribel, and D. J. Flakoll. 1983. *No me agarran viva: La mujer salvadoreña en lucha.* Mexico: Ediciones Era.
———. 1987. *They Won't Take Me Alive.* Trans. Amanda Hopkinson. London: The Women's Press.
Beverley, John, and Marc Zimmerman. 1990. *Literature and Politics in the Central American Revolutions.* Austin: University of Texas Press.
Burgos, Elizabeth. 1985. *Me llamo Rigoberta Menchú y así me nació la conciencia.* Mexico: Siglo Veintiuno.
Cabezas, Omar. 1982. *La montaña es algo más que una estepa verde.* Mexico: Siglo Veintiuno.
———. 1986. *Fire from the Mountain: The Making of a Sandinista.* New York: New American Way.
Chanfrault-Duchet, Marie-Francoise. 1991. "Narrative Structures, Social Models, and Symbolic Representation in the Life Story." In *Women's Words: The Feminist Practice of Oral History,* ed. Sherna Berger Gluck and Daphne Patai. New York: Routledge.
Franco, Jean. 1988. "Beyond Ethnocentrism: Gender, Power, and the Third-World Intelligentsia." In *Marxism and the Interpretation of Culture,* ed. Cary Nelson and Lawrence Grossberg. Urbana: University of Illinois Press.
Guevara, Ernesto Che. 1968. *Reminiscences of the Cuban Revolutionary War.* Trans. Victoria Ortiz. New York: Monthly Review Press.
———. 1968. *The Complete Bolivian Diaries of Che Guevara and Other Captured Documents.* New York: Stein and Day.
Harlow, Barbara. 1987. *Resistance Literature.* New York: Methuen.
Martínez, Ana Guadalupe. 1980. *El Salvador: Une Femme du Front de Libération Témoigne.* Paris: Des Femmes.
Payeras, Mario. 1985. *Los días en la selva.* 3rd ed. Centroamérica: Educa.

Sommer, Doris. 1988. "'Not Just a Personal Story': Women's Testimonios and the Plural Self." In *Life/Lines: Theorizing Women's Autobiography*, ed. Bella Brodzki and Celeste Schenck. Ithaca: Cornell University Press.

Stevens, Evelyn P. 1973. "Marianismo: The Other Face of Machismo in Latin America." In *Female and Male in Latin America: Essays*, ed. Ann Pescatello. Pittsburgh: University of Pittsburgh Press.

Sternbach, Nancy Saporta. 1991. "Re-Membering the Dead: Latin American Women's 'Testimonial' Discourse." *Latin American Perspectives* 18/3 (Summer): 91-102.

Viezzer, Moema. 1977. *'Si me permiten hablar. . .' Testimonio de Domitila una mujer de las minas de Bolivia*. Mexico: Siglo Veintiuno.

6

QUASI-TESTIMONIAL VOICES IN CLARIBEL ALEGRÍA'S *LUISA IN REALITYLAND*: A FEMINIST READING LESSON

Sandra M. Boschetto-Sandoval

In a recent analysis of women's testimonials, Lilian Manzor-Coats (1990, 160) writes that the place of *testimonio* in relation to literature is very similar to the place the "disappeared" have within their repressive societies: "at the crossroads between history and fiction, or, better yet, at that limbo site of encounter between untold history and fiction." This site of encounter becomes in women's testimonials a site of resistance, offering the narrator/reader not only an alternative vision to history, but the possibility of her rearticulation in history. The process also foregrounds what Mary Jacobus (1979, 12) describes as feminist metafiction: a "transgression of literary boundaries that exposes those very boundaries for what they are—the product of phallocentric discourse."

Encompassing issues of testimony, memory, boundary fluidity, and feminist reading practice, Elizabeth Meese (1990, ix) points recently to the feminist desire to be inclusive and to reject the "metalogical conflict between theoretical discourses on 'women' and politically committed feminist action in the world." Convinced that criticism is best written and spoken in the dialectic of theory *and* practice, Meese chooses to engage herself with specific texts which present in her words, "reading lessons" concerning the dialectic between critical practice and practical struggle. Meese contends that when readers consider texts by women from other cultures, they not only resist the "geographical imperialism of English studies," they also engage in a subversive praxis, a complicitous negotiation between individual and collective identity.   Meese's theoretical framework refigures women's testimonial voice as defining a relationship between the consolidation of identity (individual or personal and collective/feminist) and "the politics of inclusion which threatens the notion of singular identity but appears to be politically necessary for a socially effective and responsible feminism" (Meese 1990, ix).

To read the poeticized testimonial prose/verse novel *Luisa in Realityland* by Claribel Alegría is to expose a feminist reading lesson. Here, indeed, is a text that not only straddles boundaries, but presents a kaleidoscopic approach to the question of relationships among art, politics, language, and identity.   Described as a "self-conscious antithesis to the world of 'wonderland'" (Fisher 1989), Alegría's quasi-testimonial novel attempts to invent a linguistic structure that will reach out and accommodate areas of experience (both personal and political) normally inaccessible to language.

Luisa in Realityland, a text which, according to Alegría herself, "doesn't 'fit' comfortably into accepted literary categories" (Agosin 1988), is a novel that alternates some fifty prose vignettes with approximately forty poems, all of differing lengths and formats. Rather than convey a sharp contrast between two overt discourses, one poetic, the other testimonial, Alegría's novel merely elucidates the difficulty of differentiating the personal from the political and ultimately the political from the artistic.   The language of the narrator, which constantly shifts between witnessing and self-inventing, is heterogenous, always acknowledging other discourses and establishing a dialogue with other texts. *Luisa in Realityland* exemplifies the hybrid "dialogic" and polyphonic form theorized by Mikhail Bakhtin (Holquist 1981) and, more recently, by Dale Bauer (1988, 13), who describes the dialogical imperative as a "necessary confusion": "'Confused' is the focal term: we are meant to be unsettled by these dialogues . . . just as we are meant to be unsettled by feminist criticism which seeks to shake up the critical communities which do not acknowledge the excluded margins."

Along with the interweaving of poetry, narrative, and document, the polyphonic text of *Luisa* evokes an hallucinatory realm, what Jean Franco (1985, 415) calls the "deterritorialization of feminine space." "Horrible things are happening" (15), recalls Luisa's mother in the novel. Violence and repression have brought about the violation of sacred spaces of refuge for women and children—identified by Franco as home, convent, and brothel. In *Luisa* these former "eulogized spaces" are transformed into sites of resistance: guerilla bunkers to which combatants retreat when necessary. The family home in Santa Ana becomes not only a refuge for victims of violence and massacre ("Felix"), but a hiding place, an escape hatch for revolutionaries ("Farabundo Marti"). The personal becomes political in the de-eulogized sanctuary of the home where women become signifiers of resistance. "The dead need to be remembered and to be named so they don't fall into limbo," her mother tells Luisa in "Litanies." "The increasing number of the dead began to weigh on [Luisa]. . . . The problem was, what could she do to keep the list from becoming endless?" (13). This initial recollection at the beginning of the novel is not merely a foreshadowing of Luisa/Alegría's vocation to speak for those who have been silenced. It also serves to foreground the oppositional potentialities of the women characters in/outside the novel and the praxis (theory in action of politics) which produces the very text we are reading.

Breaking *with* tradition to signal breaks *in* tradition, the structure of Alegría's text conjoins literary and sociopolitical critique. Through the interplay of narrative and verse, love and death, the reader is invited to (re)imagine, (re)invent, and (re)present a sociohistorical reality. These (re)positionings and (re)inventions also reflect a plurality of resistances. Sandwiched between the mad woman's harangue against social injustice (92) and Roque Dalton's "via crucis" (94), for example, is Alegría's own intrusion of everyday commonplaces, like love, "a torpid gesture" (93), one that enters "through the window/pirouetting on a tightrope" (80).

Along with shaping a (re)visionary revolution in the letter, Alegría's quasi-testimonial novel reflects the shift from a politics of restrictive identity to a potentially productive polyvalence. Luisa embraces a shifting and multiple identity which is in a state of perpetual transition. The images of "dismemberment" in the opening of "The Ceiba" (12) reverberate throughout the text. The "sweeping fragments" (138) which "alter [her] rhythm," "that unhinge" the narrator (125) echo in the "Final Act," wherein the little girl is transformed into a lifeless rag doll (141). While "innumerable deaths" assail, pursue, and eventually *define* the narrator in "well-planned disorder" (140), at the conclusion of the writing she has

99

"freed [herself] at last" (137). In "The Cartography of Memory," memory and imagination have conspired to "write beyond the ending," and to bring a dazzling future into potential view:

> The rainbow shatters
> the sky splits open
> rolls up like a scroll
> of shadows
> inviting *us* to enter
> and be dazzled.
> Come, love, *let's* return
> to the future.
> (152, emphasis is mine)

    Luisa in Realityland reproduces a strategy common to the majority of women's testimonials, wherein according to Doris Sommer (1988, 108) "self ultimately achieves its identity as an extension of the collective." The slippage between attention to one's own individuality (the autobiographical voice) and a focus on the social constraints of that individuality (the testimonial voice) is a reminder that life "not only continues at the margins of Western discourse, but continues to disturb and to challenge it " (Sommer 1988, 111). The illusion of singularity, "of standing *in* for others as opposed to standing *up* among them," which Doris Sommer (1988, 112-13) accuses autobiography of nurturing, is dispelled in *Luisa* in various ways. The first-person singular is not the only voice marshaled in *Luisa* to narrate a plural history. The imperializing cult of individuality and even loneliness is replaced with a collective consciousness which extends the collective potential for resistance. What the novel articulates is a quasi-subversion of the autobiographical genre, for here the autobiographer's concern is not the creation of a monolithic self, but rather the construction of the self as a member of multiple oppressed groups, whose political identity can never be divorced from her conditions. *Luisa in Realityland* mirrors, therefore, a testimonial subject construction in which a community of narrators reconstructs the life of a revolutionary subject, in this case Luisa/ Alegría. The voice and authority of the narrator, whose "body" cannot be easily located within the text, are replaced in the novel by that of a compiler whose task it is to "agglutinate" diverse sectors of the population, to merge discourse spaces and sites into

100

one collective representativeness.[1] Hence, the revolutionary subject "emerges" ultimately as the collective pueblo. The narrator's "Personal Creed" (135) is a dedicatory "standing up among" that collective.

If, as Sommer argues, testimonials are fundamentally about constructing relationships between the self and the reader, in order to invite and precipitate change (revolution), then *Luisa* is a text of complicitous readership. Meese (1990, 99) contends that in women's testimonials "there is always 'more,' some otherness that exceeds the simple projection of identity . . . the simple projection of opposites." In *Luisa in Realityland*, the reader must contend with these gaps and slippages between speech and silence as well, between the way in which the symbolic order does or does not (re)present woman, and "the effort of woman to bring herself into representation, to show herself" (99). An example of this "something more" of which Meese speaks is captured in the poem "Malinche," in which Malinche cannot be portrayed as merely perfidious or victimized, but must be depicted as caught in the inbetween of that symbolic representation.

> The child knows it all
> guesses it
> five hundred years ago
> Malinche
> handed the invader
> her continent
> handed it over out of love
> out of madness.
> He always knew it
> knew it yesterday
> when he watched
> his father's head fall
> while trying
> to tell him something.
> Treacherous Malinche
> the blossoms of her love
> dropped away
> and there remained heads
> dangling like seedpods.
> Fifty years ago
> the bewitched tree

(the Indian girl repented
and embraced it weeping)
again produced
a harvest of skulls
Izalco wept
dry tears
and the country mourned.
. . . .
The malinche tree is perfidious
The Indian girl baptized it
bewitched it.
(75-76)

Alegría represents here an "official/original" language encased in the optics of alien, marginalized discourses, languages against which the speaker speaks. The reading problem of this poem simulates woman's (Luisa's) position in general, always speaking in another language, in another relationship to the language of power. The poem can be read as a "pre-text" reflecting a dialectic of information and counterinformation. "Malinche" is in fact a "mixed blood" text, the origin and meaning of which, like the body of Alegría's narrator, remain slippery and unsettling, thus inviting further speculation and questioning. Resistance clearly accompanies all forms of domination. It is not always identifiable, however, because it inheres in the very gaps, fissures, and silences of hegemonic narratives. It is thus that Alegría's "mixed" voice functions as a form of resistance against authority.

The nonhegemonic, negotiating feminism of *Luisa in Reality-land* slips equally, then, between speech and silence, the personal and collective identities required of revolutionaries for their very survival. In its multiplicity of gestures, movements, and operations, *Luisa in Realityland* affords the reader an overarching perspective of "feminisms" which permit transgressions and "border crossings," a fluid female boundary wherein identities converge and diverge. In this extension of people, places, things, and time beyond the boundaries, feminism is not segregated from political resistance. Instead it is placed in "metonymic relationship" with it. Sommer (1988, 108) recognizes a fundamental difference between the *metaphor* of autobiography and heroic narrative in general, "which assumes an identity by substituting one (superior) signifier for another (I for we, leader for follower . . .) and *metonymy*, a lateral identification through relationship, which acknowledges the possible differences among 'us' as components of the whole." The singular in *Luisa in Realityland* represents the plural not because it replaces or subsumes the group, but because the speaker is a distinguished part of the whole. In testimonial complicity with such (ex)centric feminisms as those displayed by the prostitute in "I'm a Whore; Are you Satisfied?," by Paulina in "The President's Sheet," by Aunt Filiberta and her "flowered cretonnes," by Crazy Pastora in "The Mad Woman of the Grand Armee," and finally by the redhaired, crazy grandmother in "Granny and the Golden Bridge," the narrator challenges us as readers to recognize existing and potential relationships that extend her/our community through the text.

Even if the reader cannot identify with the speaker to imagine taking her place (i.e., in a "politically" resistant manner of speaking), the map of possible identifications through the text of *Luisa* spreads out laterally, enabling the narrator along with her readers to recognize themselves in a metonymic relationship of shared experience and consciousness. Thus, one additional reading lesson of Alegría's narrative is that we cannot identify with a single subject of the narration, but must instead entertain the difficult idea of several simultaneous points of activity, several simultaneous and valid roles.

Feminisms in *Luisa in Realityland* refigure themselves as "strategies," which, as Meese (1990, 27) contends, to remain strategic, must "adopt the clever, chameleonlike hue of the guerrilla fighter—here and then gone again." One such tactic is the narrator's refusal to engage in the consequences of linear narrative—a refusal which stands in defiance of the common expectations of the life stories of women. Prolonged, nondiscursive pauses permeate the text; madness ("Nightmare in Chinandega" and "The Blue Theatre"), silence, and nonverbal spaces offer a challenge to linearity. The overlapping of prose and verse genres also reflects a discourse imbued with a language of refusal; a negotiated "confusion" between conventional and nonconventional form, between a masculine prosaics and a feminine lyricism.

Despite the many silences and the frustrated/frustrating attempts to speak in the gaps, there is no mistaking the oral undertones of the narratives which make up the text, an orality which helps once again to account for the collective nature of *Luisa in Realityland.* The various "myth-making" aunts, uncles, and grandfathers who populate the text of Alegría's novel reflect not only the rural tradition of storytelling with roots in indigenous survival, but, more significantly, what Manzor-Coats (1990, 161-62) describes as the "defamiliarization of history into story." Paradoxically, the "reality" effect is not lessened but intensified through this process. Thus, the text of *Luisa* reflects a variety of counterdiscourses, or stories, not so much competing for authority as acknowledging that no one version of history can be ultimately authoritative.

One of the most significant feminist strategies undertaken in Alegría's novel is the simulated and extended conversation between Luisa/Alegría and the so-termed "Gypsy" who, like Luisa, straddles the fiction/reality border in *Luisa in Realityland.* In "Luisa and the Gypsy," we note that Luisa was frightened because the Gypsy is "terribly daring . . . impatient with her fears" (17). The Gypsy encourages Luisa to keep on with her painting, "and started dictating love poems to her. Since she was *illiterate*, she had to dictate them to Luisa who, as soon as she woke, would *write* them down on a special notebook she kept by her bedside" (17). Luisa is left at times unable to understand the Gypsy, this other self who speaks in the gap, who represents the silent exclusion that operates within and at the boundaries of discourse. The narrator notes of the Gypsy that "Despite her love of adventure, her wildness, . . . it is sadness that always leaves its mark on her face" (81). The extended dialogue between Luisa and the Gypsy refigures the interpellation demanded of *testimonio* between political theorists (intellectuals and professionals of bourgeois or petit bourgeois origin) and political activists (poor, illiterate working-class masses). This connection is not one of subordination or domination, but of interdependence and lateral relationship.[2] The Gypsy's compulsion to speak herself (Luisa notes "her Utopian streak and the happiness bubbling up inside her" [81]) and her insistence on secrecy, on hiding herself—an apparent contradiction of speaking and not speaking—refigures a double-voiced strategy of political interaction: theory (the speaking of) and praxis (the action of taking Luisa and her opponents by surprise). Spanning a series of contradictory sociocultural locations, *Luisa in Realityland* posits revolutionary literature as in effect involved in and constructed out of a dialectic of oppressor and oppressed, negotiating between the opposing terms of its dichotomies: literature/oral narrative and song, indigenous/elite, action/imagination.

As he or she makes his or her way through *Luisa in Reality-land*, the reader is overwhelmed by the sense that the discourse of analysis and struggle is being created in an open-ended and syncretic process of trial, error, and surprise. This freedom from predictability might be termed an exercise in decentering language, sending the apparently stable structures of Western thought into an endless flux in which signifiers are simply destabilized. Like the large canvases that Luisa paints in swatches of different colors with lines of red dots that "began dripping and running just before they went off the canvas" (79), the captioned frames which make up the prose and poetry vignettes of *Luisa in Realityland* convey no signature and no signifier. They are "half-finished" (79). As the narrator explains, for Luisa, "painting was magic . . . because she was certain that in one of the pictures she would discover the secret: suddenly, right there in the center of the painting a door would open to let her into that other reality, which until now she had only conjectured" (78).

The power of unpredictability in the testimonial discourse of *Luisa in Realityland* refigures the power of feminist discourse which depends upon its ability to remain "dislocated, without a home in culture's institutions." The location or "place" of feminist criticism, according to Meese (1990, 127), is the "'some place' of guerrilla fighters, like the *compañeros de la montaña* who steal, hide, attack, and set up camp somewhere else, awaiting the unpredictable moment when they will strike again."[3] The metanarrative poem "At the Beach" illustrates Alegría's feminist project of dislocation, contradiction, and unpredictability in perhaps the most concise form. As an exemplary "reading lesson," I include it here almost in its entirety:

> That's nothing to cry over
> come here
> I'll tell you a story if you stop crying
> the story happened in China.
> Do you know where China is?
> She shook her head
> and reluctantly drew near
>
> . . . .
>
> A long time ago, I said
> as I settled her on my lap,

far away in China
they bound women's feet
their bodies went on growing
only their feet
were imprisoned
beneath the bandages
and the poor women
could hardly walk
they had to let
their fingernails grow
until they were claws
rather than fingernails
and the poor women
could scarcely pick up a cup
to drink their tea.
It's not that they were useless
it's that their husbands
their fathers
their brothers
wanted them like that
a luxury object
or a slave.
This still happens
all around the world
it's not that their feet are bound
it's their minds, Ximena,
there are women who accept
and others who don't.
Let me tell you about
Rafaela Herrera:
with drums
with firecrackers
and flaming sheets
she frightened none other
than Lord Nelson.
Lord Nelson was afraid
he thought the whole town
had risen up
(he came from England to invade
Nicaragua)

and returned home
defeated.
Your twisted thumb
is like being a woman
you have to use it a lot
and you'll see how well it heals.
Run along now and play
don't carry sand for the others
help your cousins
to build the castle
put towers on it
and walls
and terraces
and knock it down
and rebuild it
and keep on opening doors. . . .
(50-51)

The engine of this metanarrative is, of course, the feminine telling, an irresistible dispersion/appropriation of diverse levels of discourse. Suspended between exemplar, apology, exploration, and admonition, the story-poem is both an opening onto as well as a turning away from innocence. If innocence is impossible here, it is not because of volition, but because outside forces are invading and shaping the child/mother's (mother/child's) experience. And telling is a form of survival. "On the Beach" allegorizes one of the most crucial elements of the relations among writing, memory, consciousness, and political resistance: the creation of a communal (feminist) political consciousness through the practice of storytelling.

"On the Beach" gives a new political dimension to the term and the experience of motherhood; it transcends the private sphere and invades the political one. A new discursive articulation establishes a new speaking subject. The dialogic relationship between mother and daughter, between teacher and pupil, negotiates a network of engagement, which is both theoretical and practical. Lessons from the past must be contextualized; women, like Rafaela Herrera, must be "spoken of" and exemplified. The mother-daughter relationship is necessary in the interest of collectivity and continuity. The breaking of bonds, the freeing of minds and feet remains

107

incomplete, however, without action. "Your twisted thumb is like being a woman," advises the narrator, "you have to use it a lot/and you'll see how well it heals." As the mother admonishes her child to join in the collective effort of rebuilding the castle, Alegría also prescribes a socially responsible feminism, one which "keeps on opening doors."

As we ponder the reading lesson of Rafaela Herrera and her ambiguously polyvalent "flaming sheets," we recall that resistance and women's testimonial discourse are indeed encoded in the practices of remembering, and of writing. It is the loss of one's children or imagining for them a social change and political transformation that motivates the act of writing. The testimonial poem itself, therefore, becomes the symbol for an act of love, and a tribute to the memory of those who have been silenced, and must now be spoken and written. Paradoxically, the "flaming sheets" also evoke the power of language to destroy as it creates: the work of any rewriting. The trick is not to identify the correct discourse and to defend it with dogmatic heroism but to combine, recombine, and continue to adjust the constellation of discourses in ways that will respond to a changeable reality. *Luisa in Realityland* functions precisely in this zone of indeterminacy—between voice and memory, fable and *testimonio*, legend and history, autobiographical memoir and poetic anthology—which constitutes the feminist project. This multigeneric recombination refigures a process of feminization of literature which, as in the closing lines of Alegría's "Cartography of Memory," projects into the future a "rebellious/contagious peace/a peace that opens furrows/and aims at the stars" (152).

NOTES

1. In *Luisa in Realityland*, almost all the anecdotes related in both prose and verse vignettes are quoted, overheard, indirectly authorized second- and third-hand accounts. Thus the narrator serves most obviously as scribe, as recorder, rather than as "author." This technique is not unlike what George Yudice (1985) describes as taking place in Alegría's *They Won't Take Me Alive* (1983).

2. As John Beverley and Marc Zimmerman (1990, 176-77) explain, "Testimonio gives voice in literature to a previously voiceless and

anonymous collective popular subject, the pueblo, but in such a way that the intellectual or professional, usually of bourgeois or petit bourgeois origin, is interpellated as being part of, and dependent on, this collective subject without at the same time losing his or her identity as an intellectual . . . it suggests as an appropriate ethical and political response the possibility more of solidarity than of charity."

3. Sommer (1988, 120-21) clarifies that one of the most fascinating features of women's testimonials is their "unpredictable pattern. . . . As working-class or peasant women involved in political, often armed, struggle, the subjects of these narratives move about in a largely unmapped space. Or it is a space on which competing maps are superimposed, where no single code of behavior can be authoritative."

WORKS CITED

Agosin, Marjorie. 1988. Review of *Luisa in Realityland* by Claribel Alegría. *Christian Science Monitor* (March): 20.

Alegría, Claribel. 1987. *Luisa in Realityland.* Trans. Darwin J. Flakoll. Willimantic, Conn.: Curbstone Press.

Bauer, Dale. 1988. *Feminist Dialogics: A Theory of Failed Community.* Albany, N.Y.: State University of New York.

Beverley, John, and Marc Zimmerman. 1990. *Literature and Politics in the Central American Revolutions.* Austin: University of Texas Press.

Fisher, Carl. 1989. Review of *Luisa in Realityland* by Claribel Alegría, *Small Press Book Review,* (January/February), n.p.

Franco, Jean. 1985. "Killing Priests, Nuns, Women, Children." In *On Signs,* ed. Marshall Blonsky. Baltimore: Johns Hopkins University, 414-20.

Holquist, Michael. 1981. *The Dialogic Imagination: Four Essays by M. M. Bakhtin.* Trans. Caryl Emerson and Michael Holquist. Austin: University of Texas Press.

Jacobus, Mary. 1979. "The Difference of View." In *Women Writing and Writing about Women,* ed. Mary Jacobus. New York: Barnes & Noble.

Manzor-Coats, Lilian. 1990. "The Reconstructed Subject: Women's Testimonials as Voices of Resistance." In *Splintering Darkness:*

Latin American Women Writers in Search of Themselves, ed. with Intro. by Lucía Guerra Cunningham. Pittsburgh: Latin American Literary Review Press Series, Explorations, 157-71.

Meese, Elizabeth A. 1990. *(Ex)Tensions: Refiguring Feminist Criticism.* Urbana: University of Illinois Press.

Sommer, Doris. 1988. "Not Just a Personal Story: Women's *Testimonios* and the Plural Self." In *Life/Lines: Theorizing Women's Autobiography*, ed. Bella Brodzki and Celeste Schenck. Ithaca: Cornell University Press, 107-30.

Yúdice, George. 1985. "Letras de emergencia: Claribel Alegría" *Revista Iberoamericana* 51/132-33: 953-64.

7

MAPPING A NEW TERRITORY:
LUISA IN REALITYLAND

Marcia Phillips McGowan

A drienne Rich (1979, 35) offers a useful frame of reference for *Luisa in Realityland* in defining "re-vision" as "the art of looking back, of entering an old text from a new critical direction."[1] Re-vision, Rich says, "is for women more than a chapter in a cultural history: it is an act of survival." As the reader follows Luisa on her Alice-like journey, she sees that traditional literary forms are unable to contain Luisa's quest for survival, that several genres are ransacked along the way, and that the route Claribel Alegría chooses for *Luisa* maps a new territory. This territory not only encompasses the "myths and obsessions of gender," but discovers a new "tradition in which political struggle and spiritual continuity are meshed" (Rich 1986, 176, 187).

Reviewers of *Luisa in Realityland* have called it a "magical-realist memoir," "an autobiographical odyssey in prose and verse" (Volpendesta 1987, 24), and "an autobiographical novel alternately written in verse and anecdotal prose vignettes" (Forché 1987, 3). Its book jacket calls it an "autobiographical prose/verse novel" (Alegría, 1987). Alegría admitted to me in an interview that "though some people call it a novel . . . I don't know what to call it; it is a very special book" (McGowan interview 1987).[2]

When she told me the story of Julio Cortázar and his wife Aurora's urging her to record her memories, Alegría said of the experiences of her childhood which she includes in *Luisa,*

"I didn't think those things had any value whatsoever," but that "it is true that by depicting the things that happened to me . . . my 'magical reality,' (because I think that in Latin America, as García Marquez has said very well, all the reality is magic) . . . in describing that, I was also describing the political and social situation of my country as . . . a continuity. . . . And you know that I didn't realize this until I finished the book and then I read it, and then I read some reviews, but it was something that was there, and it was subconscious. (McGowan interview 1987)

This meshing of the personal and political can be found throughout *Luisa*, not only in the prose vignettes, but also in the poems, which Alegría regards as "political poems": "They are love poems," she has said, "love poems to my people" (McGowan interview). It is worthy of note that this meshing of the personal with the political, while very much a fact of current Latin American literature, has always been germane to feminist literature as well. Feminist poet and critic Rich (1986, 180) explains that as early as 1956 she experienced "a rejection of the dominant critical idea that the poem's text should be read as separate from the poet's everyday life in the world. It was a declaration that placed poetry in a historical continuity, not above or outside history." While this declaration might seem less than startling to the Latin American reader, to whom testimony, as well as fiction and poetry, have become as inseparable from politics as the Gypsy from Luisa, in the academies of North America old ideas about the apolitical purity of poem as text are still very much in the ascendant. It is predominantly feminist and minority literature which insists on the importance of *context* as well as text.

My reading of *Luisa in Realityland* is informed by a North American feminist perspective which honors text but also honors context as paramount to the discovery of cultural traditions. I agree with Carolyn Forché's remark (1987, 3) that the accumulation of poems at the end of *Luisa* becomes a "complete utterance of one woman's struggle to preserve her past and redeem her present." It is this redemptive power that raises *Luisa* out of the realm of ordinary autobiographical discourse and gives it the power of testimony, as well as qualities of the novel of woman as artist—a female *Künstlerroman*.

In the past ten years, much important critical work has been done in the genre of autobiography which has broadened traditional definitions to the point where an unorthodox work such as *Luisa* can be encompassed by the term. Although the protagonist is named Luisa, Alegría is clearly drawing on her own experience as a child. So thin is the line between Luisa and Claribel that their husbands share the same name, and they share the same time and history. Although the prose passages are most often cast in the third person, at least one prose vignette ("Wilf [3]") begins in the first person plural: "We never saw Wilf again" (Alegría 1987, 19). By temporarily abdicating the use of third person, Alegría projects into Luisa's experience not only herself but all of those with whom she interacted at that time in El Salvador. In counterpoint to the third person prose vignettes, she casts her poems predominantly in first person; in the poem "I Like Stroking Leaves" (Alegría 1987, 18) she asserts

> and the earth is my body
> and I am the body
> of the earth
> Claribel.

Claribel, not Luisa. And so, at least temporarily, any arbitrary distinction between fiction and memoir or "fact" is erased by the removal of the Luisa "mask," and the experience is related, as in traditional autobiography, as that of the author. But in a work in which reality is magical, anything can happen. If Alegría is, after all, to borrow Carolyn Heilbrun's term "writing a woman's life," she is, to some extent, writing it symbolically, with the collective experience of a generation of Central Americans and a generation of women in mind.

In *Writing a Woman's Life*, Heilbrun cites feminist critic Nancy Miller in addressing the need for stretching traditional conventions of autobiography to encompass women's lives (Heilbrun 1987, 18-19):

> Unlike the reading of the classics—or of men's lives, or of women's lives as events in the destinies of men—which always include "the frame of *interpretations* that have been elaborated over generations of critical activity," reading women's lives needs to be considered in the absence of "a

structure of critical" or biographical commonplaces. . . . It all needs to be invented, or discovered, or resaid.

It is in light of this need that I suggest we examine *Luisa*, which invents a new form of autobiographical discourse, incorporating elements of fiction, poetry, and testimony and allows the writer a measure of control over her life—control which is rare in women's writing. As Heilbrun has noted (1988, 16-17), "because many women would prefer (or think they would prefer) a world without evident power or control, women have been deprived of the narratives, or the texts, or the plots, or examples, by which they might assume power over . . . their lives." The text of *Luisa in Realityland*, in its insistence on self-discovery within a personal and political framework, offers its writer control over her life through re-vision.

Lest we think that Alegría's version of writing a woman's life is not a radical re-vision, we must remember, as Jill Ker Conway points out (Heilbrun 1988, 25), that

> there is no model for the female who is recounting a political narrative. There are no recognizable career stages in such a life, as there would be for a man. Nor do women have a tone of voice in which to speak with authority . . . the expression of anger has always been a terrible hurdle in women's personal progress.

Though Conway here seems to be defining "politics" in a career context, its application may be broadened to encompass the shifting of power relationships in a new generation of women in Central America, who, as Alegría has said, "are liberating themselves through the liberation of their country" (McGowan interview 1987). *Luisa* is a work which is acutely aware of power relationships and different kinds of oppression, a work which, while often elegaic and testimonial, unashamedly embodies the anger of its author, as in "Operation Herod" (Alegría 1987, 35):

> For each dead child
> ten guerillas are born
> from each one
> of these mutilated bodies
> the virus of fury sprouts

114

it is dust
it is light
multiplying itself
the stifled tears of mothers
water it
and the Herods die
riddled by worms.

This is the prophetic anger of a revolutionary in exile—a woman who, as yet, cannot return to her country, except through memory, but can find words to express betrayal, anger, and revenge. Alegría's ability to transcend her anger is due largely to her ultimate belief, alluded to in "Personal Creed" (Alegría 1987, 135),

in the resurrection of the oppressed
in the Church of the people
in the power of the people
forever and ever
Amen.

In her vision those who have disappeared "will come back/ to judge their slayers," as she one day will return to her country, completing her own life cycle, to embrace her ceiba: "the circle is open/ I must still return/ to close it" (12). The circle is, of course, a traditional female symbol of completion, fulfillment. Until the time of return, as Alegría points out in "Tropical Birdland," although Luisa wants to be "a *chiltolta*, a *clarinero*, a *zenzontle*," she is "only a buzzard with stubby wings/ who limps through time/ wasting away" (Alegría 1987, 26). The dead, the tortured, weigh heavily upon her: "Don't come any closer," the poet tells the young Luisa in "From the Bridge," "there's a stench of carrion/ surrounding me" (140).

"From the Bridge" is a poem of self-confrontation, in which the poet in the present confronts past images of herself, addressing them in the second person:

you learned the consolations
of philosophy
before understanding
why you had to be consoled (138)

115

The poet asks her younger self, images of whom parade before her, to stop at the point when her arms fill with children:

> it is easy to distract yourself
> with a mother's role
> and shrink the world
> to a household.
> Stop there
> don't come any closer
> you still wouldn't recognize me
> you still have to undergo
> the deaths of Roque
> or Rodolfo
> all those innumerable deaths
> that assail you
> pursue you
> define you
> in order to dress in these feathers
> (my feathers of mourning)
> to peer out
> through these pitiless
> scrutinizing eyes
> to have my claws
> and this sharp beak. (139)

But as much as she might bemoan the agony of peering out with her "pitiless/scrutinizing eyes," it is these eyes which enable her to share with us a vision not only of the past, but also of a redemptive future.

Clearly *Luisa* is more than the fairly typical experimental venture that Alan West (1989, 253) attributes to the Latin American writer, who, as Borges once noted, "moves freely beyond European national traditions and, therefore, combines at will a variety of styles and forms." In an essay in *Breaking Boundaries: Latina Writing and Critical Readings*, Eleana Ortega and Nancy Saporta Sternbach (Horno-Delgado et al. 1989, 17) have referred to a genre "still to be defined and still emerging, which specifically articulates Latina experience," drawing on "the Latina as storyteller," and situating "the speaking voice in a genre somewhere in between poetry and fiction, blurring the line between the short story and the novel, between

116

conversation and literary discourse." Certainly, Alegría is a storyteller, but unlike Latina writers in the United States, she is not "blurring the line between the short story and the novel," but between fiction and autobiography. If we concede a conversational quality to her prose, it springs from direct quotation and dialogue; in her poetry a conversational quality springs from apostrophe or direct address.

More useful, it seems to me, in trying to understand the wonderfully anomalous structure of *Luisa*, is Paul John Eakin's explanation of the shifting boundaries between autobiography and fiction in *Fictions in Autobiography: Studies in the Art of Self-Invention*. Eakin (1985, 3) contends that "autobiographical truth is not a fixed but an evolving content in an intricate process of self-discovery and self-creation" and that "the self that is at the center of all autobiographical narrative is necessarily a fictive structure." The autobiographers he discusses (1985, 7)—Jean-Paul Sartre, Mary McCarthy, Henry James, and Maxine Hong Kingston—"freely avow the presence of fiction in their art," and so, I am sure, would Alegría, for in one of the first prose vignettes, "The Myth-making Uncles" in *Luisa* we are told, "In Luisa's family there were many fabulous liars, including herself, of course" (Alegría 1987, 53). One of Luisa's uncles, who has never left Santa Ana, manages to convince himself, the French consul, and many friends not only that he has studied in Paris, but that he has met Henri Bergson and travelled with him to the south of France. This is a liar, a "myth-maker," a fictionist extraordinaire. And so is Alegría, whose magical reality includes ghosts, a deaf-mute woman who can "communicate with everyone in town" (84) and whose cane Luisa and her husband Bud keep in their house in Deyá, and six charming deaf-mute dwarfs who rent the house that once belonged to the deaf-mute woman, which passes, eventually, through Luisa and Bud's intermediary hands.

Luisa's lies are generally honorable, not only in the tradition of the storyteller, but also in the tradition of her father, who lies to safeguard Farabundo Martí, and in the tradition of the Chilean girl who lies at the bidding of a prisoner who would rather be tortured and killed than have her acknowledge the truth—that she knows him—to the enemy. However, Luisa's lies can be mischievous, as well, as when she denies her own identity in the short story "Eunice Avilés" and tells a man who is a painter that she, too, is one, though she regards herself as a failed painter and has abandoned this avocation. Seemingly out of control, she heaps lie upon lie until she

117

sends him to Mikonos with the hope of meeting her there. "Good grief! Why did I do that," she asks herself when he is gone, then consoles herself by thinking, "Maybe something nice will happen to him on the island, and if it hadn't been for my absurd fibs he would never have gone. Besides, who knows? He may find the Gypsy waiting for him when he arrives" (Alegría 1987, 116).

Clearly, Alegría places herself within the tradition of story-tellers as "liars." Yet if we concede both a lie and an autobiography to be fictive constructs, we can understand why William Maxwell, whose *So Long, See you Tomorrow* has "equal claims," according to Eakin (1985, 7), "to being a memoir and a novel" can say, "In any case, in talking about the past we lie with every breath we draw." Eakin says (1985, 17), in alluding to Mary McCarthy's "A Tin Butterfly" in *Memories of a Catholic Girlhood*, that

> autobiographical truth is not a fixed but an evolving content, what we call fact and fiction being rather slippery variables in an intricate process of self-discovery. In view of the complex interrelationship between the remembered incident and its expression in art, we must discard any notion of the juxta-position of story and commentary as representing a simple opposition between fiction and fact, since fiction can have for the author . . . the status of remembered fact.

Adding to this comment Elizabeth Bruss's contention that "there is no intrinsically autobiographical form" (quoted in Eakin 1985, 20), anyone acquainted with the variety of works customarily identified as autobiography should recognize that *Luisa* seems to fit rather easily into this genre despite, or perhaps even because of, its many fictions. It is not, however, simply an autobiography, but a peculiar-ly female autobiography, not only in form, but in many of the issues it confronts.

In examining women's autobiographies through the centuries, Estelle Jelinek notes (1980, 17) that though men's autobiography is most often chronological, orderly, directional, and possessed of a linear narrative, women's autobiography rejects these characteristics. Jelinek has found that "irregularity rather than orderliness informs the self-portraits of women." Jelinek adds, "The narratives of their lives are often not cronological and progressive but disconnected, fragmentary, or organized into self-sustained units rather than connecting chapters.[3]

Although there might at first seem to be no discontinuity in *Luisa in Realityland,* the more discerning reader can perceive interrelationships not only through the numbering of certain prose vignettes, but also through the symbolical connections of each prose vignette with others and with the poetry. Images of blood, trees, birds, claws, violence, mirrors and photographs, circles, masks, monsters, water, the sun, and the rainbow appear throughout *Luisa.* Indeed, it is largely through these symbols that the work moves toward transcendence and redemption. *Luisa in Realityland* is structured symbolically in a manner similar to Virginia Woolf's *To the Lighthouse* and Maxine Hong Kingston's *The Woman Warrior.* In each of these works, it is through images and symbols that the author's identification with place becomes most clear.

The first poem in *Luisa,* suffused with longing, asks,

> How was my ceiba?
> the one facing the park
> the one to which
> I made a promise? (11)

Alegría senses the map of her homeland in the foliage of the tree which she longs—despite its size—to encircle in an embrace. She must return "to close" the circle, though, as in the Catholic ritual Stations of the Cross, "the final station/ is always the hardest" (11). If the tree signifies home, it is "strange plants" growing defiantly through bulldozed earth to which she attributes the "Seeds of Liberty" (95) which must free her country from centuries of oppression. I have already spoken of the author's identification with the earth in "I Like Stroking Leaves." In "Epitaph" the poet wants no gravestone, but "fresh grass/and a flowering jasmine" (68). By "Autumn Bonfire" it becomes clear that she so closely identifies with her tree that she feels able to speak for it, as indeed, she speaks, through transcription, for the Gypsy who appears in her dreams:

> And now everything is covered with smoke
> my roots
> my leaves
> my back

all burning in the fire
of this autumn
dying suddenly
in another body
amid a feast of flames
and murmurs. (132)

The roots of the tree, the author's roots,

. . . are freedom
and death
and labyrinth
the beginning
and the end (133)

Alegría and her roots are inseparable, light and dark, yin and yang.
Even as they split apart,

above the clear abyss
of a bonfire
they search
tangle together
separate
explode in sparks
like an outburst of cries
and are nucleus
and memory
and tomorrow. (133)

Through the vision conveyed by the image of the tree, Alegría
achieves simultaneity of past, present, and future. Through the
presence of the poems, which, as Suzanne Ruta (1988, 61) has so
aptly noted, have an incantatory presence, and "like a Greek chorus,
deepen the reach of a prose chapter," Alegría achieves not fragmentation, but integration of some of her major themes: time, identity,
continuity, exile. In fact, this is a work in which the identification of
the author with her land is total. Not only does she, oracle-like,
speak prophetically for the land, but the land, through pathetic
fallacy, "speaks," as in "The Volcanoes," to the muchachos (106). In
"Seeds of Liberty," the identification is so complete that

>The *muchachos*
>the plants
>climb toward the future
>toward the sun. (96)

The balance of such positive images juxtaposed against such horrible images as the bulldozers flattening, ripping, tearing into El Salvador's crust enables the reader to perceive in Alegría not only the agony of exile, but the hope of return. Alegría does not allow the reader to lose sight of the fact that hope can grow from anguish, that a moment can be beautiful and also cause pain. She balances images of anguish and joy until it seems, as Alan West (1989, 256) has noted, that her poems themselves are like trees, "where many things have fallen out of the branches (gods, illusions, friends) and yet a few stubborn leaves remain 'like steel propellers/resisting.'"

Such balance belies the impression that women's autobiography has developed in "discontinuous forms." *Luisa*, which might at first glance seem to be fragmented, is a highly integrated work of art, one which draws upon the public as well as the private nature of women's lives, and takes seriously the possibility that many feminist writers are currently exploring, of "expanding the possibilities of formal autobiography" (Juhasz 1980, 237).

One way in which Alegría expands the possibilities of formal autobiography is through adding testimonial elements to *Luisa in Realityland*. *Testimonio*, oddly enough, appears in her poetry as well as in her prose. As John Beverley (1985, 15) states, "*testimonio* is not . . . fiction. We are meant to experience both the speaker and the situations and events recounted as real. The situation of the narrator in testimonio is one that must be representative of a social class or group." What is unusual and innovative in *Luisa* is that although the entire work, in the sense of testimonio, bears witness to the horrors of living in a particular time and place, the first person narration most often occurs in the poetry, and the *heroine* of the work is the transcriber of the experience. It is the illiterate Gypsy, the easy inhabitant of Luisa's dreamworld, who dictates the poetry for Luisa to transcribe. And the poetry (in "Operation Herod") bears witness to the oppression of a people:

>In my country
>some time ago

```
the soldiers
began killing children
bruising the tender flesh
of children
tossing babies
into the air
on bayonets. (35)
```

For a fuller discussion of testimonio in *Luisa*, the reader should consult Sandra Boschetto's essay in this anthology. It should be noted, however, that both the first-person poems and third-person narrative prose vignettes convey the impression of "bearing witness," for if in the poetry we hear a first-person voice often juxtaposed against other voices, in each prose vignette, the third-person narrator most often insists that the protagonist speak for him- or herself. This testimonial quality is first evident in a poetic fragment from "The Rivers":

```
The terrain in my country
is abrupt
the gullies go dry
in the summertime
and are stained with red
in the winter.
The Sumpul is boiling with corpses
a mother said
The Goascaran
the Lempa
are all boiling with the dead. (88)
```

Testimonio is also present in a prose fragment addressing Chilean repression in "The Blue Theatre":

"There is nothing to be afraid of," [the guard] said, "all you have to do is say yes or no when I ask you a question. Bring him in," he ordered the first man.

"There were only two chairs covered in blue plastic. The guard sat down in one, and I was left standing. A few seconds later, two more guards in hoods entered, dragging a young man between them." (111)

Each experience is personalized, yet is indicative of a wider experience in a country that has been so often brutalized by "a heavy boot/ with foreign hobnails" ("Not Yet" 55).

The surrealistic episode of "The Blue Theater" seems all too representative of the brutality of the oppressor toward the oppressed. The voice in the poetic fragment also "speaks for, or in the name of a community or group." Each of these episodes "evokes an absent polyphony of other voices . . . " (Beverley 1989, 16). Beverley says that testimony is, to use Umberto Eco's slogan, an "'open work' that implies the importance and power of literature as a form of social action. . . ." His essay suggests, as does much of feminist criticism, that there are experiences in the world today that would be betrayed or misrepresented by the forms of literature "as we know them" and that testimony is a response to the inadequacy of conventional literary forms to give representation to social struggle (Beverley 1989, 25, 12, 11).

To elaborate in greater detail the feminist autobiographical elements in *Luisa*, Heilbrun (1988, 96) contends that, "the woman who writes herself a life beyond convention . . . has usually recognized in herself a special gift without name or definition. Its most characteristic indication is the dissatisfaction it causes her to feel with appropriate gender assignments." We see Luisa at a very early age beginning to chafe at the constraints of her sex. In "Taking the Vows" Luisa and her friend Isabel act as maids of honor for Sor Ana Teresa, who is going to be "married to God": "The mother superior approached the pew where Sor Ana Teresa knelt, removed her bridal veil, and with a huge pair of shears hacked off her lovely chestnut hair just above the ears." After that Father Agapito announces that she has "died to the world" (31). It becomes clear that Luisa does not see the priests and nuns as God's exemplars in this act of submission to patriarchy: "'Why didn't God show up?' Luisa asked herself. "If he had, I'll bet he wouldn't have let them cut off all that lovely hair'" (32). When questioned about this story, Alegría replied,

> This submission of the nun, this cutting of her hair, this renouncing to the world is very much like it used to be in El Salvador to be a woman. To be a woman, to be born a girl was already a submission. For instance men, always, didn't like to have little girls; they always wanted little boys, because little boys were going to do something. . . . But little girls,

123

no. . . . To be born a girl was like . . . all of this hair [being cut] and dying to this world. (McGowan interview 1987)[4]

In "First Communion" Luisa participates in another patriarchal religious rite which the women of her household tell her is "the most important day of her life" (38). She decides that her wish upon this occasion is well worth a sacrifice, and after taking the host in her mouth, she prays,

> "Dear little Jesus . . . I don't want to be married; I don't like the way men treat women, but I do want to have a baby, Dear Jesus, and Chabe says that only married women can have babies. So that's why I ask you with all my heart to let me get married, and as soon as I have my baby, to let my husband die." (39)

Clearly, Luisa has grown conscious of the treatment to which men often subject women through members of her family like Aunt Filiberta, who arrives at Luisa's house "at least three times a year" in an ox-cart with all her children because of Uncle Alfonso's having beaten her again. Luisa has also refused to believe, in "I'm a Whore; Are You Satisfied?" in the collective wisdom of a society which tells her, "Whore was a bad word. Whores were bad women" (23). Instead, after entering the antiseptically clean and chastely decorated room of a whore who gives Luisa caramels and after recognizing the whore's humanity, Luisa tells her cousin, Carlos, who reiterates society's stereotype, "You're the one who's bad" (25), and runs toward home. It is Luisa's curiosity, her refusal to accept the so-called "wisdom" of her elders in matters of sex and gender, as much as her determination to speak for those who have been silenced, that foreshadows her vocation as a writer.

One poem, in particular, in *Luisa in Realityland*, illustrates Alegría's awareness of the oppressive effects of machismo in her society and of male domination of women cross-culturally.[5] In "At the Beach," the adult Luisa is comforting a little girl who has been hurt by her boy cousins. She tells the girl a story of how, in China, women's feet were bound and their nails were let to grow "until they were claws." She explains,

It's not that they were useless
it's that their husbands
their fathers
their brothers
wanted them like that
a luxury object
or a slave.
This still happens
all around the world
it's not that their feet are bound
it's their minds, Ximena,
there are women who accept
and others who don't. (50-51)

Then she tells the story of how Rafaela Herrera frightened Lord
Nelson into defeat by using firecrackers and flaming sheets. She
concludes, unforgettably:

Your twisted thumb
is like being a woman
you have to use it a lot
and you'll see how well it heals.
Run along now and play
don't carry sand for the others
help your cousins
to build the castle
put towers on it
and walls
and terraces
and knock it down
and rebuild it
and keep on opening doors.
Don't carry sand
let them do it
for a while
let them bring you
buckets full of sand. (51-52)

Certainly, there is a feminist consciousness at work in *Luisa*, a consciousness which acknowledges the damaging effects of male domination, machismo.

We have already seen that there is in Alegría what Rich (1986, 184) calls "an organic relation between poetry and social transformation." In *Luisa in Realityland*, the life of the artist, herself, is submerged in a narrative which emphasizes and identifies with the collective lives of her people, the life of her country. Like the autobiographies of Emmeline Parkhurst, Dorothy Day, Emma Goldman, Eleanor Roosevelt, and Golda Meir, Alegría's fails "directly to emphasize [her] own importance, though writing in a genre which implies self-assertion and self-display" (Spacks 1980, 13). As Linda Huf (1985, xx) notes,

> women have frequently balked at portraying themselves in literature as would-be writers—or as painters, composers, or actresses, who, as self-portraits of their creators, are invariably surrogate authors. Unlike men, women have only rarely written artist-novels; that is, autobiographical novels depicting their struggles to become creative artists—to become, as the Romantics had it, as gods.

In many respects, *Luisa in Realityland* is a portrait of the artist as a young woman. Luisa exhibits many characteristics of the artist-heroine. She is "stalwart, spirited," and seemingly "fearless" (Huf 1985, 4). Luisa, like many contemporary artists in the female *Künstlerroman*, "is torn not only between life and art but, more specifically, between her role as a woman, demanding selfless devotion to others, and her aspirations as an artist, requiring exclusive commitment to her work" (5). She refuses to distract herself "with a mother's role/ and shrink the world/ to a household" (139). Innumerable deaths "pursue" and "define" her. The Gypsy, who dictates poems to Luisa, disappears for several years and comes back only when Luisa stops having children and takes up painting. The Gypsy functions as more than the traditional muse; Luisa is the transcriber of the Gypsy's poetry.

Huf (1985, 153) declares that today's artist-heroine "sees herself as having been reborn—as an artist." Certainly, there are many images of rebirth in *Luisa in Realityland*. Water is a dominant image. In "The Rivers," Alegría says of El Salvador's dead: "the dead sail down/ and the sea receives them/ and they revive" (89). In her poem "Rediscovering America," she invites her love to "settle/ into

a world/ that is ours/ it's a river/ that flows/ and is filled with voices"
(117). The poet declares,

> This is my world,
> love,
> but different;
> a second birth
> a new world. (118)

And in "The Cartography of Memory," Alegría repeats seven poems
that have appeared earlier in *Luisa*; seven, the magic number, the
number of the colors in the rainbow, an image of hope and promise.
The single candle which illuminates Luisa's view of Wilf and of her
small world in the first vignette becomes by the final poetic sequence
diffracted, through the prism of art, the prism of the Gypsy and her
"iridescent soap bubble," into a spectrum of color capable of
bridging the past, present and future. As the last poems, in their
repetition, complete the circle that was begun in "The Ceiba,"
Alegría, through paradox, maps a new territory and offers us her
final re-vision:

> Once more there'll be peace
> but of a different kind.
> The rainbow glimmers
> tugs at me
> forcefully
> not that inert peace
> of shrouded eyes
> it will be a rebellious
> contagious peace
> a peace that opens furrows
> and aims at the stars.
> The rainbow shatters
> the sky splits open
> rolls up like a scroll
> of shadows
> inviting us to enter
> and be dazzled.
> Come, love, let's return
> to the future. (151-52)

NOTES

1. A longer version of this essay is forthcoming in *Letras Femeninas* in 1994.

2. Interview with Claribel Alegría, October 1987. When I told her that I thought her mixture of prose and poetry an experimental technique that worked remarkably well, she agreed, saying, "I felt that the poetry was needed in order sort of to blend everything that I have there. It was very much needed." To my query about her view of *Luisa* as a work in which "political struggle and spiritual continuity are meshed," Alegría replied, "yes," but added that it had been "done almost subconsciously."

3. Jelinek (1980, 17) asserts that "The multidimensionality of women's socially conditioned roles seems to have established a pattern of diffusion and diversity when they write their autobiographies, and so by established critical standards, their life studies are excluded from the genre and cast into the 'nonartistic' categories of memoir, reminiscence, and other disjunctive forms."

4. Alegría is very much aware of the feminist struggle in Europe and North America and has stated that she admires it, but she emphasizes that the issue of hunger will have to be "solved" in Central America before feminism can advance beyond where it has presently evolved (McGowan interview 1987).

5. Alegría has said,

> *Machismo* is a thing that is very terribly rooted . . . in all Latin America, in Central America. Even women who have important jobs have to wait on men in Cuba, Nicaragua, El Salvador. This is a very hard thing to eradicate . . . and I don't know how many generations it's going to be until men understand . . . (McGowan interview 1987).

When I asked if her travels have revealed to her what is shared cross-culturally among women, she replied, "a sense of oppression," and she sees as a common strength that "we all are struggling to gain the same liberation," as well as a shared interest in peace.

WORKS CITED

Alegría, Claribel. 1987. *Luisa in Realityland.* Trans. Darwin J. Flakoll. Willimantic, Conn.: Curbstone Press.

Beverley, John. 1989. "The Margin at the Center: On *Testimonio* (Testimonial Narrative)." *Modern Fiction Studies* 35/1 (Spring): 11-26.

Eakin, Paul John. 1985. *Fictions in Autobiography: Studies in the Art of Self-Invention.* Princeton: Princeton University Press.

Forché, Carolyn. 1987. "The Ghosts of a Central American Girlhood." *Los Angeles Times* (15 November): 3-10.

Heilbrun, Carolyn G. 1988. *Writing a Woman's Life.* New York: Norton.

Horno-Delgado, Asunción, Eliana Ortega, Nina M. Scott, and Nancy Saporta Sternbach, eds. 1989. *Breaking Boundaries: Latina Writings and Critical Readings.* Amherst: University of Massachusetts Press.

Huf, Linda. 1985. *A Portrait of the Artist as a Young Woman: The Writer as Heroine in American Literature.* New York: Ungar.

Jelinek, Estelle C., ed. 1980. *Women's Autobiography: Essays in Criticism.* Bloomington: Indiana University Press.

Juhasz, Suzanne. 1980. "Towards a Theory of Form in Feminist Autobiography: Kate Millett's *Flying* and *Sita*; Maxine Hong Kingston's *The Woman Warrior.*" In *Woman's Autobiography: Essays in Criticism*, ed. Estelle C. Jelinek. Bloomington: Indiana University Press.

Rich, Adrienne. 1986. *Blood, Bread, and Poetry.* New York: Norton.

———. 1979. "When We Dead Awaken: Writing as Re-vision." In *On Lies, Secrets, and Silence.* New York: Norton.

Ruta, Suzanne. 1988. "Witness to the Persecution." *Village Voice* 2 (February): 61.

Spacks, Patricia Meyer. 1980. "Selves in Hiding." In *Women's Autobiography: Essays in Criticism*, ed. Estelle C. Jelinek. Bloomington: Indiana University Press.

Volpendesta, David. 1987. "Surreal Estate." In *In These Times* (16-22 December): 24.

West, Alan. 1989. "Latin American Writing: Language and Spies, Resistance and Redemption." AGNI 28 (April): 248-65.

INTERVIEW

Interview. 1987. Marcia Phillips McGowan with Claribel Alegría. October. Broadcast over radio station WECS at Eastern Connecticut State University.

8

AWAKENINGS: ORAL AND WRITTEN DISCOURSE IN *DESPIERTA, MI BIEN, DESPIERTA*

Cheryl Horton Riess

A large corpus of Latin American literature is overtly political.[1] Texts ranging from Ciro Alegría's *El mundo es ancho y ajeno* (Broad and alien is the world) to Rodolfo Walsh's *Operación masacre* (Operation massacre) have denounced injustices and called for social reform. For many writers, the role of the writer in society includes "a moral imperative to speak out on issues of national concern—or when this is not feasible, to encode political dissent into the pages of 'creative' literature" (Meyer 1988, 7). Claribel Alegría continues this tradition in both narrative and poetic works. Her short novel, *Despierta, mi bien, despierta* (Awake, my love, awake), provides testimony to the disintegration of Salvadoran society while at the same time tracing the evolution of the role of women in Latin American society.[2]

Alegría sees political commitment in literature as "seldom a calculated intellectual strategy . . . a visceral reaction to the corner of the world we live in and what it has done to us and the people we know" (Meyer 1988, 308). It is "like a contagious disease" which inevitably infects one's writing, and obligates writers to communicate their own view of the world. As a writer who has witnessed and communicated the political upheavals of her own country (El Salvador) and region (Central America), Alegría's writing has been infected by this disease. She struggles, therefore, to incorporate political concerns into her writing by dividing it into two categories: the "literary-poetic" and "crisis journalism" (Meyer 1988, 309).

It is impossible to separate these types of writing, as *Despierta* demonstrates. Alegría's political commitment is evident in the text through direct reference and allusion to the violent civil war that divided El Salvador for over a decade between 1980 and 1992. At the same time, *Despierta* denies being classified as a documentary or journalistic text. There is no overt effort in the novel to document specific incidents, nor is there any pretence that the events narrated are other than fictional. The intimate vision portrayed in the narrative accentuates a duality which is sustained throughout the novel. As it exposes the political violence of the times, the text reveals a woman's struggle to gain a unique personal identity based on her own, rather than others', expectations. This process of self-definition is inextricably intertwined with the process of growing political awareness which can be traced in the novel.

This duality within the text of *Despierta* underscores the combination of political commitment with other human concerns which is especially prevalent in the work of Latin American writers, especially works which examine women's role in society from a feminist perspective. Latin American feminism differs from its counterparts in more developed regions of the world because the women in Latin America face challenges of a different nature. In Latin America, women have been excluded from the arena of political debate until recently, remaining instead in roles rejected by some feminists as "the domestic and the maternal as icons of womanhood. Latin American feminism seems to start from within those boundaries and extend them outwards, creating new images and new parameters" (Bassnett 1990, 3).

According to the Mexican critic Sara Sefchovich (1983, 15),

> La escritura de las mujeres se ha configurado como una salida, una lucha contra el silencio y contra los patrones que impone la sociedad. Es expresión de frustración, de aburrimiento, del encierro en un ámbito limitado y en una tradición social y religiosa que asfixian, de la atención concentrada en la familia y de la imposibilidad de salir al mundo y respirar en él a sus anchas.

> (Women's writing has been configured as an escape, a struggle against the silence and against the roles imposed by society. It is the expression of frustration, of boredom, of

being enclosed in limited surroundings and in a smothering social and religious tradition, of the attention concentrated on the family and of the impossibility of going out into the world and breathing freely.)[3]

Despierta is a struggle against the silence and limitations imposed by society. The novel recounts the story of Lorena, a middle-aged Salvadoran woman who is married to Ernesto, the wealthy owner of several slaughterhouses. With the encouragement of her daughter, Lorena takes a writing course at the university, where she meets and has an affair with a young revolutionary, Eduardo. The affair provides Lorena with a refuge from the increasingly overt social violence which finally destroys her family and her affair.

The narrative pursues the personal as well as the political awakening of Lorena through an intricate web of written and oral discourse. The metaphor of the web is proposed as a model in the text itself, as Eduardo sits in writing class and watches a spider spinning its web around a trapped fly. When the fly is secured, Eduardo tries to shift his attention to the lecture, but his attention remains trapped in the web (10). The image of the web is applicable to both the crumbling sociopolitical situation in which the story is set and the relationship which envelopes Lorena, Ernesto, and Eduardo. Ernesto's role is that of spider, while Eduardo assumes the role of the trapped fly. Lorena is best described as the web itself which binds the other two together.

The relationship between oral and written discourse in the text forms an intricate web of power relations as well. The oral language conveys a sense of immediacy. As portrayed in the text, oral language is natural, spontaneous speech, spoken and expressed without apparent calculated forethought. Because of its presumed spontaneity, oral discourse lacks authority. Written language in the text, on the other hand, is deliberate, manipulative, and carries a great sense of its own authority. As a deliberate act, written discourse exerts a power over both the story narrated in the text and the testimony it presents for readers.

Far from being a simple opposition between oral speech and written word, the discourses are trapped in a multifaceted struggle for power. This struggle for supremacy creates a dialogue within the text. The competing voices, or "language worldviews" (Bakhtin

1984, 184), engage in a dialogic relationship in which each questions, evaluates, and influences the others.[4] At the beginning of the narrative, the dominant voice is that of the social hierarchy, the wealthy businessmen and the government, represented by Ernesto. The privileged position of this worldview is challenged by Eduardo's revolutionary discourse which seeks to usurp the political privilege, and, ultimately, by Lorena's developing discourse.

The text of *Despierta* is the authoritative written discourse which encompasses all other verbalizations present in the text.[5] Several other forms of discourse exist within the text, each carrying out a distinct function in the dialogue which communicates the story to the reader. In a strict sense, to speak of oral discourse in a written text is impossible. Novels, as written and published artifacts, are made up of written language. The narrative of the text communicates through the reading process, eliminating the oral quality of language. Within the fictional world, however, oral discourse is an integral component of the communication process: characters talk to each other, talk about each other, even talk to themselves. Often, speech is a fundamental mode of conveying thoughts, emotions, and opinions within the text. On the textual level, oral discourse is represented by quoting characters' dialogue or recording their thoughts. The text becomes a transcription of dialogue and thought, which, paradoxically, retain an orality, a lively immediacy, within the written discourse.[6] In this way, it is possible, even necessary, to discuss oral discourse in the novel.

The interaction of written and (represented) oral discourse in the text accentuates the separate narrative levels present in the novel. It is impossible to forget that *Despierta* is a conscious, deliberate written discourse. However, in the world created by the story, oral discourse dominates. It is the mode which the protagonist employs to navigate her world, and her primary mode of expression. For Lorena, the oral must come before the written, since the written is a reflection of the oral. Oral discourse conveys Lorena's actions and decisions. The protagonist "voices" her decisions and realizations in the text.

Within the narrative, a series of incidents compels the protagonist to question the traditional woman's role which she has been fulfilling. When she realizes that Ernesto failed to stop along a highway and help a nude man whose bullet-ridden body is found the next day, she also acknowledges that he is, indirectly, responsible for the death. On her way to her mother's house, after having read the notice of the death in the newspaper, Lorena repeats to herself, "Culpable de esa muerte. . . . Emboscada o no emboscada debimos haberlo ayudado" (Guilty of that death. . . . Ambush or no ambush we should have helped him) (16). Lorena reveals her concern about the change in Ernesto's attitude in a conversation with her mother: "Es como si de pronto . . . un odio enorme se hubiera apoderado de él. No es el mismo de antes. Desconfía de todo el mundo" (It is as if suddenly . . . a great hatred had taken him over. He is not the same as before. He doesn't trust anyone) (22). When Lorena accompanies her mother to distribute food among the poor, she hears from a woman at the church about a massacre of workers at a large ranch. Lorena becomes increasingly involved with the Catholic church's efforts to help the poor, which Ernesto has forbidden her to do. After Ernesto receives an anonymous note telling him about Lorena's affair with Eduardo, confronts her, and strikes her across the face, she pensively rubs her face: "cobarde, infeliz, cómo te desprecio. . . . No puedo pasar otra noche en esta casa" (wretched coward, how I despise you. . . . I can't spend another night in this house) (60). As a definitive step toward independence, Lorena packs a suitcase and goes to stay at her mother's house.

Written discourse works within the text to formalize the occurrences reported in oral discourse. The most developed written discourses contained in the text include the *novelucha* (Lorena's fledgling novel) and her diary, which reinforce the primacy of written discourse by focussing attention on the writing process itself. In addition, there are references to other works of literature, and to newspaper articles. Citing other literary works, as well as journalistic articles, calls attention to the importance of deliberate writing in the narrative. At the same time, these references document the protagonist's development of a self-referential identity and connect the fictional world to the "real world" context of contemporary Salvadoran society. The works mentioned attempt to communicate through the writing process, whether their intention be to report an act of violence or to create a fantasy world. The stress placed on the conscious act of writing focuses attention on the writing process of the text as well.

The news articles also provide cues to the worsening social circumstances that surround Lorena's search for identity and provide a catalyst for her actions. The society in crisis furnishes the context within which Lorena's story develops. It creates the atmosphere of *carnival*, which is

> the place for working out, . . . a *new mode of interrelation-ship between individuals*, counterposed to the all-powerful socio-hierarchical relationships of noncarnival life. . . . Carnival brings together, unifies, weds, and combines the sacred with the profane, the lofty with the low, the great with the insignificant, the wise with the stupid. (Bakhtin 1984, 123)

The disintegration of society permits the status quo to be undermined and creates the opportunity for the protagonist's search for identity and political responsiveness. The dialogic process is revealed as Lorena "is able to assert her defiant voice through carnival, the masquerade, the parody of the 'official' lives she leads" (Bauer 1987, 13). Social chaos is parallelled by the interplay between written and oral discourse. Written discourse strives to maintain control within the text, while oral discourse struggles to assert itself, through its very naivete, as the dominant mode of expression.

The protagonist's affair with a young revolutionary causes confusion within her which compels her to redefine her image of herself.[7] The affair allows Lorena to feel she is part of the push for social change. At the same time, it offers her a temporary asylum from the social upheaval (she never participates in revolutionary action) and from personal turmoil she is experiencing. The process of gaining independence remains incomplete. When her lover goes into hiding, he suggests that she visit her children in Europe as a way of protecting her from the violence. Her lover takes over the role of protector that her husband had fulfilled until this point. The revelation of the affair to her husband represents a definitive step in the identity process. Lorena gains a new resolve to control her own life when she leaves her husband. The final step in the search for her own identity occurs when she finds the decapitated head of her lover that has been placed in her car. Though her first reaction is extreme anguish, the death of her lover signifies the possibility of total independence in her self-definition. It eliminates male dominance in Lorena's personal life and frees her to take the opportunity to redefine her identity in her own terms.

Lorena tries to resolve the inner turmoil by writing a novel. Her novelucha takes on a dual role within the text of *Despierta*. A love story, it turns out to be too autobiographical for comfort. Her relationship with Eduardo is, quite obviously, the anecdote which she attempts to transform into fiction. The correlation between Lorena's affair and her novel, or between life and text, is made explicit in the narrative when the protagonist reviews her novelucha and decides "no hay duda que Estela se parece mucho a mí. . . . Tendré que disfrazarla mejor" (there is no doubt that Estela is a lot like me. I'll have to disguise her better) (32). The conscious effort of writing a disguised version of her relationship with Eduardo obliges Lorena to acknowledge the reality of the affair. Writing about her affair marks a step along the path to an independent identity, since "the woman writer uses her text, . . . as part of a continuing process involving her own self-definition" (Gardiner 1982, 187). Lorena recognizes that the novelucha has all the failures of a first novel; it is overly sentimental and the description is too telegraphic, but "todos estaban de acuerdo en que manejabas el diálogo bastante bien" (everyone agreed that you manipulate the dialogue pretty well) (51). The critique of the narrative in her writing class also emphasizes the manipulation of language that constitutes written discourse.

Lorena's diary, a document that she keeps under lock and key, complements the novelucha by reflecting Lorena's emotional reactions to the things that are happening in her life. It represents a self-acknowledgement of the changes in Lorena's life. Once again, written discourse fulfills a formalizing function in the narrative. Because of the emotional charge attached to the things she writes about in the diary, it has a direct connection to Lorena and her life. It seems more honest than the novelucha, since there is no apparent effort made to disguise events or emotions. The least structured and controlled of the written discourses in the text, it more closely resembles oral discourse. The proximity of the diary to oral discourse also creates the illusion of a shortening of the distance between narrator and protagonist, and between narrator and reader.

One of the most notable uses of language is the anonymous note sent to Lorena's husband which reveals her affair with Eduardo. Significantly, it is a written discourse which determines the protagonist's future. For Ernesto, the anonymous written discourse is more believable than his wife's oral denial. Throughout the confrontation, there is no vacillation in Ernesto's conviction that Lorena is having an affair. The authority given the written work over the oral is complete and unchallenged, especially since the oral reply is spoken by a woman. The revelation of her affair represents a definitive step in the identity process. Lorena can not remain with her husband once he strikes her across the face. Lorena gains a new resolve to control her own life. Her husband has lost his control over her, and his anger concedes that fact. Ultimately, written language seems to have accomplished what oral language could not: it frees Lorena from her husband's control.

Inversely, the final step in the search for a self-defined identity is acknowledged by Lorena's scream when she discovers her lover's decapitated head in the front seat of her car. Her oral (and very natural) response to the horrendous sight carries multiple connotations. For a split second, orality reigns supreme. Her scream announces her repulsion at the sight as it denounces the violence which surrounds her. The reason for the beheading remains ambiguous, since the text of *Despierta* ends at this scene. The abrupt final scene of the narrative avoids closure and prompts a series of questions. Did Eduardo die because he was a revolutionary, or because he was Lorena's lover? Was his head left in her car to warn her not to become involved in the political struggle for power, or as a gruesome revenge taken by her husband? Likewise, the protagonist's response remains unknown. Does the death signal failure in her quest for an independent identity, or does the death strengthen her resolve to leave her husband? A final question is left unanswered as well. Is Lorena's scream her final, impotent oral discourse, or is it a scream of liberation? Perhaps it signifies that she is free from domination, both by the men in her life and by the written discourse which tells her story, but which is unable to reproduce the scream.

This scene suggests that all discourse is futile as a response to that kind of violence. In the end, no single form of discourse dominates. Oral and written discourse are engaged in a never-ending dialogue which is open to interpretation. The reader, therefore, is confronted with an ambiguous ending which must be resolved. In this case, the reading process becomes a "first step toward revisioning and rearticulating voice" (Bauer 1987, 15). The reader is invited into the atmosphere of carnival created by the ambiguity of the narrative; convention has been suspended. The reader engages the text in a dialogue which re-examines the role of oral and written discourse on both the intratextual and extratextual levels.

The inversion of discursive control on the intratextual level recalls attention to the dialogic nature of the text. While oral discourse is muted, it undermines the authority of written discourse by its very representation. Written discourse must recognize oral language in order to subsume and represent it. Thus, an "oral" voice remains in the text. As Bauer (1987, 7) notes, "Language, then, is no longer merely a carrier of theme, but is a theme itself. . . . Thus, by experiencing the otherness in the text, we can grasp the powers which either restrict or subvert that otherness." In this case, oral discourse functions as the "other" for the written text.

The narrative voice plays a pivotal role in the text by bridging the distance between written and oral discourse. Gardiner's suggestion (1982, 187) that "novels by women often shift through first, second, and third persons and into reverse" is exemplified by Alegría's text. There are numerous shifts in narrative person, as the opening sentence indicates: "Qué lata, me olvidé de comprar tinta verde, abriste el cuaderno de tapas también verdes. . . ." (What a nuisance, I forgot to buy green ink, you opened the cover of the notebook, which was also green) (7). Just as oral discourse is subordinated by written discourse, the first-person protagonist's expression is subsumed by the third-person narrator and incorporated into the second-person narrative.

This narrative voice engages the protagonist in a dialogue in which Lorena is muted. Her thoughts and words are embodied in the words of the "other." The muted dialogue between narrative voice and protagonist generates the oral tone which permeates the text. Throughout the reading process, there is a tension created by the give-and-take of the narrative voice and the protagonist, a conversation in which readers fill in the blanks.[8] Readers experience this dialogue from the vantage point of the narrative voice. It is as if the reader were eavesdropping on a conversation between narrator and protagonist looking over the narrator's shoulder, or with an ear pressed against a door to hear the conversation on the other side. While able to "hear" the action, the reader remains a witness. In essence, the reader assumes the role of audience, or public, which receives the "testimony" of the witnesses: the protagonist and the text. Since readers of *Despierta* interact only with the text, written discourse is the sole means of discovery. Oral discourse has become muted at this level and can only be represented in the text.

The muted dialogue may well constitute an internal dialogue in which the protagonist is both "self" and "other." The "other," represented by the second-person narrative, is necessary for an examination of the "self." However, the unfolding of the protagonist produces two unequal entities. The narrative voice holds power over the "self" by narrating thoughts, conversation, writings of the protagonist; Lorena can keep no secrets from the "other." In addition, the narrative voice reveals that it is on a narrative level superior to that of the protagonist by narrating the actions and thoughts of other characters in the third person.

The multifaceted relationship between the narrative voice and the protagonist parallels the protagonist's role in society. Addressing the protagonist with *tú*, rather than by name, eliminates her personal identity. The female character assumes a generic role which permits an association with a generalized woman's role in society. The protagonist becomes the muted "other" which challenges prevailing social norms. The narrative correlates oral language with the protagonist's role, indeed the woman's role, as a subordinate voice and position. Being placed in a marginal position requires that the women's voice contest the dominant voice's authority if any change is to occur. "This internal clash of competing voices creates the split between the authoritative and the internally persuasive, between the desire to conform and the desire to resist" (Bauer 1987, 7).

Within her fictional world, the protagonist's family provides a basic security that enables Lorena to dabble in writing while at the same time it is her cage, that from which she must escape to attain her own identity. She must free herself from her husband's domination and her passive role in her marriage and in society. She must stop defining herself using man as the only reference point. She must find and assert her own voice; engage the other voices in dialogue. Her quest culminates in the realization that she must awaken to the political realities of her society, as well as take responsibility for defining her own identity. This political awareness is traced in the text through the evolution of written discourse. Meanwhile, the protagonist attains her identity as a self-reliant individual by developing her oral discourse.

Despierta denounces woman's place as a marginal figure in Latin American society and the sociopolitical situation in El Salvador and Central America. The text resists being "condicionada a la obediencia, la sumisión, la reproducción de los valores sociales en el seno de la familia (conditioned into obedience, submission, the replication of social values in the heart of the family)" (Sevchovich 1983, 14). By subverting the apparent dominant-submissive relationship between written and oral discourse and revealing the complex interdependence of the two, Alegría engages the dominant social and political structures in a struggle for power, both political and linguistic. *Despierta*, the call to awaken, invigorates Alegría's quest to fulfill her "writer's commitment" (Meyer 1988, 308).

NOTES

1. See González Echevarría (1985) and Meyer (1988) for a discussion of the sociopolitical aspects of Latin American literature.

2. Hereafter, the title *Despierta, mi bien, despierta* will be shortened to *Despierta* in the text.

3. All English translations that follow quotations are my own and will differ from any published version. Page numbers given are for the original citation.

4. In Bakhtin's model, the concepts which constitute the worldview "must clothe themselves in discourse, become utterances, become the positions of various subjects expressed in discourse, in order that dialogic relationships might arise among them" (Bakhtin 1984, 183).

5. In the current discussion I use *intratextual* to refer to the storyline of the novel. The actions, thoughts, and words of the characters would all be included in this level. *Textual* is used to refer to the written text of the novel, the physical artifact that we read. Here, of course, only written language exists. The *extratextual* level refers to the relationship of the written text to the world outside of it. Readers interact with the text at this level through the reading process. Gerard Genette's explanation and analysis (1980) is especially useful in developing a terminology which facilitates the discussion of narrative levels. Rimmon-Kenan (1984) also provides a concise summary of narrative levels.

6. See Edward Said (1983) for a lengthy synthesis on the issue of oral versus written language. Said draws on a variety of works including those of Paul Ricour, Michael Riffaterre, and Nietzsche. Much of the discussion is based on Michel Foucault's theories of power relationships. For a feminist critique of Foucault's work, see Benhabib and Cornell, (1988).

7. Judith Kegan Gardiner (1982, 191) contends that "the sexually active women heroes are not guilty, nor do they find sexual love redemptive. At best it offers women temporary warmth and sensual exhilaration; more often, it confuses women and alienates them from themselves." Lorena views her affair with Eduardo as a pleasurable asylum from the rest of her life.

8. This statement implies that the role of the reader is a participatory one, a concept informed by reader-response criticism. For an introduction to this orientation see Thompkins (1981).

WORKS CITED

Alegría, Claribel. 1986. *Despierta, mi bien, despierta.* San Salvador: UCA Editores.

Bakhtin, Mikhail. 1984. *Problems of Dostoevsky's Poetics.* Ed. and trans. Caryl Emerson. Minneapolis: University of Minnesota Press.

Bassnett, Susan, ed. 1990. *Knives and Angels: Women Writers in Latin America.* London: Zed Books.

Bauer, Dale. 1987. *Feminist Dialogics: A Theory of Failed Community.* Albany: State University of New York Press.

Benhabib, Seyla, and Drucilla Cornell, eds. 1988. *Feminism as Critique: on the Politics of Gender.* Minneapolis: University of Minnesota Press.

Foucault, Michel. 1972. *The Archeology of Knowledge.* Trans. A. M. Sheridan Smith. New York: Pantheon.

Gardiner, Judith Kegan. 1982. "On Female Identity and Writing by Women." In *On Writing and Sexual Difference,* ed. Elizabeth Abel. Chicago: University of Chicago Press, 177-92.

Genette, Gerard. 1980. *Narrative Discourse: An Essay in Method.* Trans. Jane E. Lewin. Ithaca, N.Y.: Cornell University Press.

González Echevarría, Roberto. 1985. *The Voice of the Masters: Writing and Authority in Modern Latin American Literature.* Austin: University of Texas Press.

Meyer, Doris, ed. 1988. *Lives on the Lines: The Testimony of Contemporary Latin American Authors.* Los Angeles: University of California Press.

Rimmon-Kenan, Shlomith. 1984. *Narrative Fiction: Contemporary Poetics.* London: Methuen.

Said, Edward. 1983. *The World, the Text, and the Critic.* Cambridge: Harvard University Press.

Sefchovich, Sara. 1983. *Mujeres en espejo, I.* Mexico: Folios Ediciones.

————. 1985. *Mujeres en espejo, II.* Mexico: Folios Ediciones.

Thompkins, Jane P., ed. 1981. *Reader-Response Criticism: From Formalism to Post-Structuralism.* Baltimore: Johns Hopkins University Press.

9

THE INTERNAL REVOLUTION: STRUGGLING WITH AND AGAINST THE SELF IN "FAMILY ALBUM"

Margaret B. Crosby

"Revolution begins with the self, in the self."

—Toni Cade Bambara
Black Feminist Thought (229)

Postmodern theorists demolish the classical Cartesian concept of a stable and integrative self—one that is synonymous with conscious-ness, meaning, and truth—and argue instead for a multiple, frag-mented self. "Family Album," a novella by Claribel Alegría (1991), is about the fragmented self. The protagonist, Ximena, exemplifies a division between the inner child and outer adult selves. This division is further fragmented by her own cultural identity as an upper-middle-class, Salvadoran-Nicaraguan woman and by her relationships with her husband, nanny, and other family members. As Ximena explores these plural selves, she develops a deeper understanding of her family and life and, in so doing, constructs a new identity. When she confronts her fears as well as the disparity between her familial values and the nature of Central American reality, her political and social consciousness are awakened. While the main action of "Family Album" takes place in Paris, a subtext occurs in Managua, Nicaragua, in 1978, on the day Edén Pastora seizes the National Palace in a concerted effort to overthrow the Somoza regime. Ximena's fragmented self and the construction of her subjectivity emerge out of these diverse settings.

144

Jane Flax (1991, 26) asserts that "Gender is a central constituting element in each person's sense of self and in a culture's idea of what it means to be a person." The conflict between Ximena's private aspirations and the public roles that society constructs for her as a woman, that is, wife and mother, becomes immediately apparent when Ximena expresses her personal desire to be a writer to her great aunt, Mamita Rosa:

> "Mamita Rosa, you're a saint, and now that you're about to die I want you to ask the Virgin to grant me three wishes. . . . That I get away from here, that I love my husband very much, and that I become a writer."
> "I'll ask for the first two, but not for the last. I don't like the way poets live."
> "But Mamita Rosa. . . ." (75)

Although Ximena objects, the fulfillment of all three wishes is impossible because they cannot exist in triplicate, and so give birth to a divided self. Since Mamita Rosa discourages Ximena from becoming a writer and later on dies, Ximena forgets about her aspiration and conforms to the role Central American society allots to women. She marries and becomes a housewife who spends most of her time at home and lives an isolated and sheltered existence, disconnected from the real world. Lidia Curti (1992, 150), in commenting on the association between women and narrative, contends that, whether women watch or read fiction at home, "the restricted space of the home . . . can be considered a female ghetto, a solipsistic world that is outside action, outside history [and] outside . . . pubs . . . [It is] the space of lack, of the negative, of being a non-man-[womens'] ontological existence, their being there, with themselves, in a voiceless intimacy." Curti's image of the home as a passive "female ghetto" where women engage in a "voiceless intimacy" with their televisions or novels, suggests the isolation, silence, and boredom that characterize Ximena's life as a housewife.

Ximena lives in Paris with Marcel, her French husband, who views Latin America as a marginalized Other and who seems bored and uninterested in her family there. Although Marcel and Ximena have been married for fifteen years, Ximena attributes the fact that they have no children to her undeveloped maternal instinct and to her doctor's diagnosis that she has the "uterus of a small girl" (118).

Ximena implies what patriarchal society believes, that motherhood changes a girl to a woman and that, without having a child, Ximena is incomplete, immature, and lacking. Moreover, we see a split in her adult self. There is the gendered self that conforms to societal expectations, yet sees herself as incomplete because she is not a mother, and there is the self that aspires to move beyond silence into speech by becoming a writer.

"The act of writing," says Gloria Anzaldúa, "is the quest for the self, for the center of the self, which we women of color have come to think as 'other'—the dark, the feminine . . ." (Anzaldúa 1981, 169). The writer that Ximena wants to be, but never becomes, suggests her desire to discover the self. The self is located in her relationships with family, in language, and in desire—the ontological struggle for wholeness. Lacan believes that "knowledge of the world, of others and of self is determined by language, and it is language that constitutes us as a subject" (Sarup 1989, 7; 9). Accessing language through writing is a means by which Ximena can discover and/or reconcile the "other," or the multiple selves within her. Writing is also a way to break the silence that characterizes her life as an upper-middle-class, Salvadoran-Nicaraguan wife and teacher living in Paris. In this context, as a Central American woman in France, Ximena is straddling four cultures and is split between her Central American and French identities as well as between her Salvadoran and Nicaraguan nationalities. Since her husband believes that French culture is superior to Latin American culture, she represents the Other whom he disdains. Thus we see another fracture. As Germaine Brée (1988, ix) asserts, "writing provides a space within which the 'self' may best appear in its complexity, conscious and unconscious of its 'difference' and similarities with respect to the characteristics of a given culture." Because writing is not an option for Ximena, she must define her subjectivity by other means, such as the oral act of story telling.

Ximena spends much of her time recalling memories and telling stories to Marcel about her family and childhood in Santa Ana, El Salvador. Ximena, who feels like Scheherazade, says that "she has always loved having people tell her stories and that Mamita Rosa and her mother were great at it" (88). Curti (1992, 142) claims that "fables and myth have a longstanding link to gender, to the feminine. Scheherazade, in the active role of story teller, provided the means to sustain life." Telling stories enables Ximena to preserve memory,

146

to connect with the past, and to construct her subjectivity, as a social self, delineated by her familial relationships. After learning that her Uncle Sergio, a symbol of the avarice of the Salvadoran oligarchy, has disinterred her father's bones because he does not belong to Sergio's family, she begins to obsess about her "blessed family" (87) and the fate of her father's bones. Ximena's obsession with her father's bones represents a downward descent into her inner self to excavate knowledge and justice that have been buried and desecrated.

Whenever Ximena recalls a relative or family member, she moves into her inner self and into her thoughts, fantasies, questions, and memories of childhood. She retreats "into her private world, a world in which Marcel figured only as a ghost while her thoughts, memories, and Chus Ascat were as real as flesh and blood" (79). Chus Ascat, her beloved and trusted Indian nanny who spoke Nahuatl and who died when Ximena was twelve years old, speaks to Ximena from the "other Santa Ana," a place George Yúdice (1985, 962) calls the "space of death" (el espacio de la muerte). Chus can foresee a person's death and informs Ximena of the death of her Uncle Sergio and later of her cousin Armando.

In addition to being the space of death, the other Santa Ana is a place of social consciousness and empowerment for the marginalized Other. There, power relations are subverted, and those people who have no power in society get even with those who do have power, but have abused their authority. Anyone who is guilty of social injustice is punished and made to suffer for his or her misdeeds by being transformed into an ugly creature. Because Sergio has mistreated the coffee workers on his coffee plantation, he is metamorphosed into a hairy animal with hooves. His punishment is to pick "thousands and thousands of coffee beans, without help from anyone" (73). Since Felipe Cuevas took potshots at the poor kids "who climbed up his jocote tree when they were hungry and looking for fruit," he is changed into a "huge vulture and can only eat rotting carrion" (74). For his punishment, the children he killed throw stones and make fun of him, and they will not leave him in peace. The other Santa Ana, however, also provides peace to those who help achieve social equality and justice. Ximena's father, who fought to effect social change in Nicaragua, is very happy there: "His cheeks are ruddy and he rides around on the sorrel mare he brought from Esteli" (106).

When Ximena is in her private, inner world, she asks Chus many questions about her relatives and their relationships with each other. Chus, who sees Ximena's family realistically, hesitates to tell her the truth because she knows Ximena will not understand the racist, exploitative, and hostile nature that characterizes some of her family members. We see the emergence of Ximena's child-self in her naiveté and limited understanding of the power relations that structure El Salvador and the rest of Central America. Ignorant of the greed that motivates her Uncle Sergio and Aunt Lupe, Ximena wonders "where on earth did Uncle Sergio get his obsessions from?" (71). Since he characteristically does strange things like celebrating his own funeral or preserving his amputated leg in cognac, there is a certain predictability to his behavior that renders it harmless. Used to his behavior and bizarre antics, Ximena is not surprised, nor does she get upset. She does not even get angry at him for disinterring her father's bones, but instead remains completely loyal to him because he is part of her family.

Feminist critic Minnie Bruce Pratt, in reflecting upon her childhood and the town in which she grew up, admits that her understanding of her childhood home is childish and limited. Much of the safety of her childhood, she says, was because Laura Cates, a black servant, was responsible for her, while her memory of a safe place to be was based on places secured by omission, exclusion, or violence and on her submitting to the limits of that place (Pratt 1988, 25-26). Pratt's observations closely parallel Ximena's life experiences. Both women achieve a sense of safety from their nonwhite care-takers—Laura Cates and Chus Ascat—who create a home with familiar, safe, and protected boundaries. Pratt's and Ximena's understanding of the places in which they were raised is childlike and immature; they see only what they were taught to see and are shaped by what they did not see or did not notice. Furthermore, both Pratt and Ximena passively abide by the established order of their home towns without ever questioning or criticizing the omission, exclusion or violence that existed there. For example, we see violence in the life of Felipe Cuevas, who used to shoot at the poor kids who climbed the tree in his yard and who was hacked to death. Omission and exclusion are demonstrated by Aunt Lupe, Sergio's wife. Because Sergio had many illegitimate children working as peons on his estate, Lupe would write irrational newspaper articles "saying there should be laws to prevent illegitimate children from inheriting, as this was an affront to religion and morality" (75). Lupe feared that the children might diminish the inheritance of her own two sons. Through Chus Ascat and Ximena's observations and perspective, Alegría shows how the safety in Ximena's family and neighborhood was in reality an illusion secured by exclusion, terror, fear, and subservience.

In order for Ximena to break through to her own liberation and greater understanding of herself, she has to "struggle with herself, against herself" (Pratt 1988, 35). In other words she must acknowledge her ignorance and fears and realize how *she* is implicated in the injustices perpetrated upon the people who are not like her. As a privileged woman, Ximena finds it easier to erase all trace of compassion for the majority of people who are not as fortunate as she is than to get involved in effecting social change. Unaware of the privileges her social class affords her, Ximena adopts what María Lugones (1990, 51) calls a "disengaged stance," one in which she "stands outside of the racial state and ethnocentric culture, looking in." From her position she argues that the disengaged stance is a "radical form of passivity toward the ideology of the ethnocentric racial state which privileges the dominant culture as the only culture to 'see with' and conceives this seeing as to be done non-self-consciously." From her position she argues that the disengaged stance is a "radical form of passivity toward the ideology of the ethnocentric racial state which privileges the dominant culture as the only culture to 'see with' and conceives this seeing as to be done non-self-consciously." From this position of distance and disengagement, Ximena avoids understanding the racist and ethnocentric attitudes that characterize her social class while, at the same time, ignoring her complicity in the perpetuation of these attitudes. Ximena's upper-middle-class status, then, creates another split in her sense of self. Furthermore, she finds it is easier to deny than to admit that her whimsical, eccentric, old uncle is really a despot whose "latifundio" is a "microcosm of patriarchal relations" (Palmer 1989, 76). It is also less threatening to think of his madness as foolish enthusiasm, rather than as an example of dementia, inhumanity, and barbarity. Since she lives in Paris, far away from the "family," and the death, destruction, and despair of the war in Nicaragua, Ximena is relatively unaffected and has no need to change. Yet by remaining intellectually blind to the problems in her countries, she is complicit in the oppression of other people, until

Armando gives her a reason to change and shows her "a new way to be in the world" (Pratt 1988, 42).

It is Armando's political discourse and passionate commitment to the revolutionary struggle that impresses Ximena and motivates her to change. When she is with Armando, we see her moving outward, away from her inner, private world and into the external realm of social, political, and ethical awareness. Armando, a former guerilla with the Sandinista National Liberation Front (FSLN), and now the diffuser and translator of FSLN propaganda in Paris, informs Ximena of the changes occurring in Nicaragua. Ximena resists Armando's excitement about the Sandinistas' gain in power and pessimistically asks, "What can a few ill-armed kids do against a National Guard equipped with sub-machine guns and tanks, helicopters and planes? Thousands of young men are going to die, only to have Yankee Marines land on our soil once again" (83). Armando opposes Ximena's pessimism and confronts her indifference: "Thousands of Nicaraguans have died unnecessarily since the Somoza dynasty took power. But they are the silent dead, Ximena, does that make it easier for you to forget them? . . . We have to fight on until we win" (83-84). Ximena is not convinced of the need to change. Even though she thinks Armando is "hopelessly overexcited," his words remind her of her obsession with her father's bones, and she begins to wonder if there are more important things to think about, such as Armando's son, Mario, who is trapped inside the Nicaraguan palace.

Armando challenges Ximena's strong need to be loyal to her family. He shows her that Uncle Sergio's greed "is not the exclusive monopoly of Santa Ana" (96), but characterizes the economic system all over Central America. He assures her that yes, "you can turn against your own family," especially when they are part of the problem. Attacking her complacency and attachment to material wealth, he criticizes her indifference:

> "It's your attitude that bothers me, . . . you were raised in that sea of misery, and you've erased all trace of it. . . . Don't you ever feel even the least bit uncomfortable? What have you done to help your people? You're very complacent, Ximena, your creature comforts are too important to you." (97-98)

When Ximena gets defensive and wants to know what she should do, Armando tells her "to show more interest, to stop being quite so blasé, to explain the problem to Marcel, to talk about it to her friends, to raise it as a topic in school" (98)—in other words, to get involved and to talk about the problem with other people.

We begin to see a change in Ximena when Armando discloses his own commitment to the guerrilla movement. As he describes his experiences of moral suffering, incarceration, torture, humiliation, and self-doubt, Ximena is moved and impressed. "True revolution," he explains, "comes from within, it is a solitary and intimate internal revolution that moves us to take a first step that can only be taken in silence of one's own accord" (111). Hearing Armando's stories and seeing the emotional pain they cause him again makes Ximena wonder if there are more important things to do in life than to worry about burying her father's bones, particularly when her father died twelve years ago.

Literary critic Margaret Higonnet asserts (1989, 81), "In literature of the civil wars, it is virtually a rule that the external conflict, which serves as a catalyst of social change and narrative sequence, also becomes a metaphor for inner conflict and the experience of inner emigration." Although the Nicaraguan revolution serves as a catalyst for social change in "Family Album," it does not function as a metaphor for Ximena's inner struggle, but rather as the impetus that leads to her personal change. The comparison Armando makes between marriage and death functions as a metaphor for Ximena's inner struggle:

> "It's the same thing to join the FSLN. . . . You have to make your commitment and *wed death*, . . . I know how the decision to *marry death* suddenly sets you free. You leave aside cowardice and fear for your precious skin, and you're incorporated into an audacious, invincible organism" (111) (my emphasis).

For the Nicaraguan who commits to the revolutionary struggle and weds death, she or he overcomes fear and is able to concentrate on the task on hand: "the destruction of Somoza and all he represents" (111). For Ximena to confront her family, to face her fears and to examine her "infantile obsessions" (111) is to be like the guerrilla who weds death. Once she "leaves the fear behind . . . everything

151

else becomes a lot easier" (119). She is free to achieve new goals, and the obsession with her father's bones ceases to control her. Lacan posits that "the discourse within which the subject finds its identity is always the discourse of the Other—of a symbolic order which transcends the Subject and which orchestrates its entire history" (Sarup 1989, 29). After hearing Armando's testimony, the discourse of the Other, and watching him express deep-seated passion and feeling for his work in the guerrilla, Ximena's awareness is raised, her consciousness is awakened, and she is convinced of the need to help her people. She commits herself to the FSLN and to the creation of a new Nicaraguan society. Armando ironically comments, "aside from [translating and distributing FSLN information bulletins], I spend my time awakening political consciousness in the souls of bored housewives such as yourself" (99).

Ximena's awakening brings growth, maturity, and the transition to adult womanhood. We see that she no longer acts like an immature child, but accepts the responsibility of a woman who is developing a sense of self. This is exemplified by the scene in the text where Ximena stares at her reflection in the boutique window and asks herself if she dare go through with her commitment to help Armando and the FSLN. The reflection smiles back and nods affirmatively. This scene suggests Lacan's mirror stage, in which the child recognizes herself as a self. Moreover, "the self," according to Lacan, "is always finding itself through reflections in the Other" (Tong 1989, 221). Ximena finds herself through the reflection of Armando, the Other. That is, by listening to his personal testimony and his discourse on social justice, she develops a social and political self. She admits that her "infantile outlook on life" (118) had stemmed from her fears of taking responsibility, growing older, and relinquishing material possessions. Her dramatic changes cause her to redefine her values. Now that she has a more realistic perception of the world and a moral response to Nicaragua's problems, she is no longer obsessed with the whereabouts of her father's bones. Her concentration is directed instead to questioning the meaning of dictatorship, hegemony, death, despair, and hope in Central America:

> Children crying with hunger are far more important. . . . Will Marcel understand this? That it's far more important to breathe fresh air, an air unpolluted by conquistadores or military despots and by overseers? That it's much more

important not to be gassed by the stench of the rotting room? (118)

Ximena's awakening also results in a greater understanding of her relationship to her family. Able to look at the Salvadoran side of her family more realistically, Ximena no longer protects them just because they are her blood relatives. She refers to her "dreadful family" (106) and admits to Marcel, "my family divides into people who take and people who give" (88). When she thinks about the Nicaraguan side of the family, she recognizes that a long history of resistance and struggle for social justice characterize them: "her great-uncle Zeldón, her father fighting alongside him and later alongside Sandino, Armando in prison for three years. And now Mario" (83). It is with this side of the family that she now identifies.

When Armando decides to return to Panama, he resigns from his job and makes Ximena the FSLN resentative in Paris. Before leaving Paris, he gives her the photo album that his wife, Maruca, gave him when he was incarcerated. First, the album represents the "passage from genealogical ties of filiation to the collective bonds of affiliation" (Harlow 1987, 116). Ximena realizes that Sergio has uprooted her past by disinterring her father's bones and that his corrupt desire for power and wealth are the same as those of Anastasio Somoza. Having this awareness, she stops being loyal and lets go of her familial ties to him and to the other relatives who share the same values. In joining the FSLN, she acknowledges her affiliation with the collective struggle to help her people. Second, the album signifies solidarity in the way it circulates among and between family members. Maruca gives the album to Armando who, in turn, passes it on to Ximena who is keeping it for now, but will probably pass it on to someone else in the future. Third, the album symbolizes knowledge and power. As Ximena learns more about the Nicaraguan side of her family, she gains knowledge about herself. The album contains a photograph she has never seen before of her father standing among the aunts, uncles, and forty-eight cousins. There are photographs of her new family in the FSLN which include photos of Maruca, Mario, and the commandoes. Possessing a record of family history, such as the photo album, empowers her and gives her a stronger sense of pride and commitment; it expresses the emergence of a collective self. Finally, the album foreshadows Armando's death, since his face is excised from every photograph.

Ximena hears Chus Ascat say, "He won't be long in coming" (121), which means he will not be long in coming to the other Santa Ana, the space of death.

Ximena returns to the safety of her inner, private world, where she processes her changes. In the voice of her child-self, she asks Chus how to say certain words in Nahuatl. We see the repetition of "child" which Ximena asked how to say earlier in the novel. Then, instead of asking how to say "bed," as she did before, Ximena asks how to say "cradle," suggesting a return to her Nicaraguan origin and to her father's roots. The last word Ximena asks how to say is "guerrilla." Here we see the expanding consciousness of a child into an adult and the implication of outward movement toward higher values and the broader realm of political, social, and ethical truths. Since "guerrilla" connotes multiple meanings—for example, strength, resistance, commitment, liberation, justice, solidarity, war, violence, and death—its meaning evokes a political identity for Ximena, as well as her embrace of violence and death and the end of everything her immediate family has taken for granted or valued.

In conclusion, Alegría juxtaposes the protagonist's fragmented self and subsequent intellectual awakening with a political subtext to show how war is a catalyst for personal change. Alegría constructs Ximena's subjectivity through her gender, class, ethnicity, family relationships, and access to language. In so doing she shows Ximena's transition from ignorance and indifference to awareness and social responsibility. Because Ximena develops a political and social consciousness of the problems in Central America, she renounces her relationship with her wealthy Salvadoran uncle and all that he represents. She also develops an appreciation for her Nicaraguan family history, one that is rooted in resistance movements and the struggle for social change. Although she now sees her family and understands Central American reality in a more complex way, the "struggle with and against the self" is not over. Given the potential danger of her political work and affiliation with the FSLN, her life is in jeopardy. Furthermore, her change in consciousness signifies the loss of Armando through death, the end of her materialistic life style, and quite possibly the termination of her marriage. It appears that Ximena is not conscious of these losses or the potential threat of losing her own life. At the end of the novella, we see Ximena speaking to Chus from her child-self, a position of innocence and wonder. After committing herself to helping Armando and the revolutionary cause, she says, "All of us are changing. This old world of ours is transforming into something unknown" (115).

WORKS CITED

Alegría, Claribel. 1991. *Family Album*. Trans. Amanda Hopkinson. Willimantic, Conn.: Curbstone Press.

Anzaldúa, Gloria. 1981. "Speaking in Tongues: A Letter to 3rd World Women Writers." In *This Bridge Called My Back*, ed. Cherríe Moraga and Gloria Anzaldúa. Watertown, Mass.: Persephone Press.

Brée, Germaine. 1988. Foreward. *Life/Lines: Theorizing Women's Autobiography*. Ithaca: Cornell University Press.

Curti, Lidia. 1992. "What is Real and What is Not: Female— Fabulations in Cultural Analysis." In *Cultural Studies*, ed. Lawrence Grossberg, Cary Nelson, and Paula Treichler. New York: Routledge, 134-53.

Flax, Jane. 1991. *Thinking Fragments*. Berkeley: University of California Press.

Harlow, Barbara. 1987. *Resistance Literature*. New York: Methuen.

Higonnet, Margaret R. 1989. "Civil Wars and Sexual Territories." In *Arms and the Woman*, ed. Helen Cooper, Adrienne Auslander Munich, and Susan Merrill Squier. Chapel Hill: University of North Carolina Press, 80-96.

Lugones, María. 1990. "Hablando cara a cara/Speaking Face to Face: An Exploration of Ethnocentric Racism." In *Making Face, Making Soul. Haciendo Caras*, ed. Gloria Anzaldúa. San Francisco: Aunt Lute Foundation Books, 46-54.

Palmer, Paulina. 1989. "Patriarchal Relations." In *Contemporary Women's Fiction: Narrative Practice and Feminist Theory*. Jackson and London: University of Mississippi Press.

Pratt, Minnie Bruce. 1988. "Identity: Skin Blood Heart." In *Yours in Struggle*, ed. Elly Bulkin, Minnie Bruce Pratt, and Barbara Smith. Brooklyn: Long Haul Press, 11-63.

Sarup, Madan. 1989. *Post-Structuralism and Postmodernism.* Athens: University of Georgia Press.

Tong, Rosemarie. 1989. *Feminist Thought.* Boulder: Westview Press.

Yúdice, George. 1985. "Letras de emergencia: Claribel Alegría." *Revista Iberoamericana* 51/132-33 (July-December): 953-64

PART THREE

EXTRALITERARY CARTOGRAPHIES

The relationships of literature with other discourses are various and complex. For example, literature has sometimes consciously attempted to achieve the effects of painting, to become word painting, or has tried to achieve the effects of music or photography, to turn into music, to provide only "negative exposures." At times poetry has even wanted to become sculpturesque. More concretely, we may define the comparable elements of literature and other discourses—whether visual or aural—as complexity, integration, and rhythm. In the extraliterary cartography of Claribel Alegría these elements are conceived as a multiplex scheme of dialectical relationships, often working to transform the "art" they have entered. The excursive project which underlies this "new poetics" appears to subvert the evolution of a successful system of terms for the analysis of literary works. What we may capture in the works of Alegría, therefore, is the form of an intricate pattern of coincidences and divergences rather than neat parallel lines.

It is perhaps with this scheme in mind that Kathleen March admonishes that "literature being written mentally or physically from a war zone makes demands for new evaluatory methods and criteria." According to March, the Fantastic as a subversive literary genre of denunciation in Alegría's "Family Album" is not purely "literary" but "experiential," serving to underscore "real" problems of visibility or invisibility.

The visibility or invisibility of pain and the bringing of that experience into language is the problem with which Nina Molinaro contends in her essay. Pain, etymologically implicated in "penalties" and "punishments," has no fixed form of its own, its original role lying outside of literature. The relationship between the discourse of pain and that of literature, however, is prefigured in the truth-bearing document that *testimonio* imitates. Pain, as both method and discourse, is also part of the "unwriting" experienced in Alegría's narrative. Previous writings of history, as well as subjects, are undone as new ones are attempted and eventually emerge.

Jo Anne Engelbert's examination of the "extraliterary dimension" of the New World elegiac tradition as defined by Alegría leads her to compare Alegría's poems to *arpilleras*, "vivid scraps of personal experience commingled with verses by poets and artists who were witnesses to the common struggle." Alegría's poetry inhabits what Engelbert terms a "precarious zone," one more extensive with departure than tradition.

Finally, Celia Catlett Anderson offers us a reading lesson of a different sort. Here, we discover that lines separating literature for adults and children may blur in several significant ways. More importantly, the "required politics" of literature lead Anderson to examine one of Alegría's texts within the pedagogical context of the classroom, where aesthetic and moral, literary and spiritual issues must contend. Thus Alegría, through her complex chart of extraliterary relationships, may attempt to show her readers "how to grow from childhood to adulthood without becoming a mere imitation."

10

THE REAL AND THE FANTASTIC IN THE POLITICAL DISCOURSE OF "FAMILY ALBUM"

Kathleen N. March

B ecause it is a rather brief work, Claribel Alegría's "Family Album" might seem deceptively simple. However, it actually exhibits an extraordinary complexity, which derives from a fundamental contrast. That contrast or, in a certain sense, contradiction, is created by the author's use of the fantastic in a text that has a clear political commitment. For this reason, the imaginary or unreal content is foregrounded against a context that is not only formed by concrete historical circumstances, but which also takes a stand that is characteristic of an intensely sincere involvement with the striking reality these same circumstances represent. This apparent contradiction in terms, or in perspective, will be the focus of the following essay. I will attempt to show in what ways the opposition in question works to both intensify and negate reality, a process which ultimately enhances the characteristics of this very reality, and in so doing also calls into question some features of the fantastic as defined by Todorov (1973). At the same time, it more comfortably satisfies Rosemary Jackson's assessment of literary fantasy (Jackson 1982). We shall see that the point or paraxial region (cf. Jackson 1982, 19) at which the real and the imaginary ultimately merge or mirror each other is the human experience of death.

The protagonist who centers "Family Album" is Ximena. Her world, in terms of temporal and spatial constructs with their corresponding experiences, is a clearly contradictory one, yet there are elements from each sector superimposed upon the other. These gradually modify the meaning of the titular phrase, calling into question the process of representation and the limits within which it occurs through asking *who* is in the album and to *what* family does the album belong? The use of photographs to focus the central theme of the text is consonant with the statement of Jackson (1982, 43):

> The topography of the modern fantastic suggests a preoccupation with problems of vision and visibility, for it is structured around spectral imagery: it is remarkable how many fantasies introduce mirrors, glasses, reflections, portraits, eyes—which see things myopically, or distortedly, as out of focus—to effect a transformation of the familiar into the unfamiliar.

The album is the text within which the physical representation is inserted; the work "Family Album" is the metatext within which the problems of visibility, invisibility, and vision are placed in contact with the extraliterary plane.

Ximena alternates between memories of her childhood in Third World Central America (which, although not directly stated in the work, is El Salvador) and her present life in the modern, urban, European setting of Paris. The two locations, which correspond to two chronological periods of her life, are certainly very different, materially, linguistically, and spiritually. Nevertheless, while the Central American past might seem remote, the force of its influence on the protagonist is very real; her contact with it through memories, phone calls, or letters implies a greater involvement on her part in those remote family affairs than she seems to afford her daily activities in the foreign city she barely notices (and, in fact, will come to reject near the end of the work).

It is particularly in terms of spatial coordinates that the real and the fantastic elements first intersect and become manifest. Santa Ana is portrayed as the place where Ximena's family members lead a closed, conservative existence, tacitly structured around Catholicism, since they attend to such a great degree to social norms. One way in which the Christian religion is indirectly causative of the family's grotesque behavior is seen in the way it does not prepare them to deal with mortality and has allowed them to focus on the final resting place of the dead rather than on treatment of the living.

One result is Uncle Sergio's need to first fetishize his own final moment by annually lying in his prepared coffin and subsequently create a ritualistic solution to the partial loss or death represented by his amputated leg. The grandmother's rebuff of religious resignation is symbolized in her deathbed desire to urinate on pure white gladioli. This world of suffocating family ties and degraded Christian beliefs is framed, in a sense, by the question of where the bones of Ximena's father will be "allowed" to rest, what space they are to be allotted. This controversy becomes grotesquely infantile by the end of "Family Album."

As spiritual occupant of an imaginary space that is associated with the geographical Santa Ana (El Salvador), Chus is the counterpoint to Ximena's middle-class family. The main character's former nursemaid has nothing else in common with them; her calm descriptions contrast with the baroque rituals developed to supplement Christianity's inadequacy. Chus, as the guardian for alternative perspectives, is Ximena's point of contact with the *other* Santa Ana. In true fantastic fashion, the latter is the afterworld, or world of death, but it is not characterized in terms of the fear for the supernatural or unknown, as is common in this literary modality. Rather, it is a natural space, a locus where social differences are leveled. This is signified first and foremost by the manner in which the former servant now functions as Ximena's *nahual,* or spiritual guide, and as an informed observer of that alternative space. Moreover, except for occasional phone calls with bad connections, Chus is the predominant representative of Ximena's original world, the only one who has accompanied her to Paris and whose communication is based on the relationship's positive aspects: childhood innocence, natural knowledge, and openness. Although she provides the potential for a different perspective, initially she does nothing special to help Ximena shed her passive, intranscendental role of secondary school teacher in a foreign country. The indigenous Chus thus facilitates the first step toward contact with an alternative reality, which is not in direct keeping with what could have been an eerie photographic motif representing the supernatural or fantastic world of the dead, but which functions instead as a reverse portrait, a negative exposure, of a starkly real one. Chus's soothing discourse also contrasts with the family's jealous, agitated one, and she reveals the falsity of "family" concerns, as she helps convert aunts, uncles, cousins into caricatures, their lives meaningless beyond the grave because their self-centered natures had already rendered them meaningless during their lifetimes. Called "la otra Santa Ana" (the other Santa Ana) in the text, Chus's world is a mirror to the real Santa Ana; her internal or spiritual space enhances and provides a clearer focus of the other one, a part of which has been silenced or made impossible by class differences.

Ximena's family, with its closed spaces (Sergio's boxes, interiors, repossessed houses), its childhood and childishness (senile transgressions, silly squabbling), is decaying morally, just as Sergio's body is literally becoming dismembered, or just as Aunt Tula's entire body is undergoing degeneration due to the excessive consumption of alcohol. The rottenness is not at all subtly symbolized by the *tufo* or foul odor, that pervades everything, emphasizing the grotesqueness of this atmosphere and inferring that even the family members who are still living in reality inhabit a burial ground. Only Chus, who is not a family member, escapes the implied degeneration and is located in a liberated territory of fantasy. If this were the extent of Ximena's family and the authorial intent were not consciously related to an extraliterary reality, "Family Album" would remain fundamentally in the realm of amusing eccentricity, which characterizes the Santa Ana seen by the protagonist's patronizing French husband, Marcel.

However, the heretofore unknown makes its appearance in Ximena's anodyne existence in the form of her cousin, Armando. His presence eventually forces her to redefine her concept of family and her relationship to it. The intrusion of her cousin's world into hers is represented in primarily two ways: a family album, with its special characteristics, and a new form of discourse, one centered not on blood ties in the sense of a genetic link, but on ties related to blood as it is conceived and shed. This is the family Ximena scarcely knows, has never seen in fact, and which Marcel cannot accept because its space is not "familiar" to him, as Armando affirms:

> Marcel will never understand our problems, unless he goes to Central America and feels them in his own flesh and bones. He has to live with them, until they seem as familiar and unconditionally horrible as the Eiffel Tower. (97)

Jackson (1982, 48) states that fantasy is the representation of the invisible, the writing which brings forth or calls attention to that which is not normally perceived:

> Themes of the fantastic in literature revolve around this problem of making visible the un-seen, of articulating the un-said. Fantasy establishes, or dis-covers, an absence of separating distinctions, violating a 'normal', or common-sense perspective which represents reality as constituted by discrete but connected units.

This is precisely what Armando does: he brings an album showing the unseen, or rather, that which cannot be seen, because it has disappeared. The simple yet forceful paradox lies in the fact that the photos that have mysteriously disappeared are a reference to the people who had actually disappeared in Nicaragua, El Salvador, and other Latin American countries. In Alegría's work, these people's invisibility is made perceptible by the very absence of a tangible image—the force of nothingness which sets a new situation in motion. The family, and the family album, are spaces within which roles and individuals are recognized; it is a social structure, the *esplace* defined by Alain Badiou (1982) as the arena within which society functions and the pieces move about. The missing photographs belong to persons no longer participating within that territory, either because they have met their death or because their political commitment forces them to leave the familiar esplace to enter a new, counter-, reality.

Armando states that the photographs disappear, but only suggests that the album is "embrujado" (bewitched). The two cousins hesitate over an explanation for the phenomenon, as Todorov suggests characters frequently do before a manifestation of the fantastic. And since the inexplicable situation of the missing portraits is never resolved, it also conforms to the Todorovian definition of the purest fantastic form while, judging from their comments, the characters merely see it as an uncanny event that has a possible reading or representation in reality. Although it is motive for discussion, it is not a deterrent to subsequent action.

At this point a comparison of family circumstances emerges: the narcissistic Santa Ana residents are rooted in their material bodies, seeming even more present (and malodorous) in death.

Hence the leg that is not disposed of, the aunt whose cadaver is made to pass as living, the bones that are bothersome enough to some to require digging up and moving elsewhere. The other side of the family is barely noticeable, is not easily located, and indeed is totally disappearing, leaving no remains behind. The photographs, or rather the absent photographs, represent them in allegorical or figurative fashion, although this is a function which Todorov would contend weakens the fantastic. The purpose of "Family Album," however, is not to serve as an exercise of the imagination, in order to identify some evil force at work, but to have the blank spaces serve as referents or signs marking a starkly real phenomenon.

Because of the contrast Armando signifies, Ximena begins to reassess her concept of "family," while she contemplates her own condition as a barren woman, her "childish uterus" that makes it impossible for her to have offspring. The implication is that her view of life is underdeveloped, immature, and, when combined with her statement that she once loved Peter Pan and the idea of never wanting to grow up, quite escapist. This escapism is reinforced by her spouse's treatment of her as well as, initially, the spiritual intimacy she sustains with her former nursemaid from childhood. Armando redefines not only family ties, but also the parental role for her, as his paternal pride in his son Mario is based chiefly on the youth's commitment to the revolution. The father thus "gives" his son to society, despite the danger that he might die in guerrilla activity. The focus on this side of the family is an open, outward one, a linking with the collective experience of the country which renders personal details vague or irrelevant, as opposed to the restrictive, calculatingly selfish individualism of Santa Ana and its gossip.

The fantastic element introduced by the politically committed character is quite intricate. What is more, without it Armando's role would be overly simple, reduced to a denunciation of injustice as in numerous works in which authorial intent may be admirable (to certain groups of readers, at least) but is detrimental to the aesthetics of a creative work. Thus, in the same way as Santa Ana's residents could have remained on the level of the folklorish, the other part of the family could have suffered from representation by a dogmatic (albeit well-intentioned) discourse. The fantastic phenomenon of the missing photographs prevents the polarized or simplified categorization of the two "family texts." As will be seen at the end of this essay, the voice of Chus is ultimately responsible for bringing the real and the unreal full circle to their final interaction and significance.

A reflection or ripple effect of the fantastic photographs is the lexicon that permeates Armando's speech, subtly but unmistakably, and which reinforces the ultimate junctures of fantasy with reality in "Family Album." Hence terms such as "fantastic" (which appears three times), "vampire" (also appearing three times), "marvel," and "miracles" help neutralize or soften the more insistent political content and lessen the conceptual dissonance between the revolutionary perspective and the "bewitched" album. Perhaps most interesting is the use of "vampire," a term clearly not meant in the literal sense and which briefly becomes the subject of discussion by Armando and Ximena. The fantastic aspect is all but drained from the word as Armando explains how Somoza literally drained the blood donated to his people after the earthquake and sold it back to the donors, reaping great profit for himself. Here, then, the fantastic changes roles; instead of referring to the unreal, it underlines the Nicaraguan reality known to be so horrible, so unthinkable, so incomprehensible, that it seems unreal and must be represented by what is outside the normal human experience. One who removes blood from others is indeed best characterized as a vampire, a supernatural figure which synthesizes the concepts of death, deceit, pleasure (Somoza's goal was adding to his wealth and therefore to his own sensual satisfaction), inescapable ubiquitousness, etc. The term signifies the deed as well as the psychological effect it has upon the victims.

Chus is the original facilitator of Ximena's acquisition of a new, political perspective, because the level on which she functions for her former charge is intimate, more primitive or instinctive. At least this holds as long as it is suggested that the protagonist has not reached true maturity. As previously observed, the servant describes an alternative existence where barriers cease to exist and moral traits are called into account; justice, in other words, is done in the other Santa Ana, as it was not in the earthly one. Chus herself is a "spirit" or supernatural character, although the narrator avoids giving her any fearful aspects and instead portrays her appearances as natural phenomena, as does Ximena, for whom she is the only known confidante. Armando, as a real character and who is still living during the time of narration, also is a facilitator of the new viewpoint his cousin will assume. His function is different, however, in the sense that he is linked less to a place of final justice ("la otra Santa Ana") than to one characterized by an ongoing struggle (Nicaragua). The stark, tragic present of Armando, Mario, and others like them complements and completes Chus's articulatory status of past and future. Yet the two planes merge. This occurs when the nursemaid affirms that Armando will soon arrive in "the other Santa Ana," meaning that his return to Nicaragua will result in his death. However, it is worth noting that this return to the homeland and its resistance movement simultaneously indicates his incorporation into the family, on his own terms.

In a process that runs parallel to Armando's political conversation and Chus's comments about the family back home, Ximena experiences growth. While she continues to seek information from her spiritual guide, by the end of the work, the definitions she requests increase in complexity as well as emotive content. She wants first to know how to say *niño* (child) in Nahuatl, then *cuna* (cradle), and then *guerrillero* (guerrilla fighter). These are terms for which she wants more than a translation; she strives to understand the meaning. Chus, her indigenous informant, is supposed to provide the answers. Interestingly enough, the Nahuatl word for the first two terms is given, but for the third, "guerrillero," there is no answer. Perhaps there is an implication that such a concept does not exist in the native language, as violence such as that now experienced in Central America was not part of the preconquest experience. In any event, the absence of such a term is not an indication of linguistic inadequacy, but a way of leaving the text open for further reading. This too is frequent in the fantastic, which resists closure. In effect, the fantastic is at its purest when no resolution is provided as to the real or imaginary nature of the events portrayed by a specific literary discourse, whether it be that of characters, narrator, or implied author. In a sense, then, a word such as *guerrillero*, which has no relation at all to fantasy, is left for future understanding, as if it might designate an unexplained manifestation, a marvelous or uncanny being, associated with a reality yet to materialize. Conceivably there could be another tenuous link with the fantastic in that to the external observer, the guerrillero or guerrillera is often invisible (when clandestine), or disguised as someone else in daily life. There are multiple thematic, stylistic, and ideological relationships in this work.

The final page of "Family Album" is a different sort of text, combining the discourse of modern media (the official story, one might say) with the initial textual territory of the signifying ancestral bones. However, the narrative has since passed through the filter of political awakening. In this one-page segment, Somoza, who at the time of the narrative present is politically very real, and historically an "incredible" tyrant, must escape from the new political esplace with his own family skeletons. He is thus linked to the grotesque family of Santa Ana and its self-centered decadence. Now, too, Ximena begins to call all Central America a *pudridero*, a mausoleum or place where people rot into nothingness, which constitutes a rewriting of the term's earlier reference to the familial sphere so that it acquires the status of a politically motivated metaphor.

According to Todorov (1973, 60), the fantastic not only cannot be allegorical or metaphoric, it cannot have a poetic reading or be present in poetry. Yet Alegría's text manages to retain a poetic rhythm through lexical repetition and especially through terms bound to the semantic field of death (therefore offering suggestions of the supernatural or unknowable) and others pertaining to extraordinary phenomena. Mirrors, negatives, negations of each other, the two worlds of Ximena's family constantly clash as they try to fuse into a single entity. Armando even points out a parallel: religious vows and the vows taken by revolutionaries to fight for freedom despite the risks to self and loved ones:

> You have to make your commitment and wed death, just like the nun. You know you're laying your life on the altar and from then on your skin won't matter a scrap to you: you've offered it up for those who will survive to enjoy a better future. (111)

Ultimately, the extraliterary reality prevents the disappearing photographs from dissolving into an adventure through the author's imagination. The lack of explanation for the occurrence can be seen as the displaced denunciation of the historical lack of explanation surrounding the many persons who have disappeared during the course of contemporary Central American history. Yet naming the cause, even in its monstrous manifestation as vampire, is not enough, and Armando knows this (35), for he decides to heed his own advice and return to the struggle. Both he and Chus affirm that Ximena's father would be pleased at the fall of the horrendous dictatorship, in another step toward the coalescing of the contemporary revolution with ancient, indigenous values.

What does this all signify for the interpretation of the fantastic in literature? Jackson (1982, 3) says early on in her study that fantasy "is a literature of desire, which seeks that which is experienced as absence or loss." As a literary modality associated with absences, the fantastic is indeed appropriate for the portrayal of the constant disappearance of people in Latin America and, specifically, in Central America. The paradox, as noted, derives from the fact that the fantastic as a mode or technique and a fictive signifier is here pointed toward a very real signified. The fact that the disappearances from the family album are not designated as such, but rather as "cut out photographs," renders just a bit more tenuous the linguistic connection that, as Todorov (1973, 76) observes, is at times the source for the occurrence of the fantastic in creative writing.

Jackson (1982, 4) affirms that fantastic literature, by tracing the edges or outlines of what is silenced, suggests the basis upon which a cultural order rests. One would have little difficulty in substituting "cultural" with "political" in the case of "Family Album." The statement of Bellemin-Noël (1971, 112-13) that the fantastic "names the unnameable" is also appropriate for the text in question, although the reason for the inability to provide names for the disappearance or the disappeared in "Family Album" is not likely to be the one this critic had in mind. Also relevant is Hélène Cixous's statement (1973, 68) that the uncanny (we have seen that the characters' reactions to the absent photographs is that it is odd) is the rehearsal of the encounter with death, which is pure absence. Finally, Jackson (1982, 175; 180) concludes that the fantastic is the "art of estrangement, resisting closure" and in so doing, it moves forward, dismantling the real and its categories. This is entirely the situation of "Family Album," in which Ximena's world as she has seen it until then undergoes profound restructuring. In the end, she not only sees things differently or for the first time (we once again note that the fantastic is an experiential and literary modality closely associated with vision), she also gives them different names and in so doing gives herself a name, a purpose in life. She inherits Armando's briefcase, finds the political pamphlets and decides she should translate them for distribution. And she will call Marcel to tell him of her new reality, her new identity, her new maturity: "guess who's the new FSLN representative in Paris? I am." (119) In so doing she discards one language (that of traditional Santa Ana) for another, and replaces silence (equivalent to passivity, uselessness, complicity, repression) with affirmation of self, but a self related to others and committed to participating in a collective cause.

Todorov's statement that the literary fantastic leaves us two equally unsatisfactory notions—reality and literature—is seconded by Jackson (1982, 37):

> By offering a problematic representation of an empirically real world, the fantastic raises questions of the nature of the real and unreal, foregrounding the relation between them as its central concern. It is in this sense that Todorov refers to fantasy as the most literary of all literary forms, as the quintessence of literature, for it makes explicit the problems of establishing reality and meaning through a literary text.

Because that meaning has in "Family Album" a well-defined political identity, the fantastic aspects are even further foregrounded as differing from the real. In fact, they come to be modified by their counterreferent, so that in a sense they are less revelations or a questioning of reality than, paradoxically, its affirmation and representation. Just as the real comes under constant dialogical attention (Jackson 1982, 36), the ontological definition of the unreal comes into play. If, as Bessière (1974) claims, the fantastic is the most artificial and deliberate narrative, it is even more of an artifice in the politically committed text which strives to denounce true conditions as unjust as well as play up their incredible nature.

Underlying these more unique or innovative functions, the disappearing photographs embody the way the fantastic "draws attention to difficulties of representation and to conventions of literary discourse" (Jackson 1982, 84). The process understandably extends to the extraliterary discourse as well and ultimately the difficulty is assigned to a specific cause: the repression of a violent government which enforces a law of silence around deaths, causing them to remain unexplained, making people invisible or their location unknown. These circumstances clearly carry elements of the unreal, invisible, mysteriousness. If fear is a frequent (albeit not required) feature of the fantastic work, one can also see that the constant fear and danger suffered by Nicaragua under Somoza (and by El Salvador or Guatemala, among other countries) in a sense turns the entire population into walking dead. The soldiers who patrol the rural areas and torture civilians without reason, sometimes in public and just as often in private, are as great a source of fear for the general populace as the Siguanaba or Cipitio. In fact, they are a reality much more to be feared than those mythical figures, because their treatment of the people is infinitely more inhuman and monstrous. This is, of course, a lateral text, but the authors and readers are always keenly aware of its existence.

While the fantastic may be used to question the concept of character (and therefore, of the self as a coherent whole), in a Central American setting such as that of "Family Album," one senses that the individual's identity is not being called into question seriously. In other words, here Todorov's designation of one category of the fantastic as that of "I—not I" themes is less applicable, precisely because one of the purposes is to define and discover the meaning of a complete family. The series of disappearances forms a group whose fate is due to a shared ideology; they are a family based not on genealogical ties but on solidarity, on commonality of purpose and collective commitment. They are the representatives of the rational world, while Santa Ana and Somoza signify the hyperbole of greed, the former remaining on the level of the grotesque because their concerns do not extend beyond the family, while the latter irrationally attacks those he does not know. The human experience of death provokes fear, which in its irrational effects leads to the creation of monstrous beings, although a dictatorship like those of Nicaragua's three Somozas is hardly a product of anyone's fantasy. The political discourse of "Family Album," which is not that extensive, thereby includes metadescriptive, metaphorical terms not intended for literal interpretation or perhaps not even for evoking a sense of the uncanny, but rather meant to be a rational, political identification of the natural psychological effect on the population. On the other hand, the reader is left to make the easy connection between the unexplained photograph disappearances and the real, physical effect of government mistreatment of the populace.[1]

This discussion does not address every aspect of the fantastic as it appears in "Family Album," nor has this been its purpose. Its goal has been to illustrate some of the complexity of Alegría's narrative, while keeping in mind that literature produced in contexts of survival and resistance—this includes literary modalities such as the fantastic—can be an integral part of the revolution against social injustice. The author Roque Dalton wrote that he had arrived at the revolution through poetry, from which one would infer that revolution would be located in the poetry as well. This would account for the reversal of literary techniques, the difference in their effects, the need for a diverging critical stance in order to achieve accurate evaluation. In short, literature being written mentally or physically from a war zone makes demands for new evaluatory methods and criteria on all participants: writers, readers, and critics. In a parallel manner to Armando's evaluation of Marcel, some critics have affirmed that there is no way to understand these works, which are resistance literature (cf. Harlow's [1987] discussion of this term), without having been inside. If that is physically impossible, there is another way, another sort of text: that of history. In "Family Album" it is a family history of exploitation and violence leading to civil war, genocide, and nearly every incredible atrocity humans commit in their unbelievable need to satisfy their desires. National history renders individual family histories ridiculous, because it exposes their pettiness when the members turn inward to try to satisfy their own needs above all others'. This process of exposure has been made possible precisely by the use of the unreal because, as Jackson (1982, 180) concludes,

> The modern fantastic, the form of literary fantasy within the secularized culture produced by capitalism, is a subversive literature. It exists alongside the real, on either side of the dominant cultural axis, as a muted presence, a silenced imaginary other. Structurally and semantically, the fantastic aims at dissolution of an order experienced as oppressive and insufficient.

In a final overview of "Family Album," it thus becomes clear that neither Santa Ana nor the revolution, Ximena's Salvadoran family or her Nicaraguan one, holds its own without the septum and diastolic pulse that is represented by the fantastic elements of the text. One might laugh at the Uncle Sergios and Aunt Petronilas, or mourn the losses Armando describes, but the heart of the matter is located in their intersection and transfusion. It is a heart that points toward justice as a potential result. That the indigenous woman

Chus is the final voice of this *other* Santa Ana is consonant with the vindication today by various Latin Americans, including A. Roa Bastos and works such as *Hijo de Hombre* (Son of Man), of the revolution as an effort to settle accounts for and with those who were the victims of brutal invasions and conquests centuries ago. There is one overtly political discourse which knows how to present the other vision, but indigenous and fantastic modalities are able to represent it in a way that finds a space within even more resisting readers. Together, in works such as "Family Album," which combine them, a new text is created, and it betrays neither of the originals while going beyond its own brief extension precisely on the strength of this cross-fertilization. Alegría, Argueta, Dalton, and other Central American authors illustrate in what ways their national literatures can simultaneously be imaginary, visionary, and denunciatory: how they can and do have a vital role in their societies.

NOTES

1. A brief comparison is in order: just as major shifts occur in the fantastic as used in this Central American narrative, so do they take place with feminism. Although this is not seen in "Family Album," the concept of feminism's nature and purpose is called into question in other works, notably Gioconda Belli's novel *La mujer habitada* (House of woman). The usual feminist discourse simply does not fit, or at least must undergo alterations in the context of a people's revolution. Like the "I—not I" question, the female-male interrogation is frequently not the one foremost among the minds of the *compañeros* (comrades) as involved in armed resistance. This does not invalidate feminist discourse, just as the fantastic as Todorov and others see it is not invalidated. However, the context that is defined by the very real danger of a horrible death and survival requires the help of all. There can be little discussion of household tasks and equal employment opportunities when one's home has been razed and per capita income totals barely a few cents a day, when the entire family works, including young children. In the introduction to *Lovers and Comrades: Women's Resistance Poetry from Central America*, Amanda Hopkinson (1989, xxii) writes: "As a major area of struggle is against a monolithic external enemy (the United States),

women cannot afford to adopt a separatist stance against the male half of their population."

WORKS CITED

Alegría, Claribel. 1991. "Family Album." In *Family Album*, trans. Amanda Hopkinson. Willimantic, Conn.: Curbstone Press.

Badiou, Alain. 1982. *Théorie du sujet*. Paris: Éditions du Seuil.

Bellemin-Noël, Jean. 1971. "Des Formes fantastiques aux thèmes fantasmatiques." *Littérature* 2 (May): 103-28.

Bessière, Iréne. 1974. *Le Récit fantastique: La poétique de l'incertain*. Paris.

Cixous, Hélène. 1973. "La fiction et ses fantômes: Une lecture de l'*Unheimliche* de Freud." *Poétique*, 10, 199-216.

Harlow, Barbara. 1987. *Resistance Literature*. New York: Methuen.

Hopkinson, Amanda. 1989. *Lovers and Comrades. Women's Resistance Poetry from Central America*. Trans. A. Hopkinson and members of the El Salvador Solidarity Campaign Cultural Committee. London: The Women's Press.

Jackson, Rosemary. 1982. *Fantasy: The Literature of Subversion*. London: Methuen.

Todorov, Tzvetan. 1973. *The Fantastic: A Structural Approach to a Literary Genre*. Trans. Richard Howard. Cleveland: Case Western Reserve University Press.

11

THE LANGUAGE OF BODILY PAIN AND THE FICTION OF CLARIBEL ALEGRÍA

Nina L. Molinaro

"They cut off my voice
So I grew two voices
in two different tongues"
                    —Alicia Portnoy

"Physical pain has no voice,
but when it at last finds
a voice, it begins to tell
a story."   —Elaine Scarry

One of the most visible and prolific writers of Central America, Claribel Alegría is also a vocal commentator on the political turbulence that has characterized that region for the last several decades. Alegría considers herself first and foremost an activist, aspiring to convey the difficult and ultimately destructive realities of Nicaragua and El Salvador, two countries engulfed by what she terms "fratricidal tragedy" (Forché 1984, 12), a tragedy controlled, in turn, by foreign imperial interests, namely the United States.   Living in voluntary exile for much of her adult life, Alegría essentially views her writing as the act of collecting ghosts (Yúdice 1985, 953), a position made manifest by her attitude towards language; in an interview with Forché (1984, 11), she observes that "all too frequently I feel that words are growing sterile, that I am reconstructing and extrapolating a memory, an empty evocation of the themes that I prefer to deal with." Her comments also aptly summarize one of the challenges posed by testimonial literature: to make undeniably objective, and hence referentially valid, to the reader, the subjectivity of another person (or community), whether that subject be the author, the author's assumed persona, or a fictive character.   John

174

Beverley (1992, 10) incisively elaborates the peculiar position of testimonial literature:

> el testimonio es y no es una forma "auténtica" de cultura subalterna; es y no es "narrativa oral"; es y no es "documental"; es y no es literatura; concuerda y no concuerda con el humanismo ético que manejamos como nuestra ideología práctica académica; afirma y a la vez desconstruye la categoría del "sujeto."

> (testimony is and is not an "authentic" form of subaltern culture; it is and is not "oral narrative"; it is and is not "documentary"; it is and is not literature; it agrees and does not agree with the ethical humanism that we use as our practical academic ideology; it affirms and simultaneously deconstructs the category of "subject.")[1]

In Alegría's work, this dynamic overlaps with an investigation of the possibilities for individual, and often overtly feminine, self-assertion, memory, and creative expression; as Yúdice (1985, 956) notes of Alegría's *They Won't Take Me Alive,* "se dan las condiciones para convertir el sujeto en disolución o desaparición en un sujeto emergente" (the conditions are made available to convert the dissolving or disappearing subject into an emerging subject). The emerging subject of which he speaks corroborates a message of increased political awareness for the community at large.

Because much, if not most, of her work portrays the conflictive situations of El Salvador and Nicaragua, the social realities that she attempts to translate frequently feature a representation of the excessive forms of physical control exercised by a repressive government, such as imprisonment, torture, disappearance, and murder. Although an assessment of psychological and emotional pain traverses much recent Latin American literature, a similar examination of physical pain, a constant in testimonial literature, is rare. Elaine Scarry suggests that this may be the case because physical pain, pain that originates in and expresses through the body, effectively shatters language by resisting objectification; of all the sentient experiences, pain is unique in that it is not *of* or *for* anything beyond itself. Pain also occasions a division between self and other, a division that springs from its unsharability as "that which cannot be denied and that which cannot be confirmed" (Scarry 1985, 4). The experience of pain radically separates the person in a state of pain from the person who observes someone else in a state of pain. This separation comes to inhabit the language constructed around its existence; "physical difference is translated into a verbal difference: the absence of pain is a presence of world; the presence of pain is the absence of world. Across this set of inversions pain becomes power" (Scarry 1984, 37). Language is thus rendered insufficient to communicate intense physical pain and instead turns it into an effect of power.

By the same token, although art typically extends the visibility of its referents, the invisibility of pain remains virtually uncontested. One of the principal sites that responds to this invisibility is, precisely, testimonial literature because it offers a forum for those who speak on behalf of others in pain. Literature of testimony tends to arise during times of political instability as an antidote to the monologic presence of a dominant ideology, as a voice for those who have been systematically stripped of their voices. One way to effectively deprive a sentient subject of her voice is, as has been argued above, through divorcing voice from body. Thus, pain is associated with the power to manipulate a person's ability to make his or her experience accessible to others; the agency absent in pain reasserts itself in the fiction of power, and "the sheer material factness of the human body [is] borrowed to lend [a given] cultural construct the aura of 'realness' and 'certainty'" (Scarry 1985, 14). In the two most dramatic political events involving widespread pain, torture and war, the fiction of power is maintained through an obsessive display of false agency which substitutes for the object of pain.

How to bring the experience of pain, an intentional state lacking an intentional object, into language? Scarry (1985, 164) suggests that the site of this "making" properly lies in the act of imagining, which she describes as "an intentional object without an experienceable intentional state." It is through imagining that pain is extended to the point at which it acquires an object and is transformed into a self-modifying, self-eliminating phenomenon. Much testimonial literature underwrites a dynamic based on imagining physical pain into language, on providing it with an object, on converting pain into a story. With this in mind, let us now turn to four narrative texts by Alegría that fasten on, to varying

176

degrees and with differing results, the state of physical pain and its conversion into language. Narrative would seem to lend itself to such an analysis because the genre of narrative, and especially the subgenre of testimonial narrative, evinces language that is purposefully mimetic and, thus, more potentially objectifiable. Intentionality determines and, conversely, challenges the function of testimonial literature in telling a certain story in which the story includes an acknowledged desire to assign to pain a false agency (for example, the power of a given regime) and/or an equal desire to imagine language that will convince the reader of the reality of pain. Alegría's fiction occupies various sites along the continuum established between the two desires.

Alegría's "Family Album" and *Despierta, mi bien, despierta* (Awake, my love, awake) present two examples of the ways in which the language of pain successfully resists objectification.[2] In both texts the communication of pain is condensed by superimposing its correlative death; the former text metaphorizes the negation that inheres in pain while the latter text literalizes the same experience. "Family Album" recounts the story of Ximena, a Salvadoran woman living in Paris with her French husband, as she develops an awareness and acceptance of her political responsibility toward her homeland. The action of the novel begins, significantly, with a phone call from Ximena's uncle Sergio who celebrates his own funeral annually, thus articulating one of the many ways in the novel that the potential for physical pain is effectively anticipated and neutralized before it can divide subject and object. The story of pain elides linguistic representation by substituting a describable and repeatable practice, the funeral, isolated from its context.

The "family album" of the title alludes to the family photo album belonging to Ximena's cousin Armando, the only article he brought with him from his imprisonment in Nicaragua to his political exile in Paris. When Ximena notices that many of the faces in the photographs have been cut, Armando explains that his wife erased the faces for security reasons because "all the missing faces belong to comrades in the guerrilla" (109). He then amends his statement to intimate that the faces belong to only those friends who were assassinated or tortured to death, and that he does not know who is responsible for deleting their faces. The missing faces of the revolutionaries, the visible loss of their identities, hints at a split between subject and object, but their pain is assimilated and

177

dispersed through Armando's vague descriptions of his political activity and his unwillingness to articulate a specific cause.

At the end of the novel Armando departs, with the financial aid of Ximena, for Panama to participate in the Nicaraguan resistance, and she later opens the album to find that the face of her cousin has mysteriously and methodically been cut out of each of his family photos. The implication is that Armando has died, or will die, fighting for a noble cause. The specificity of pain, however, is abstracted to the level of symbol, confirmed by the novel's dual ending: Ximena asks the ghost of her nurse Chus, who periodically appears in the novel to offer advice, "And *guerrilla*, Chus, how do you say guerrilla?" (122). The novel concludes with a newspaper clipping detailing Somoza's forced exit from Nicaragua on 18 July 1979. The desirability of political resistance eclipses the specificity of pain. Physical pain appears only incidentally in the novel, assumed rather than described, and physical torture, a definitive presence in Armando's life, is reduced to its implements, as illustrated by his elaboration of the various means of torture, or its result, which replaces the state itself. Language projects the causes and effects of pain, as opposed to the experience, in order to identify the enemy to the reader and manipulate her sympathies accordingly.

In *Despierta, mi bien, despierta,* the female protagonist once again acquires a sense of her political self and a realization of her previous duplicity, refracted through her affair with a militant leftist student who is murdered at the close of the novel. The initial passage in which Lorena, the wife of a conservative millionaire businessman, tries to begin to write her story is succeeded by her reading of a newspaper account of the death of a man that she and her husband had passed on the highway the night before. The man had appeared completely naked with "el rostro desfigurado por el horror" (his face disfigured by horror) (15), a situation which provoked dissimilar responses on the part of Lorena and her husband; Lorena's husband purposefully ignored the man, whereas Lorena pleaded to stop and assist him. The newspaper account minces no words in its version of the event: "'Ayer se encontró el cadáver de un hombre desnudo muerto a balazos en el kilómetro 30 de la carretera San Salvador-Santa Ana (Yesterday the body of a naked man dead from bullet wounds was found at Kilometer 30 on the San Salvador-Santa Ana highway)" (15). Lorena's resulting anguish and guilt initiate the process of self-doubt that culminates in

178

her decision to leave her husband and reject the privileges he has offered her. The concluding lines of the novel dispel any notion of idyllic escape: seeing a parcel on the seat of her car, Lorena opens it to find her lover's head "con los cabellos revueltos y el rostro lívido [que] te miraba con ojos desorbitados" (with its hair messed up and its livid face [which] looked at you with bulging eyes) (75).

As with "Family Album," physical pain is abstracted in the name of maintaining the fiction of political power and collapsing the distinction between self and others through a rhetorical posture of unity. In the first incident, pain occurs somewhere outside the narrative, between Lorena's subjective experience and the objective newspaper report. In the second, pain is also inferred retrospectively; from the body part, described in chillingly human terms, the reader extrapolates to the act that caused pain and concomitant death. In both texts, the protagonist filters the physical pain of others through her evolution of an ideological stance and her accompanying adherence to a fiction based on power. As readers we are left to infer pain from covert causes, aligned with the abuses of repressive governments, and, more to the point, from metaphorical and literal effects. Imagining an object is unnecessary because any physical pain is successfully absorbed in the emotional crises of the protagonists.

They Won't Take Me Alive and "The Blue Theatre" (one of the vignettes in *Luisa in Realityland*) are much closer to articulating a language of pain in their combination of the fiction of power and the imagination of a suitable object of physical pain. Of the four narrative texts, *They Won't Take Me Alive* furnishes the clearest instance of testimonial literature, according to Margaret Randall's traditional definition of the genre (Randall 1992, 21-23). The text takes as its principal subject the life and death of a Salvadoran revolutionary, identified only as Eugenia, and involves "testimonies" from her husband, her sister, other members of her family, her comrades, and her direct superiors. The narration of Eugenia's evolution from a member of El Salvador's comfortable middle class to one of the highest ranking women in the guerrilla organization of the Frente Farabundo Martí para la Liberación Nacional (FMLN) offers an exemplum of ideological fervor and dedication; her sense of duty and civic responsibility is praised and her actions deemed worthy of emulation.

Notably, the primary incident of physical pain happens not to Eugenia but to her sister Marta, who is nine months pregnant when she is captured by the Guardia Nacional on 18 October 1978. After the guard's repeatedly beating her and threatening rape, Marta goes into labor almost immediately: "[they] went down the line hitting us. They beat my back with a rifle butt. I started going into labor, but didn't say anything about it to them" (84). She is taken to a hospital, delivers her baby with the help of a sympathetic doctor, and "disappears" for several days until someone recognizes her and alerts her family to her whereabouts.

Unlike in the previous two cases, Marta tells her story orally to a transcriber who presumably copies down her spoken words and makes them directly accessible to the reader. A unified ideological vision underwrites the document, making any personal development secondary to a presentation of the details and facts that compose Eugenia's life. As in "Family Album" and *Awake, my love, awake*, the fiction of political power is transformed into a reality, but, unlike the two previous texts, it need not be proved or elaborated. Organized resistance assumes primary importance, and the narration of Marta's physical pain is coopted to that end. It is, however, highly significant that the pain of torture is fully integrated into the pain of childbirth, the latter replacing the former as its object. The language of pain expresses its negation by displaying an image of creation. Imagining leads to the articulation of a parallel experience that, in the end, subsumes the original pain, that converts its effect to one of productivity.

In the last text, a short narrative sketch entitled "The Blue Theatre," included in *Luisa in Realityland*, the language of physical pain moves toward a more comprehensive imagining. The title of the short text refers to a blue lit stage in Chile commonly used for torturing political prisoners. The sketch concerns a woman's memories of watching her friend tortured. Alejandra explains her current insomnia to her friend Luisa by saying that a blue neon light on the next street keeps her awake. She then recounts the story of the blue theatre. Incarcerated for unspecified political crimes, Alejandra was taken to the blue theatre where she was asked to identify a friend. Upon receiving her negative reply, the torturers cut off the prisoner's ears, fingers, and hands, as she was forced to watch. The text ends when Alejandra remembers receiving the news that her friend had died: "At some point I fainted and awoke in my cell. The guard told me Sergio had died, and it was my fault, because if I had said the truth they might have let him go" (112).

Once again an observer reacts to the pain of another person, and the dichotomy between subject and object remains intact. Pain is once again referred to its causes in order to maintain the fiction of power, which is itself embedded in a denunciation of injustice and inhumanity. In this last example, however, the process of imagining associates past with present, giving pain an object and a medium of expression. Language relates a story of pain in which the collaborative visibility of spectacle, temporal as well as spatial, and object coincides to make meaning, to communicate the incommunicable. Physical pain separates Alejandra's memory from its referent, but her memory of another's pain emerges as a story, as the object of that pain.

Together the four texts discussed serve to outline a continuum of the kinds of language created around the communication of pain. At one end lies the metaphorization of pain in "Family Album," its a priori conversion into a figure that presents an object with no visible state, photographs with no recognizable identity. Further along the continuum lies *Awake, my love, awake* in which pain is translated, also a priori, into experiences located before and after pain. In both, the protagonist's developing self takes precedence over another's physical suffering. Language conveys the story of unified subjectivity, as opposed to the separation of voice from body. In the last two texts, the narration of pain abandons the subject in order to enter into the process of objectification; bodies in pain are displayed more fully, and their display involves imagining narrative objects for a story that resists communication. "The Blue Theatre" evinces the clearest literalization of the experience of pain; although the narration is doubly filtered through the memories of an observer, the body in question remains other, an object irrevocably separated from its voice. In all four cases, however, the experience of pain eventually finds language, albeit someone else's language, and language inevitably finds pain. The "two different tongues" of Alegría's fiction finally testify to the silence of their speakers.

NOTES

1. All translations of quoted material from the original Spanish into English are mine unless otherwise noted. Beverley provides an excellent introduction both to the critical politics of testimonial literature and to the twelve subsequent essays that compose the issue of *Revista de Crítica Literaria Latinoamericana* 18/16 (1992), which is dedicated specifically to testimonial literature.

2. Most of the existing scholarship on Alegría's work focuses on either her poetry or her best known novel, *Cenizas de Izalco* (Ashes of Izalco), neither of which is included in the present study. In addition to the sources cited in the essay, see Seymour Menton (1988).

WORKS CITED

Alegría, Claribel. 1986. *Despierta, mi bien, despierta*. San Salvador: UCA Editores.

————. 1991. *Family Album*. Trans. Amanda Hopkinson. Willimantic, Conn.: Curbstone Press.

————. 1987. *Luisa in Realityland*. Trans. Darwin J. Flakoll. Willimantic, Conn.: Curbstone Press.

————. 1987. *They Won't Take Me Alive*. Trans. Amanda Hopkinson. London: The Women's Press.

Beverley, John. 1992. "Introducción." *Revista de Crítica Literaria Latinoamericana* 18/16: 7-18.

Forché, Carolyn. 1984. "Interview with Claribel Alegría." *Index on Censorship* 13/2: 11-13.

Menton, Seymour. 1988. Review of *Despierta, mi bien, despierta*. *World Literature Today* 62/2: 256-57.

Randall, Margaret. 1992. "¿Qué es, y cómo se hace un testimonio?" *Revista de Crítica Literaria Latinoamericana* 18/36: 21-45.

Scarry, Elaine. 1985. *The Body in Pain: The Making and Unmaking of the World*. New York: Oxford University Press.

Yúdice, George. 1985. "Letras de emergencia: Claribel Alegría." *Revista Iberoamericana* 51/132-33 (July-December): 953-64.

12

CLARIBEL ALEGRÍA AND THE ELEGIAC TRADITION

Jo Anne Engelbert

I n his book on Jorge Manrique, Pedro Salinas defines the poet's relation to literary tradition through an extended analogy. Literary tradition, he says, is comparable to "what in natural history is called *habitat*, the zone capable of sustaining life." The poet, he observes, is born to a particular tradition and lives and breathes and creates within its boundaries; the savage acquires the elements of his song by listening to the shaman; the modern poet does do by poring over Horace and Baudelaire. Poetic creation only occurs within the poet's tradition. "Allí es donde crecen las variadas hechuras de la creación poética, complicándose según la tradición se acrece en volumen y densidad. Fuera de esa zona no hay más que el grito inarticulado del cuadrúmano, o el silencio inefable." (That is where the varied creations of poetic art thrive, growing more elaborate as the tradition increases in volume and density. Outside that zone there is nothing but the inarticulate cry of the primate or ineffable silence.) (Salinas 1947, 115-16.)

In a happier time these pronouncements, like those of T. S. Eliot in "Tradition and Individual Talent," had the ring of eternal verities. To reread them now is to realize how deeply the Latin American writer's relation to tradition—always problematic—has been affected by events of the past fifty years. Salinas's untroubled definition of tradition as "natural habitat" and Eliot's conviction that while tradition could not be inherited, it could be "obtained"—albeit at the cost of "great labour"—make us nostalgic for a simpler era.

183

For Central American writers identified with the forces of change, the question of tradition reached a crisis in the cultural genocide of the period called La Matanza (The Massacre). In 1932 the government of General Hernández Martínez moved against the indigenous peasant population of El Salvador in a campaign of systematic mass killings. Thirty thousand people were killed in a brief period, and the persecution was so horrific that the indigenous population sought to make itself invisible, abandoning forever native dress, customs, and languages. "Indians as a distinct group vanished after 1932:   hounded for any feature that might mark them as 'savages,' they had to shed their distinguishing characteristics in order to survive at all.   Names, clothes and habits were changed, native languages and traditions suppressed. . . .   It became a crime to be a native Salvadoran" (Hopkinson 1987, 18; 14).   Intellectuals who identified themselves with the victims eventually found themselves among the host of Latin American *apatrides*, (those without a country) a group so large and so generalized in this hemisphere, Carolyn Forché (1985, xiii) observes, as to "move many Latin Americans living abroad to question the validity of the term 'exile' in the modern world."

For many Central American writers, the aftermath of La Matanza precipitated a rupture with respect to the past that compromised their relation to many aspects of Hispanic literary tradition. Mined by successive betrayals of history, the former "habitat" became treacherous terrain.   Few elements of the tradition Salinas had defined so serenely remained untainted, and writers of Claribel Alegría's generation did not presume that somewhere there existed a tradition they might simply "obtain" by dint of "great labor."

Ruben Darío was the last great Central American poet who could confidently assume the entire tradition of Western literature. Salinas attributes to him a citizenship that transcends mere latinity. His country was "that of the world's great humanists . . . not *pluripatria*," a word marred by the idea of number, but *magnipatria*, a space with "no limits but the vision and dreams of mankind" (Salinas 1948, 44).   Salinas does not exaggerate.   In his elegy to Verlaine, for example, Darío commands sonorities encompassing Greek mythology and the Christian mass, the Spanish baroque and French symbolism; the entire repertoire of Western tradition is his to invoke.

In contrast, an elegist of our times who would memorialize the slain peasantry of El Salvador exists in a no-man's-land, the wild zone described above by Salinas, "where nothing is heard but the inarticulate cry of the primate." Alegría inhabits precisely this precarious zone, and the anguished cry predicted by Salinas can indeed be heard in her poetry: "In her poems," says Forché (1982, xi), "we listen to the stark cry of the human spirit, stripped by necessity of its natural lyricism, deprived of the luxuries of cleverness and virtuosity enjoyed by poets of the north." If Alegría's poetry is stark, if she has stripped and deprived it of ornamentation, it is because she has chosen to forge a poetics on the narrowest possible base, eschewing any traffic in the coin of the culture of domination. The role she has chosen for herself as poet is an extraordinary one: "Soy cementerio apátrida" (I am a cemetery, I have no country), she writes; she is the memorialist of the forgotten, the repository of her rosary of souls. In five decades of Central American poetry deeply preoccupied with the theme of death, Alegría has emerged as a sensitive and original elegist, a role which in all literary traditions has been universally reserved for males. In the process she has helped to forge a New World poetics of solidarity, providing a model for elegizing the nameless and the dispossessed. In order to form a clear idea of the magnitude of her achievement, we need to consider briefly the nature and function of elegiac poetry and its critical relationship to previous tradition.

I should make it clear that I am using the term *elegiac* in the broad sense that includes not only the lament of an individual for the death of a loved one but the expression of grief "originada por un acontecimiento triste para una colectividad entera" (arising from a sad event which affects an entire community collectively) (Camacho Guizado 1969, 4 n).

The Hispanic Elegiac Tradition

Few genres have a greater claim to a literary tradition or a more clear and functional need for one than the elegiac tradition. There are many reasons why this should be so, chief among them the fact that the writing and recital of elegiac poetry remains a ritualistic act that has an extraliterary dimension for both the individual mourner and the community. Rilke called the elegy "that vibration which charms us and comforts and helps," recognizing the genre's restorative function. By providing a form for language to enact its work of mediation, elegy aims to restore order to life after the chaotic interruption of death. Although it is a reflection on death, elegy is also, inevitably, a reflection on life that leads the mourner and the community of mourners toward catharsis, resolution and reconciliation.

Elegy has the power to mediate, to bridge the devastating dysfunction of separation, to link the survivors to the deceased and to one another and to unite all in a larger design of human continuity. This quasi-sacramental function gives the elegy unique textual authority. It is tempting to speculate that in patriarchal societies the role of elegist may once have been seen as a kind of sacerdotal activity appropriate to males.

In his excellent book *La elegía funeral en la poesía española* (The funereal elegy in Spanish poetry), Camacho Guizado (1969, 22) stresses the social function of elegy:

> The funereal elegy is essentially social in nature in the sense that it reveals a human attitude *toward the other.* The occasion of the poem is always someone's death, a fact which definitively determines its structure and makes it almost obligatory that the poem reveal the worldview, the beliefs, customs and ideas of an era, the social status of the poet and the deceased and prevailing conceptions of reality, life and death; all of these factors determine the *sign* that death shall have for this community of survivors.

Obviously, then, a text privileged among all others, figuring not only the shared sorrow of the moment, but prefiguring and mediating the death of the mourners themselves.

In consoling the bereaved the elegy addresses complex emotional needs with a directness infrequent in other genres.

> In every elegy one may discover a consolation; that is, the laments, the imprecations against death constitute a kind of indirect consolation, providing a means of catharsis for pain and grief. The very act of writing a poem on the death of a loved one is a way of objectifying the tragic event, of purging oneself of passion and thus finding consolation. (Camacho Guizado 1969, 16)

Salinas believed that elegiac literature is always, in the last analysis, a protest, a struggle against death, "una lucha con la muerte." Even the elegist whose message is one of serene resignation subverts his or her own message, Salinas (1947, 48) insisted, by the very act of writing:

> Even when poets write of acceptance in the face of death, they belie their own words. The best and noblest form of resignation is silence, and words are spoken here, precisely, in order that something not perish: words themselves—that they may survive that very death whose acceptance is being extolled.

But even the "individual" elegy inevitably has a communal dimension, and, as with any authentic sacrament, the efficacy of the elegy derives in part from a sense of expectancy on the part of all participants, from their common understanding of the meaning of the rite through long experience with its forms, its function, its allusive language and transcendent significance.

Because this is so, the elegy almost as a matter of course self-consciously evokes its own literary tradition, displaying conspicuously the healing sign of continuity. From the melancholy flute songs of ancient Greece to the solemn lyrics of Propertius and Ovid, from the cropped flowers of the pastoral elegy to the lilacs of Whitman or the poppies of Miguel Hernández, the elegies of Western tradition have constantly and deliberately sought to activate the resonance of their forebears.[1]

The Spanish elegiac tradition, one of the richest and most ancient in Western literature, begins with laments, "embedded like diamonds," as Wardropper (1967) puts it, in epic poems. In the *Cantar de Roncesvalles* Charlemagne, overwhelmed with grief at the death of his brave young nephew Roldán, cries out in pain and incredulity, giving rise to what will become an increasingly significant genre. In unbroken sequence, each age produced elegiac poetry enriching the genre's repertoire of tropes, systems of allusions, and codes. By the Middle Ages, Charlemagne's simple apostrophe had evolved into a genre already having many formal requirements.[2] As the genre continued to develop, the repertoire of stylistic features increased along with a constellation of topics and themes. When Machado asks in a familiar elegy, "¿ a dónde fuiste, Darío, la armonía a buscar?" (where did you go, Darío, in search of harmony?), his question has the resonance of centuries. Without tracing the *Ubi sunt?* to its classical origins, but thinking only of the Hispanic tradition, we can find this structure in laments by Juan Ruiz, the Marqués de Santillana, Jorge Manrique, the Romancero, Garcilaso, and Bocángel, as well as in such modern poets as Juan Ramón Jiménez, García Lorca, and Dámaso Alonso.

In the vast tradition of Spanish elegy, strikingly few poems are expressive of collective rather than individual sentiment. Camacho Guizado's comprehensive study devotes scarcely ten pages to this aspect of the genre. Nevertheless, the experience of war—particularly the massive tragedy of the Spanish Civil War—gave rise to a collective sensibility in certain poets. In "Cementerio de Morette-Gliéres, 1944," for example, José Angel Valente creates an entire stanza from the names of the fallen, and concludes, "all the bodies are/ a single burning corpse" (Camacho Guizado 1969, 395). Today, in the opinion of Camacho Guizado (1969, 339), there are few Spanish poets who would not subscribe to the words of Blas Otero: "It is man who interests me, not as an isolated individual, but as a member of a collectivity existing in a particular historical situation."

The persistence through time of specific formal elements is a significant aspect of the genre. The fundamental consistency of the elegy across the millennia is quite independent of humanity's changing views of death and the destiny of the deceased: the Western elegy in its expressive possibilities serves Ronsard and Shelley as well as it serves Unamuno and Juan Ramón Jiménez. For the elegy, as Wardropper (1967, 11) points out, does not depend on philosophical or theological tradition but on its own *literary* tradition. Few traditions are more opulent, more varied, or more venerable.

Jorge Boccanera is perhaps the only commentator who has attempted to include the indigenous literatures of Latin America in an account of the elegiac genre. In the introduction to his anthology *El poeta y la muerte* (The poet and death), Boccanera (1981, 10) characterizes this elusive substratum of Central American literature. "For the indigenous peoples of Mesoamerica," he tells us, "death was never a line of demarcation as it is in Christian tradition. In Nahua poetry, for example, life and death are two sides of the same coin; there are no frontiers between one and the other." The elegiac genre was well represented in the poetry of Mesoamerica, as the collections of Angel Garibay, José Alcina Franch, Miguel León

Portilla, and others have revealed. This highly conventionalized poetry stresses the transitoriness and illusory quality of life ("We came only to dream./ It is not true, it is not true that we came to live upon the earth;/ our hearts will sprout and grow again,/ the buds of our hearts will once again unfurl") (Alcina Franch 1957, 84). In the Aztec city-states of the fifteenth century, poets gathered in closely knit societies at court to reflect, to improvise, and to invoke the departed. Many poems of that era express the belief that the communion of the fraternity of poets will persist uninterrupted in the next life, that poets will continue to make verses together "alongside the drums," after death.[3]

Boccanera (1981, 10) calls attention to the Mesoamerican belief in the efficacy of poetry. "The poem," he tells us, "like the the warm heart of the sacrificial victim, has the power to revive the myths that gave origin to the world." With the Conquest this poetic sensibility, like so many other aspects of indigenous culture, was eclipsed. "America's native sensibility had to go underground," says Boccanera (1981, 13); "Christ and the apostles took the place of Huitzilopochtli and the 400 brothers of the moon." Although it is impossible to demonstrate a continuity of literary tradition, the elements of an underlying indigenous sensibility help to account for certain constants of Central American poetry. The preference of the indigenous tradition for a less individualistic, more collective poetic persona, its distinctive view of life and death, its sublime faith in the efficacy of the word, and its ancient ideal of an eternal community or fraternity of poets are all elements in evidence today in the region's elegiac poetry.

A New Elegiac Sensibility

In the post-Matanza era, elegiac poetry in Central America is eloquent through stark simplicity. The great cathedral organ of Hispanic tradition is sparingly intoned or renounced in favor of an unamplified voice that is at once personal and collective. Death in the Central American isthmus is not *cortés*, as elegized by Manrique; Death as personified by Alegría is the implacable god Tlaloc demanding blood; his victims are the dispossessed, stripped of land, customs, dress, language, and history. The language of elegy must faithfully reflect this; a lament for the children of the Woman of the

River Sumpul must of necessity be as pure as water, uncompromised by reliance on the codes of power.

It is not merely the diction of elegy which is problematized by La Matanza, but the very function and nature of this poetry. In the very midst of chaos, who can pretend to comfort, to reconcile? Who perceives an order to be restored or a power capable of restoring it? Classical resignation and spiritual quietude are often replaced in this latitude by exhortation to action. Boccanera (1981, 15) observes, "En pueblos donde la represión y Muerte son ya una costumbre de la barbarie, la poesía pasa de la elegía a la denuncia, de la clandestinidad al exilio, y nada contra la corriente para no perecer ahogada en la sangre del pueblo agredido" (In countries where repression and death have become the praxis of barbarity, poetry moves from elegy to denunciation, from clandestinity to exile, and swims against the current in order not to drown in the blood of the oppressed). In Central America, Alegría and others are creating a new elegiac tradition that does not merely denounce but which essays a new response to the human needs of the bereaved. Its elements are a rigorous sobriety of expression, identification with the oppressed, a poetic persona that is collective rather than individual, and a sensibility that reflects New World beliefs and values. A fundamental departure from received tradition is the emergence of the female elegist.

Some religious communities, as a symbolic gesture, renounce the luxury of instrumental music. "For orthodox Jewry the absence of musical instruments is regarded as a symbol of the absence of the departed glory of the Temple and a reminder of the tragic history of a people scattered over the four quarters of the globe" (Tobin 1961, 166). Similarly, in Alegría's poetry the absence of verbal opulence signifies somber remembrance and complete identification with the subject.

The normal recourses of poetry fail under the weight of this subject matter. Manuel Sorto writes (quoted in Guillén 1985, 131),

> El sangrerío es grande
> demasiado grande
> para medirlo con metáforas.
> Ninguna alucinación se le parece.

(The river of blood is immense
too great
to be measured in metaphors.
No hallucination can equal it.)

The inadequacy of metaphor to the expression of horror is what
Neruda alludes to when he writes, "The blood of the children/
flowed out into the streets/ . . . like the blood of the children"
(Forché 1985, 257).   No comparison, no simile, no linguistic
elaboration can equal the efficacy of the poet's naked, unmediated
voice recounting concrete experience. Alegría never speaks about
death in the abstract, nor does she speak about "the dead." Rather
she speaks, with maternal tenderness, of "mis muertos" (my dead).
In her fictional autobiography *Luisa in Realityland,* she recounts the
childhood ritual of nightly prayers for her dead and recalls her dread
of omitting the name of a single individual whose soul, on her
account, might fall into limbo. As she grew older she added name
after name to her rosary of souls until the list threatened to become
interminable (Alegría 1987, 13). Even now, she tells us (Alegría 1981,
91), her paradise in Mallorca fills with phantoms after dark, the
ghosts of all her dead.

As in the indigenous tradition alluded to above in which
"death was never a line of demarcation," Alegría blurs and dissolves
boundaries. Her dead mingle promiscuously with the living; they
come and go at will, appear in the street, vanish in the mist. But it
is in life, not in death, that she wishes to remember her host of souls.
"Tu muerte me cansa," she tells her father, "Quiero olvidarla ahora/
y recordar lo otro" (I am weary of your death,/ I want to forget it for
a while and remember all the rest) (Alegría 1981, 95). The faces she
holds in memory are vibrantly alive; her father's, for example
(Alegría 1981, 96):

Tu vida y no tu muerte:
tu rostro aquella tarde
cuando llegaste humeando de alegría
y alzándola en vilo
le anunciaste a mi madre
que ahora sí,
que ya es seguro,
que le salvé la pierna
a Jorge Eduardo.

(Your life and not your death:
your face that afternoon
when you came in beaming with joy,
held it up for all to admire,
and announced to my mother
that yes, finally, it was certain
that you had saved Jorge Eduardo's leg.)

There are no panegyrics in this poetry. Alegría does not speak *about* the dead; rather, she speaks *to* them with the naturalness of everyday conversation. "Remember that hot day," she asks her father, "when we stole the only watermelon/ and wolfed it down, just the two of us?" (Alegría 1981, 96). She imagines her mother at the age of twelve, face flushed, braids flying, performing a stunt on her roller skates. In the timeless zone of memory she asks her (Alegría 1981, 122),

¿ Cuándo perdiste
esa alegría?
¿ Cuándo te convertiste
en la muchacha cautelosa
que colgó los patines?

(When did you lose that joy?
When did you become
that cautious little girl
who put away her roller skates?)

The dead invoked by Alegría are disconcertingly active; they do not, cannot, rest. They rise and leave the cemeteries to seek justice; they mount guard, harass the living, lie in ambush, ready to accost the passerby. Gesticulating, winking, waving, they pursue the poet, desperate to tell their stories. Their rage is palpable:

nadie sabe decir
cómo murieron
sus voces perseguidas
se confunden
murieron en la cárcel
torturados

192

Se levantan mis muertos
tienen rabia

(no one can say
how they died.
Their persecuted voices are one voice
dying by torture in prison
My dead arise, they rage.)
(Forché 1982, 55)

They are legion; they form a solid wall that reaches from Aconcagua to Izalco. In desperation the poet struggles to hold them all, to retain them in memory lest they fall into the limbo of oblivion. But they are too many; she cannot contain them all: having described herself as a cemetery apátrida, she says that her dead "no caben," (they do not fit). *Presentes* (present in spirit), like the ghostly guerrilla fighters in poems by Roberto Obregón or Roberto Sosa who rise at night to fight alongside their companions, these dead in their anger "continue the struggle" (Alegría 1981, 157-58).

In her book *Poetry in the Wars* Edna Longley observes, "The 'I' of a lyric poem does not egocentrically claim any privilege as structuralists would have it. Strategically individualist, but truly collective, a poem suppresses self in being for and about everyone's humanity" (Longley 1987, 17). The particulars of Alegría's poetic persona—her loneliness, weariness, even the fungus between her toes—are often links to the collective subject (all of the lonely, weary, pauperized expatriates living in Madrid got fungus infections in the public baths where everyone went to "scrub off the stench exile" (Forché 1982, 28). Her poems do not so much suppress self as transform and transcend it; her progressive identification with those who have fallen in the struggle becomes more and more intense with the passage of time. In poem after poem she identifies herself with those who have suffered or died in the struggle. She submerges herself in the collective historical subject and her voice is one with the chorus, the river of voices raised in protest:

Ya no es una la voz
es un coro de voces
soy los otros
soy yo

es un río de voces
que se alza
que me habla de la cárcel
del adiós
del dolor
del hasta luego
se confunden las voces
y los rostros se apagan
quién le quitó a ese niño
su alegría?

(It is no longer a voice
it is a chorus of voices
I am the others
I am myself
it is a river of voices
that is rising
that speaks to me of prison
of goodbyes
of suffering
of so long for a while
the voices blend together
the faces dissolve
who snatched the smile
from that little boy?)
(Alegría 1981, 172)

"Sorrow," the longest and most powerful of Alegría's elegiac poems, actually takes the form of such a chorus or river of voices. Dedicated to Roque Dalton, "Sorrow" is one of the most original and profound elegies in Central American poetry. An entire poetics of solidarity could be extracted from its strategies for voicing a collective lament. The poem is an *arpillera* pieced of fragments, vivid scraps of personal experience commingled with verses by poets and artists who were witnesses to the common struggle.[4]

"Voces que vienen/ que van" (Voices that rise and are gone), the poem begins. We recognize them from familiar phrases— "cuando sepas que he muerto/ no pronuncies mi nombre," "verde que," "puedo escribir los versos más tristes," "me moriré en París" (when you know that I have died/ do not speak my name) (green,

I want you green) (tonight I can write the saddest verses) (I will die in Paris) (Forché 1982, 18). Besides the fraternity of poets—Dalton, Lorca, Neruda, Vallejo, Antonio Machado, and Hernández—others identified with the cause are invoked as well. Victor Jara appears and Violeta Parra, Che Guevara, and Sandino. Their words are stitched together in a graphic representation of solidarity, appliquéed upon the strong fabric of the poem's personal statement. The poem's eight sections are eight stations of the course of mourning. The invocation of the voices is followed by the recollection of a dusty pilgrimage to the grave of Lorca ("no te pusieron lápida/ no te hiceron el honor/ de arrancar los olivos/ combatientes/ torcidos") (They didn't give you a grave marker/ they did you the honor of tearing up/ the twisted, the stubborn olive trees) (Forché 1982, 24). The third section evokes the sense of loss that is the experience of exile. The expatriates floating like wraiths along the cold boulevards of Madrid recognize each other by the mark on their foreheads, the hunted look in their eyes. The next three sections recount the poet's response to the "implacable news" of the death of Roque Dalton. She passes from stunned horror to an elevated experience of identification with all those who have suffered or died for the cause: in the seventh section she projects herself through prison walls to a narrow cell and lies on a cot listening in the darkness to the screams of the tortured. We recall the ritual of her childhood litanies, now become an exercise in horror: "empiezo a contar nombres/ mi rosario de nombres/ pienso en el otro/ el próximo/ que dormirá en mi catre/ y escuchará el ruido de los goznes/ y cagará aquí mismo en el cano/ llevando a cuestas/ su cuota de terror" (I begin counting the names/ my rosary of names/I think about the other/ the next one who will sleep here/ on my cot and listen/ to the groaning hinges/ and shit right here in this open pipe/ hunched beneath his quota of terror). The intensity of this emotion is the poem's climax:

> Desde mi soledad
> acompañada
> alzo la voz y pregunto
> y la respuesta es clara.
>
> (from my solitude I raise my voice
> I ask and the answer is clear.)

One by one, voices call out to her in the darkness: "Soy Georgina/ soy Nelson/ soy Raúl" (I am Georgina/ I am Nelson/ I am Raúl). The chorus of voices rises, growing more and more powerful, drowning out the voice of the jailer demanding silence. She rends the veil of time that separates her from herself, from the others. Suddenly there are wine and guitars and tobacco, and sorrow has become reunion. She takes a piece of coal and scrawls on the wall, "más solos están ellos/ que nosotros" (they are more alone than we are), the only consolation this elegy can offer and the only consolation that it needs.

In this fraternity of suffering, the dispossessed have their homeland in each other. Salvadoran guerrillas often repeat, "we have our mountain [i.e., our refuge] in the people." The poets of this era find their mountain, their "habitat," in the consciousness of their counterparts in solidarity, regardless of era or place of birth.

"Sorrow"'s eighth section, an epilogue, parallels traditional elegiac form by referring confidently to the persistence of the poem itself, exactly as Salinas observed ("words are spoken here, precisely, in order that something not perish: words themselves"), with the enormous difference that the poem, in this tradition, is no longer the work of a single individual; this is its precise strength:

> existen los barrotes
> nos rodean
> también existe el catre
> y sus ángulos duros
> y el poema río
> que nos sostiene a todos
> y es tan substantivo
> como el catre
> el poema que todos escribimos
> con lágrimas
> y uñas
> y carbón.
>
> (the bars do exist
> they surround us
> the cot also exists
> with its hard sides
> the river poem

that sustains us all
and is as substantial as the cot
the poem we are all writing
with tears, with fingernails and coal.)
(Forché 1982, 43)

The poem's final words are not a pious generality but a challenge, an incitement; the function of this poetry is not to reconcile but to engage:

y surge la pregunta
el desafío
decidme en el alma quién
quién levantó los barrotes?

(and the question arises, the challenge
tell, me, in spirit, who
who, raised up this prison's bars?)
(Forché 1982, 42)

Using few of the resources of the traditional elegy, Alegría has created a poetry that approximates its weight and scope and resonance. With others of her generation, she has helped define a New World elegiac tradition, individual and collective, unmediated and profound, a poetry "for and about everyone's humanity."

NOTES

1. When Lope writes in his poem "En la muerte de Baltasar Elisio Medinilla" "Y quiere que consagre a tu memoria elegos versos," he uses a term employed by Euripides. The traditions evoked by Spenser in *The Shepeardes Calender* include not only the poetry of Chaucer but that of Theocritus, Virgil, Mantuan, and Petrarch (Sacks 1985, 38). The panegyric in *Llanto por Ignacio Sánchez Mejías* (¿Qué gran torero en la plaza!/ ¿Qué amigo de sus amigos!/ ¿Qué señor para criados y parientes!) in turn echoes that of the epic (María Rosa de Malkiel demonstrates that Jorge Manrique takes great pains to have us identify his father with the earlier ideal of the "caballero famoso," Fernán González or El Cid).

197

2. According to María Rosa Lida, by this time the rhetorical convention "already demanded of the funereal elegy: 'reflections on the topic of death, the formal lament of the survivors and a eulogy for the deceased'" (La convención retórica exigía tres partes al poema fúnebre: "consideraciones sobre la muerte, lamento de los sobrevivientes y alabanzas del difunto") (Camacho Guizado 1969, 16).

3. "Ha de seguir enlazándose la unión de los amigos, ha de seguir enlazándose la sociedad junto a los atabales" (The union of poet friends shall continue,/ the society of poets must persist beside the sacred drums) (Alcina Franch 1957, 87). The poet Nezahualcoyotl memorializes the princes who have left for "the region of mystery" and tells Prince Tezozomoctli, "Has de venir a vernos en la tierra" (You must come to visit us on earth). Centuries later, Nezahualcoyotl was to be memorialized himself in a poem by Darío, "A Roosevelt."

4. *Arpilleras* are pictures created by the appliqué of scraps of cloth on a burlap ground. This genre of needlework is closely identified with its political use by wives and mothers of the disappeared to convey their anger and grief. The making of Arpilleras is a popular Latin American handicraft.

WORKS CITED

Alegría, Claribel. 1981. *Suma y sigue* (Add and carry). Prologue by Mario Benedetti. Madrid: Visor.
———. 1987. *Luisa in Realityland*. Willimantic, Conn.: Curbstone Press.
———. 1989. *Woman of the River/ La mujer del río*. Pittsburgh: University of Pittsburgh Press.
Alcina Franch, José, ed. 1957. *Floresta literaria de la América Indígena*. Madrid: Aguilar.
Boccanera, Jorge, ed. 1981. *El poeta y la muerte: Antología de poesías a la muerte*. Mexico: Editores Mexicanos Unidos.
Camacho Guizado, Eduardo. 1969. *La elegía funeral en la poesía española*. Madrid: Editorial Gredos.
Eliot, T. S. 1964. *The Sacred Wood*. First published 1920. London: Methuen & Co.

Forché, Carolyn. 1982. Introduction to *Flowers from the Volcano* by Claribel Alegría. Pittsburgh: University of Pittsburgh Press.

———. 1985. "El Salvador: An Aide Memoire." First published 1981. In *Poetry and Politics: An Anthology of Essays*. New York: Quill.

Guillén, Orlando. 1985. *Hombres como madrugadas*. Barcelona: Anthropos.

Hopkinson, Amanda. 1987. Introduction to *They Won't Take Me Alive* by Claribel Alegría. London: The Women's Press.

Longley, Edna. 1987. *Poetry in the Wars*. Newark, Del.: University of Delaware Press.

Sacks, Peter. 1985. *The English Elegy: Studies in the Genre from Spenser to Yeats*. Baltimore: Johns Hopkins University Press.

Salinas, Pedro. 1947. *Jorge Manrique o Tradición y originalidad*. Buenos Aires: Editorial Sudamericana.

———. 1948. *La poesía de Rubén Darío*. Buenos Aires: Editorial Losada.

Tobin, J. Raymond. 1961. *Music and the Orchestra*. London: Evans Brothers.

Wardropper, Bruce. 1967. *Poesía elegíaca española*. Salamanca: Ediciones Anaya.

13

LUISA IN REALITYLAND: AN ANTIDOTE
FOR DICK, JANE, AND SALLY

Celia Catlett Anderson

Although Claribel Alegría's *Luisa in Realityland* was not written for children, its honest and vivid portrayal of the thoughts and experiences of a child in a culture permeated with revolution, terrorism, extreme poverty, and eccentric wealth makes it a touchstone in a children's literature course, a demonstration of the wide range of experience possible in young people's lives. Alegría's combination of poems and vignettes inspired by her childhood in El Salvador has proved a powerful means of revealing to North American students the experience of growing up in a war-torn Latin American country. In addition, the fact that Alegría deals with sexuality in children, with death, and with violent politics plunges students into the perennial debate about what is and what is not suitable reading for children. Finally, when compared with one of Alegría's fantasy stories written for children, the book also serves as an excellent basis for discussing the differences between writing about and writing for children. For all of these reasons I include *Luisa* among the required readings for my children's literature course.

Alegría's work is usually discussed from a feminist, postcolonial, or poststructural perspective, and, while this and the sophisticated format of *Luisa* may seem reasons to exclude the book from a children's literature course, this is not the case. Many works for children experiment with or mix genres. Certainly prose and poetry are frequently combined in fairy tales and in works by such authors as Rudyard Kipling and Kenneth Grahame. Furthermore, scholars in this field share the critical perspectives used in other areas of literature. For one thing, commentators on children's books concern themselves with the importance of positive role models and the exploration of powerlessness, issues that also concern feminist scholars. In regard to postcolonial approaches to literature, investigating what the books written for juveniles tell us about the society that produced them provides a perennial source for studying how the older generation socializes or civilizes those eternal "primitives," the young. In regard to poststructuralism, few fictions can probe the interstices of a society's constructs as thoroughly as can those presented through the viewpoint of a child character and written by an author who remembers the inquiring mind of the child.

The young Luisa's subversive innocence is a perfect example. As one of my students has written, in "the stories there seems to be an undercurrent of discovery. Children often discover more than adults with previous experience."* Recall Luisa's curiosity about the absence of a divine bridegroom during the initiation of Sor Ana Teresa into the nunnery ("Taking the Vows"). Luisa is displaying the literal-mindedness of the young, an attitude frequently exploited for its humor by children's authors. Alegría's title is, after all, a play on the title of that most famous of children's books, *Alice in Wonderland*, and when Luisa as child serves as central consciousness, she shreds the assumptions of the society she is observing in the same way that Lewis Carroll's Alice fragments, with her persistent questioning, the sanctity of Victorian mores.

Including *Luisa* among texts specifically written for children instigates a useful discussion about the nature and the presumed limits of children's literature as a genre. Professional scholars of children's literature (although they may argue in more sophisticated terms and make finer distinctions than most students do) frequently engage in the same debate that rages in my classroom when we discuss the suitability for children of books like *Luisa*. To put it in the simplest terms, the issue is whether children should be protected from or introduced to "reality" in books and whether or not children's literature has a special obligation to society's norms of morality. One of the more thoughtful considerations of the problem

---

* The following students gave me permission to use quotations from their essay answers: Franklin L. Hayes, Mary Schweitzer, Karen Patrylak, Jeffrey M. Hlavaty, and Celia Bagdonis.

that I have encountered is critic and children's author Eleanor Cameron's address, "Art and Morality" (1980). Cameron raises the issue of the insistent demand for moral meaning that is placed on authors who write for juveniles. She puts the debate in the context of the ongoing argument about the relative importance of aesthetics and ethics in literature. Critical theory during much of the twentieth century, Cameron notes, has stressed the primacy of the aesthetic and sought to divorce art from moral messages. Yet the demand that children's authors present a healthful, positive moral vision has been continuing. Citing the furor raised by "certain professionals in the world of children's literature" over Robert Cormier's grim novels for the young, Cameron asserts (1980, 41) that when reading material for children is under consideration, "the protective impulse is passionately called forth."

The debate is perennial. May Hill Arbuthnot, an early and major commentator on children's literature, found even such a classic author as Hans Christian Andersen somewhat inappropriate for the young, holding that "because of the double meaning, the adult themes, and the sadness of many of these stories, the whole collection is usually not popular with children" (Arbuthnot and Sutherland 1972, 313). By the eighth edition (1991), Zena Sutherland, then the first-listed author, is considerably less judgmental about Andersen's "sadness": "Andersen's stories have unusual literary and spiritual values, and they are, for the most part, in a minor key, melancholy and even tragic" (Sutherland and Arbuthnot 1991, 66). I would argue that both Andersen and Alegría use humor as a counterpoint to the sadness evoked by the situations they portray, and although Alegría's humor can be as whimsical as that in any fairy tale, she generally makes irony more central to the meaning of her stories than Andersen does. She demands that the reader peel away several layers of Luisa's innocent misapprehensions in order to reach the core of disorder in the society Alegría is exposing. A good example is Luisa's surface-pious First Communion prayer that the death of her future husband follow immediately on the birth of the child she desires because "I don't want to be married; I don't like the way men treat women" (Alegría 1987, 39).

Much of Alegría's power comes from the tension created by her balance of the comic and the tragic. In the dream sequence described in "The Pool," the author refers to these two central elements. In this story, Luisa is puzzled by the neck ornaments on two statues of young men:

> "Why a garland and a serpent?" she asked.
> "For humor and for sorrow," her mother said.
> "Don't ever forget this." (121)

Alegría did not forget the ghostly mother's behest in writing *Luisa*.

Alegría exhibits a wry humor, and of sorrow there are certainly enough instances in *Luisa in Realityland*, many of them connected with childhood. Alegría deals with the wounds of hunger and with actual or psychological death caused by El Salvador's long-lasting civil conflict. The hunger and malnourishment of impoverished children are sardonically revealed in two sections. The urchin Memo in "The Versailles Tenement" is finally forced to tell Luisa that he wishes her to cage and keep the white pigeon he has caught because

> "It's just that . . ." Memo twisted his filthy toes in anguish, "my ma wants to kill her because we don't have anything to eat." (34)

In "The Mejia's Dogs" we are presented with the socioeconomic cause of Memo's and other poor Salvadoran children's hunger. Thirty great danes protect a vacant mansion's orchard from fruit thieves. Not only does the fruit rot in waste, but the absent owners have a cow butchered three times a week to feed the dogs. When a truck delivers the carcass:

> The small boys from the surrounding *mesones* would crowd about the truck, and despite the shouts and the swats that the cha[u]ffeur aimed at them, they would dart in to seize scraps of meat and offal that fell to the ground. Some would leave empty-handed, while others ran off excitedly to offer their mother a length of intestine or a pancreas. (130)

That the great danes thrive while the children starve makes palpable the unjust consequences of materialistic priorities. This passage draws expressions of disbelief from my students. Hungry children can currently be found altogether too easily in the United

States, but the rich avoid proximity with the poor and, therefore, do not appear so bare-facedly indifferent to their needs. Such passages in *Luisa* are a catalyst for discussions about the facile dismissal of the very existence of underprivileged children by self-appointed censors of children's literature.

There is in North America no twentieth-century tradition of revolution, massacre, and guerrilla warfare, all of which have touched the lives of Salvadoran children. "Where Was Your Childhood Lost?" Alegría asks in the title of her poem dedicated to Daniel Frederick. She sees in the eyes of his photo

> thousands of dead children
> and dead youths
> . . . .
>
> they died tortured
> died suddenly
> died in jail (40)

Another poem, "Malinche," challenges adults who insist on children's innocent incomprehension of the world's sorrows:

> a child's drawing:
> black trees
> withered branches
> heads dangling
> like seedpods.
> "A refugee child,"
> Rosa says in her letter
> the skull facing me
> is winking one eye.
> The child knows it all
> guesses it. (75)

The child artist had seen his father decapitated, an event that none of us, child or adult, finds pleasant to contemplate, yet an event generated by what one of my students (Mary Schweitzer) designated as the treachery and the chaos of the adults around him. It is important to note that the child who actually lived through this horror was able to turn the memory into art. It is precisely art and literature as a forum for dealing with what is painful that should not be denied to children.

Katherine Paterson, two-time Newbery Medal winner, has spoken and written eloquently on permitting, even encouraging, the minor key in works for children. In her address "Wednesday's Children," drawing her title from the old nursery rhyme line that reads "Wednesday's child is full of woe," Paterson (1986, 290) identifies the Wednesday's children of the modern world—the undernourished, the war-trapped, the abused—and challenges those of her critics who hold she should not expose children to sorrowful matters:

> It never occurred to me, that I could con my readers or cheat my characters by frosting over the last chapter with happily ever after. I take very seriously the tragic dimension of human life. Every human life ends in death. I do not consider it a kindness to pretend otherwise. Nor do I believe that our children should be shielded from the world with its infinite store of wonder and fear and its immense possibilities both for good and evil.

Other voices with very wide influence continue to argue, however, for what the grown-ups have decided children ought to know. Sometimes the argument is extremely subtle and on the surface seems to be promoting opening up reality to the child. For example, Bruno Bettelheim (1977, 147) vindicates the often violent events of the tales, but he does so because the happy endings are a form of personality-integrating consolation, which is the "greatest service the fairy tale can offer a child: the confidence that, despite all the tribulations he has to suffer, . . .not only will he succeed, but evil forces will be done away with and never again threaten his peace of mind." Not surprisingly, Bettelheim is among those who find Hans Christian Andersen unsatisfactory, because some of the tales "do not convey the feeling of consolation characteristic of fairy tales" (Bettelheim 1977, 37). Jack Zipes (1983, 16), author of a number of books on fairy tales, takes exception to Bettelheim's insistence on the presence of consolation: "Like many cultural censors of morality, Bettelheim believes that only literature which is harmonious and orderly should be fed to the delicate souls of children."

Given this context, it should be easy to see why a book like Alegría's *Luisa* stands in vivid contrast to the majority of books written for children and why *Luisa* makes a good subject for debate. Though few areas are currently forbidden to children's authors, a failure to incorporate "consolation" does still draw adverse criticism. The thirty participants of a 1983 National Endowment for the Humanities Institute on Children's Literature, although they did recommend controversial authors such as Cormier, maintained (Brockman et al. 1983, 5) that "Children's literature requires a particular mixture of both honesty and consolation, and while such literature must confront reality, it must also discover meaning in chaos and despair." As a critic of children's literature, I find a satisfactory balance of "honesty and consolation" in *Luisa in Realityland*.

Allison Lurie is another author-critic who speaks out strongly for allowing a full range of subject and attitude in books for the young. Lurie (1990, ix-xi) notes that she discovered in her own childhood a division between books that "told me what grown-ups had decided I ought to know or believe" and another kind that "celebrated daydreaming, disobedience, answering back, running away from home, and concealing one's private thoughts and feelings from unsympathetic grown-ups." Lurie holds that "the great subversive works of children's literature . . . mock current assumptions . . . appeal to the imaginative, questioning, rebellious child within all of us, renew our instinctive energy, and act as a force for change." I do not know if Lurie has read *Luisa in Realityland*, but her description of "great subversive works of children's literature" is also a good description of Alegría's book.

For example, a number of the sections in *Luisa* celebrate daydreaming. Both Luisa the child and Luisa the woman move with ease between the worlds of the conscious and the subconscious or the worlds of wishes and everyday disappointments. Luisa's alter ego and muse, the Gypsy, is the clearest case of the joyous risk of inhabiting more than one level:

> Ever since Luisa was very young, the Gypsy appeared in her dreams, and the two of them would undergo incredible adventures. . . . [T]he Gypsy was terribly daring and got her into all sorts of scrapes. (17)

However, even though the Gypsy sometimes abandons Luisa, Luisa never abandons the Gypsy, crediting her with dream-dictated love poems and, by inference, the dream paintings, which become Luisa's door "into that other reality" that she could "only conjecture" when musing before actual paintings (78).

The myth-making uncles, celebrated in two sections (53 and 97), represent the type of daydreaming that, in the waking mind, intrudes as a lie. Alegría identifies her heroine with these uncles in the opening sentence of the first of these anecdotes: "In Luisa's family there were many fabulous liars, including herself, of course" (53). This jubilant dismissal of truth as an absolute good would undoubtedly disturb any overly serious guardian of children's morals (just as Huck Finn's "stretchers" have been disturbing such censors over the past century).

Lurie (1990, x) also cites "concealing one's private thoughts and feelings from unsympathic grown-ups" as a mark of subversive children's literature. That Luisa keeps her childhood world to herself can be inferred from many passages. In her encounter with a whore, for example, Luisa ignores her tennis companion Carlito's taunt "I'm going to tell your father" (24), which implies that he knows she would not tell her parents about such a thing. The secrecy is again emphasized by the woman's parting injunction, "And don't tell your mother you've been here" (25). Luisa's First Communion prayer that her future husband will die as soon as a child arrives is another example of a thought not shared with adults, and after her cousin René's death, the violent act of ripping out the doll's eyes bespeaks her inability to tell anyone in the family of her love-twisted grief. The portrayal of secret thoughts and of such grief, the half-understood although passionately felt sorrow of childhood, make *Luisa in Realityland* both a central text on childhood and a book that would be rejected by many critics and teachers who deal with selecting what children read.

Besides picturing for us hunger and the violent deaths of children or their families, Alegría portrays the psychological death that can ruin the lives of young people who are too devastated by events to cope with the opportunity for a better life when it presents itself. The story "Felix" is an illustration of such inability. "Felix," when compared with Alegría's fantasy for children "The Story of the Unhappy Willow," also provides a fine study of the differences we expect (and frequently find) between literature for adults and literature for children.

Felix is a "skinny and lovely" (61) boy, apparently an Indian as his parents were killed in the 1932 massacre. Luisa's father takes in the abandoned child, discovers that he responds well to education, and plans to keep him and launch him in some trade. Unfortunately, the boy believes a vindictive servant woman's threats that he will be punished for accidently breaking a colored-glass pane. Luisa and her brother try to persuade Felix that their kindly father will scarcely mind, but "There was nothing to be done. The maid's threat was too much, and Felix ran away, taking only what he wore on his back" (62). This is the reality that Luisa/Claribel lived with as a Salvadoran child, the reality of a companion of promise lost forever.

When, however, Alegría takes up the theme in a children's fantasy story of a forlorn child adopted into a strange home, the ending is quite different. In "The Story of the Unhappy Willow," two riverside willow trees have a son who "was small and always seemed sad." Some children who play by the river are the "only creatures who seem to make him happy" (Alegría 1989, 135). The parent willows ask a water nymph to turn their son into a human child with no memory of his past. The children then accept him as a playmate, and, when he cannot give them any name, dub him José. One boy, Andres, invites José home. José spends the night and goes to the school the next day. Here a schoolboy laughs at the willow child, who cannot say where he comes from. Distressed, José runs to the river and hides between the two willow trees, where "he cried for a long time and dug his fingers into the earth, which gave him a strange sense of comfort" (Alegría 1989, 136). Andres seeks his new friend out and again takes him home. The father questions him (albeit in a kindly fashion) about his origins and proposes that if José will tell them the names of his parents and they cannot be found, Andres's family will adopt him.

José again retreats to the river where the water nymph appears and asks why he is so sad. José explains his problem. The nymph comments that human beings are like that—untrusting, "always inventing difficulties," and queries, "How would you like to become a tree—one of these willows, for example?" The parent willows assume that their child will choose to become a tree again, but "'No,' José answered. 'All I want is to know who my parents are and to live in Andres's house and not let the police get me.'" The water nymph assures him, "'Everything is going to work out for the best'" (Alegría 1989, 141). Andres and his father return to the river, claiming—and miraculously believing—that José has always been in their family. This is now also José's memory.

"The Unhappy Willow Tree" is a wistful tale about an unfortunate outsider who is accepted into a circle of loving friends. Felix, who is merely of another social class and race, rather than of another species, cannot remain in the accepting circle of Luisa's family, because he cannot blot out the memories of his past. The injustices he has witnessed before being rescued have incapacitated him to live happily in Realityland. He cannot find any benign order behind the chaos unleashed by the 1932 revolution that cost his parents and thousands of other Salvadoran Indians their lives. It is only in the the world of spirit, of talking willows, of water nymphs and magic wishes—the world of fairy tales, of children's stories—that happily ever after prevails. Is it justice or injustice that we do to children by showing them this Elysian vision, but veiling the harshness that makes the vision an aching necessity for the human race?

Alegría herself obviously struggles with this dichotomy. In "From the Bridge," a meditation on the stages of our knowledge of good and evil, she looks back and watches the child she was evolve into the mythical birdwoman of ill omen, the Siguanaba. She is also a Cassandra figure, cursed with the bitterness of unhappy truths, calling back to a former self that can neither heed the warning nor swerve from the path leading to political and personal grief. At one point in the poem Alegría sums up the dilemma of whether to give or to withhold the knowledge of evil from the young:

> your books spoke to you
> of justice
> and carefully omitted
> the injustice
> that has always surrounded us
> you went on with your verses
> searched for order in chaos
> and that was your good
> or perhaps your condemnation (139)

In "The Final Act," the last anecdote in *Luisa in Realityland*, Alegría offers the reader another dream sequence, which ends when a live child holding Luisa's hand turns into "a lifeless rag doll" (141). On one metaphoric level, Alegría is lamenting the plight of the artist whose vibrant vision must always be conveyed through some inanimate medium, but, given a poem like "From the Bridge" and the many descriptions of blighted youth that fill the pages of *Luisa in Realityland*, on another metaphoric level Alegría is concerned with the question of how to grow from childhood to adulthood without becoming a mere imitation of life, "a lifeless rag doll." One answer may be to learn early to deal with the trials of reality.

When I use *Luisa* to raise this theory to a conscious level, my students' reactions vary from enthusiastic acclaim to shocked disbelief. The majority respond positively. One wrote, as a postscript to her essay test on *Luisa*, "I believe this to be the best novel we have read so far. It is very powerful, and I plan on reading it a few more times." Many say they would (or actually have) given it to a child to read. There is generally a consensus that certain stories in the book are likely to be more accessible to children than others and that the poetry may present greater difficulty than the prose. As another student pointed out, "The novel is structured to enable the stories to appear in childhood innocence, while later placing the moral of the tales in the form of poetry."

There are, however, inevitably a few students, like the grade school librarian, who would not allow it in her library for fear of parental reaction, and like the teacher at a denominational school, who found certain sections shocking. The latter challenged my judgment for including such a book in the course and was unconvinced by my firm justification of it on the grounds I have outlined.

The segment considered most unsuitable by the two objecting students was "Sunday Siestas" (90-91). In this story a girl and her younger brother demonstrate the sex act (learned from spying on the parents). Others in the class admitted to being uncomfortable with this one. The story "I'm a Whore; Are You Satisfied?" (23-25) was also questioned. Students do not, however, generally object to the anecdote about Luisa's morbidly romantic attachment to her cousin René, whose talk of death intrigues her and whose actual death causes her to rip out the eyes of a doll she has named after him (56-57). I judge "René" as much more problematic; it is a story I would prefer to read with a child rather than simply give for private perusal.

Some of my students apparently side with those who object to exposing children to descriptions of physical sexuality or to knowledge of prostitution, but they find emotionally disturbing romantic views acceptable fare for the young.

A number of my students do, however, grasp that Alegría is dealing with important socioeconomic themes that bind one generation with another. One older student, herself a grandmother, wrote that she found central to the book the theme of "survival, and certainly endurance, patience, courage—all the essential qualities that help teach children how to deal with the harsh realities of life." Paterson (1981, 101) says that children know "in their deepest selves that though truth is seldom comfortable, it is, finally, the strongest comfort." I will continue to use *Luisa in Realityland* in my children's literature course. Alegría's book is a valuable center for much that I wish my students to contemplate.

WORKS CITED

Alegría, Claribel. 1987. *Luisa in Realityland.* Trans. Darwin J. Flakoll. Willimantic, Conn.: Curbstone Press.

————. 1989. "The Story of the Unhappy Willow." Trans. Darwin J. Flakoll. *Children's Literature* 17: 135-41.

Arbuthnot, May Hill, and Zena Sutherland. 1972. *Children and Books.* 4th ed. Glenview, Ill.: Scott, Foresman.

Bettelheim, Bruno. 1977. *The Uses of Enchantment: The Meaning and Importance of Fairytales.* New York: Random.

Brockman, Bennet, Francelia Butler, William Moynihan, and Samuel Pickering, eds. 1983. *Children's Literature and the Humanities: A Declaration* (by 30 participants of the 1983 NEH Institute on Children's Literature at the University of Connecticut). Storrs, Conn.: University of Connecticut Press.

Cameron, Eleanor. 1980. "Art and Morality." *Proceedings of the Seventh Annual Conference of the Children's Literature Association,* Baylor University, Waco, Tex., (March): 91-97.

Lurie, Allison. 1990. *Don't Tell the Grown-ups: Subversive Children's Literature.* Boston: Little, Brown.

Paterson, Katherine. 1981. "Up from Elsie Dinsmore." In *Gates of Excellence: On Reading and Writing Books for Children* by Katherine Paterson. New York: Dutton.

————. 1986. "Wednesday's Children." *Horn Book Magazine* (May/June): 287-94.

Sutherland, Zena, and May Hill Arbuthnot. 1991. *Children and Books.* 8th ed. New York: Harper/Collins.

Zipes, Jack. 1983. "The Use and Abuse of Folk and Fairy Tales with Children." in *Children and Their Literature: A Readings Book,* ed. Jill P. May. West Lafayette, Ind.: Children's Literature Association Publications, 14-33.

AFTERWORD

Marc Zimmerman

Some years ago, driving Claribel Alegría around Chicago, I asked her if she had seen any serious criticism of her work. Not too much, she said, although she had seen one essay by George Yúdice (1985) that was very interesting indeed. I remember expressing my bewilderment and frustration over the matter, my sense that even Latin American, to say nothing of the culturally literate mainstream Anglo-American, literary critics were reluctant to take a politically sensitive Central American woman writer seriously; and my view that several serious studies would be required before her opera could be separated from the more run-of-the-mill Central American political writing and be seen as the important works they were.

It would not be long before a few other works of significant criticism would emerge in conferences or appear in print. However, it is a sad irony that only now, after Perestroika, Esquipulas II, the Sandinista election defeat, and the Salvadoran government/FMLN accords, only now, when so many have died, and when revolution is no longer on the immediate agenda in Central America, does it become clear that Alegría's works will not fade into history; only now, after so much revolutionary and counterrevolutionary discourse, ranting and posing, do these works begin to rise above the immediate, compelling circumstances of their creation and become recognized as the important achievements which they are in the contemporary Central American and broader literary landscape. Finally, it is only now, after all that has been said and done, loved and seemingly lost, that this volume appears to consolidate a virtual consensus about Alegría's work and to chart the space for her in the cultural map of contemporary literary culture.

When Sandra Boschetto-Sandoval told me that she and Marcia McGowan were going to put together this long overdue book, I was quite pleased; when Boschetto asked for my participation, I was gratified. Now, seeing the texts together and knowing of the work and care involved for them to have reached publication, I am deeply happy for Claribel, and for all those who love or will come to love her and her work. However, in the role assigned to me, as one asked to place the entire enterprise in some final perspective, I find myself somewhat in awe. For the volume is certainly a rich one, an achievement of the editors and the contributors, one that sums up many prior perspectives and insights and which, before my own small intervention, says most, if not all the things, needed to be said to introduce the writer and open the field for further explorations.

A problem for the contributors may be described as a difficulty in fully placing Alegría and her work simultaneously in a more general literary and more specific regional context. The editors, as well as Rodríguez, Horton Riess, Crosby, Treacy, and others, relate her to Central American and Third World feminism, subaltern, feminist, testimonial, and resistance literature. But essential mediational matters—Alegría as poet and as Central American and Salvadoran—seem to get less play. Only Engelbert's essay concentrates on Alegría as poet. Arias attempts to outline her movement (in anticipation, he notes of Roque Dalton and Manlio Argueta) from poetry to fiction—specifically, to what he characterizes as the new, Central American, dialogic or Bakhtinian narrative of which he himself is a prime representative and interpreter (cf. Arias 1990 and 1991). And yet it is Alegría the poet, as well as prose writer (indeed, I would argue that it is Alegría the poet *first*), who must be placed in relation to Salvadoran, Central American, and broader literary contexts in which questions of feminist and subaltern discourse, and the relations of literary genres and particular expressions, text and context may be more amply entertained.

It was as a poet that Alegría began. Without giving weight to the poetic function in her work and the relation of poetry to other literary modes as means of representing Central American realities and struggles, it is difficult if not impossible to fully chart her alterations between, and combinations of, poetry and prose, fiction and testimony, as well as her movement from private, subjective, feminine, and domestic to public, political, and feminist. How do we trace the development of Claribel's work from feminine to feminist

214

poetry, from poetry to prose, from purely interpersonal to public and political? What characterizes her move from poetry to prose and what has been the relation between these two modes, as well as between the oral and written, the testimonial and the imaginative, the positivistically realistic and the (often "more real") fantastic/magical in her work?

Of course several contributors give us some sense of these relations in their analyses. Perhaps Ruffinelli is among the sharpest here in suggesting how the poet's confrontation with history (her growing recognition of her own identity as tied to a developing regional and national crisis) impelled her. Evoking some of the older structuralist analytical frames (specifically Jakobson and Halle 1980), we could characterize Alegría's dominant developmental tendency as one in which her "visceral" reaction to the social and political world leads her discourse from initially metaphor-centered poetic norms to ones which, while never abandoning metaphor and lyricism, nevertheless are primarily characterized by the metonymic and narrative inflections that are most readily realized in prose.

Historical circumstances, largely tied to Central America itself, led Alegría to a sense that being is becoming; those circumstances (as *vanguardismo, exteriorismo,* and other post-*modernista* modes which were moving Central American poetic discourse from a metaphoric to a metonymic base) thus created a literary discursive context for a poetry that would narrate and that might, in different, extenuating circumstances, lead given writers to narrative prose. Above all, it is probably Alegría herself, influenced by life and literature outside of, perhaps even more than within, her region, who most clearly articulates this shift in her collage/volume of poetry and prose (her "portrait of a woman artist," as McGowan points out), *Luisa in Realityland.* Especially important in *Luisa* is a poem which I believe to be the subjective centerpiece of her book and her life work, "From the Bridge."

McGowan quotes this poem extensively in her essay, and makes many suggestive comments for her own purposes. For mine, the poem would require a more careful and systematic analysis in relation to the questions raised here than space and deadline time now permit. Let it suffice to say that the poem is a central autobiographical, aesthetic/political statement, tying Alegría's own development as a daughter of the Central American bourgeoisie to her achievement of self-understanding and full self-expression; it is also at the core of the movement Boschetto points to from autobiographical to "quasi-testimonial" to fully testimonial discourse. The metaphors of crossing over, of mirrors, the questions of memory, recognition, and growth are central of course not only to understanding *Luisa* but also to understanding the relation between Alegría's other fictive autobiographies and the more literary testimonial works which are part of the Alegría (and Flakoll) canon. In this context, we can only concur with Molino that the process involving the recognition of personal public history is also one of pain, a pain perhaps not unlike that of birthing, one that leads to the awakening and rebirth of Alegría's female protagonists. As Saporta Sternbach shows, this look into refracting mirrors, this often painful moment of bridgework and discovery, takes place in *Cenizas* when Carmen reads the diary her mother has bequeathed her. March and Crosby chart for us how it occurs again as Ximena experiences revelations, culminating in the magical play of images in her family album.

Drawing on Reiss's suggestive analysis of *Despierta, mi bien, despierta* (Awake, my love, awake) we might note that the bridgework involved usually means placing one representative mode of discourse against another (diary, album, television newscast, *testimonio,* or other oral modes—the list is infinite in her work) to produce a new sense of personal and collective being, a new epiphany, and indeed a new discourse mode. Just to cite one mode which Alegría I believe has not ventured, the prototype for bourgeois feminine awakening and transformation found in *Family Album* and other Alegría texts is probably Ibsen's *Doll's House*—the rebellion against patriarchy in familial and matrimonial terms, a process of discovery and struggle propelled beyond the bourgeois microworld to society at large. Here we should remember that Ibsen's Nora is not born on the day she confronts her husband, but only acknowledges an awakening that had in fact begun years before when she saved her husband's life. Nora in the private sphere (and that may tell us where Ximena's marriage may be going as she sees the family album picture fade) becomes Antigone in the public—for Ximena's moment of truth and her look into the family album (the Lacanian moment of recognition) are tied crucially to her understanding of her double role as being Salvadoran/Nicaraguan and therefore more generally Central and Latin American, as she sees her landowning Salvadoran uncle as a Creon (or more specifically a Somoza) in her own family.

This invocation of Ibsenite and Sophoclean drama through our own metonymic associations may seem thoroughly out of place; however, the Argentine film *Official Story* points to at least one other Latin American Ibsenite appropriation; and consciously or unconsciously Antigone parallels, at least, abound in recent discourse in or about Latin America (Rigoberta Menchú on the death of family members, Ariel Dorfman's first play about disappeareds are just two instances). The theme of women coming to consciousness in relation to deaths and burials of kin is a basic pattern in contemporary Latin American feminist narrative, and the predominance of this theme in Alegría's work suggests some of the key bases of Alegría's own relatedness to other Latin American writers, as well as the "cultural literacy" revealed in her work. The sense that Alegría's revolutionary and feminist, Third World, Central American drama is embedded in, and rises up out of, a familiarity with European bourgeois culture (the key, overt reference to which is Lewis Carroll) is not so much an absurd colonial imposition of mine as a recognition of Alegría's own training and grounding in that culture (not atypical for her class and time in El Salvador, as part of criolla anti-Americanism). Out of such preparation, what is Central American, revolutionary and feminist in her work then emerges.

If the reflection over past as the basis for future action is the core connection between Sophoclean and Ibsenite dramatic construction, so too is the concern with intertextuality and with the audience or "reader" response elicited by such a construction—a matter that is central to the analyses by Reiss and Boschetto, as they have been to Aristotle and Brecht in their respective eras. There can be no question in this context that Alegría begins with what came to be the prototypical bourgeois drama and extended beyond it to the collective dramas of her testimonial poliphonies—without for all that taking on, and in fact maintaining some critical distance from, Brechtian Marxist-Leninist extremes—as they achieved their Salvadoran synthesis in Roque Dalton and his contemporaries. Alegría is a writer and woman who keeps at least one foot in bourgeois, feminine culture even as she projects to worlds beyond. This apparent limitation has enabled her to speak to and affect many who have not as yet made the transitions which those who have already made might impatiently wish her work to project more aggressively. This perspective may help to explain how "From the Bridge," *Luisa*, and other works by Alegría may, as Anderson suggests, come to express and also influence developmental growth stages for young readers.

Above all, our Eurocentric references point to "From the Bridge" as a locus, or rather nexus (indeed, a crossing bridge), for internationally rooted political/ideological and aesthetic/literary transformations, as it is simultaneously a generative narrative of self-discovery and rebellion on the part of a Central American bourgeois woman. Furthermore, the poem constitutes a model for the transition from narrative lyric, to lyric narrative—tied to Ruffinelli's private/public evolution, and further tied to Salvadoran/Nicaraguan, male/female, and other binaries in Alegría's work. To draw on Greco-Roman figures Alegría does *not* mention in her interview with McGowan (but ones clearly related to her own Lacanian logic as well as Central American bourgeois educational norms), it is as if a female Narcissus were to gaze in a pool and see not only herself but her entire people in the reflection; it is as if Echo were to hear her disempowered voice now multiplied and given force as part of a polyphonic chorus of the many Salvadorans and Central Americans whose voices are finally to be heard. And, it should be added, the chorus, *el pueblo*, is not just those proletarianized and lumpenized males of whom Dalton sang so movingly, but also the many women who have suffered and struggled to bring forth a new world, a new narrative in poetry as well as prose projecting Central American being and becoming.

Clearly the poet Alegría gives a lyric base to narrative, and narrative metonymically spins out from her poetic core, embracing and exploring larger, particular historical issues. Clearly too, Central American political literature has benefitted greatly by the politicization of a writer of lyric gifts, an extensive literary education, and an already articulated poetic practice.

Alegría's early volumes of poetry require careful study in relation to her subsequent trajectory, and that trajectory has to be rethought in relation to our growing understanding of that early poetry. So little has been studied of Alegría's apprenticeship with Juan Ramón Jiménez and the impact on her work of his "poesía pura," her development beyond Central American feminine lyricism (the possible influences of Mistral, and in her own country, Claudia Lars), her possible relations with earlier politicized Salvadoran

218

women poets, or with other Central American women poets, overtly politicized or not. How much did she identify with her Central American roots in her earlier poetry? How did her relation to the generation of the 1960s (Dalton, Armijo, and Argueta) develop in Mallorca, Cuba, Uruguay, or wherever? And how, in this relation, might the younger writers of the 1960s, 1970s, and 1980s have influenced her own work, just as she undoubtedly influenced theirs?

Finally, in relation to her more recent efforts, since her residence in Managua and her world travels, how have her relations with the Sandinista revolution and the cultural struggles among writers young and old connected therewith (Gioconda Belli, Daisy Zamora, and, most dangerously, Rosario Murillo) affected her relations to Salvadoran, regional, and worldwide concerns, as (thanks to Sandy Taylor, Judith Doyle, and others) her work has been translated and she has had an enlarged forum in the U.S. and other countries?

Returning to this essay's core concerns, Englebert adds new dimensions to the still incipient study of Alegría's poetry by her focus on the elegiac dimension therein. From the point of view suggested here, this dimension must be seen as at the heart of Alegría's own particular lyricism, given the Central American circumstances which do so much to generate the reason for elegy (think of Cardenal, all the poems to fallen heroes in workshop, guerrilla, and other kinds of Central American poetry)—and which may project elegy to actual and fictionalized testimonios about those who have been killed. The question of recognition emerging from a confrontation with death is central, again, in "From the Bridge" and in the transition from lyric poetry to lyric narrative which would be Alegría's itinerary.

To cite my own previous work on these matters (Zimmerman 1988; Beverley and Zimmerman 1990) we may initially posit Alegría as typical of the educated Central American women writers from "good families" who began early to write a lyrical, subjectivist, and traditionally "feminine" poetry, only to break through toward the new militant, Left political literature that emerges with younger poets like Dalton, Argueta, and José Roberto Cea during the rise of the international and Central American countercultural movement in the 1960s and 1970s. Clearly, Alegría's *Cenizas* and *Luisa*, novels of the 1960s, are major moments of this shift, with 1932 as the key historical date for the birth of her own politicized poetics, just as it is for Dalton and others (cf. "Todos," in Dalton 1974). Her elegiac poetry about the death of Dalton (a figure she never met) is symptomatic of the growing transition in her writing and her growing identification with El Salvador's 1960s "generación comprometida" (committed generation). That connection is of course strengthened by the political conjunction of the late 1970s culminating in the Sandinista victory and then her reaction to word of Monseñor Romero's death, as given her by Roque's friend, Robert Armijo.

Salvadoran Left literature, as developed by the 1960s poets, had represented at least a *search* for a broad, revolutionary movement in function of the nation and "the national question." Hence its efforts to reach *in poetry* toward a national narrative, to establish a line of "progressive" heroes (Morazán, the Indian rebel Aquino, Farabundo Martí), to adumbrate a roughly linear historical process leading to some kind of socialist salvation—a quest best articulated in Dalton's *Historias prohibidas del pulgarcito* (1975). Hence, too, the effort in the years after Dalton's death—and most notably in the work of Argueta, Armijo, Cea, and several others—to redirect a primarily urban (intensely secular and male-centered) poetic instrument in the direction of more rural (religious and woman-centered) concerns.

The irony of the Salvadoran literary Left was that while its theoretical and literary discourses, including poetry, were primarily articulated in the city, the revolutionary process itself fared far better in the countryside. Furthermore, while the ability to fight the military depended on all sectors and the ample participation of women, the literary system, dominated by poetry, was particularly male-centered. These facts suggest why most Salvadoran poetry, even of the Left, continued to function as a minority and often machistic discourse in the national culture as a whole, and how far it actually stood from representing all the sectors required for a successful revolutionary process or for at least constituting a potentially revolutionary "national popular" in the Gramscian sense.

With respect to the question of women's and specifically feminist poetry, Salvadoran literature prior to Claudia Lars includes nineteenth-century figures like Antonia Galindo and Ana Dolores Arias, but there were no women poets whose work became part of the normative literary canon. In the 1930s, Communist party member or fellow traveller social poets wrote poems about *la mujer india* (the Indian woman), or *la mujer proletaria* (the proletarian woman). But on the whole, the most "progressive" male writers (i.e., most writers before the 1970s) succumbed to and/or struggled with a machismo that was not only inscribed in the culture, but was given a kind of legitimacy in the early constructions of revolutionary selfhood associated with the Cuban Revolution: the concepts of the "new man," and the image of the *barbudos* (the bearded ones), of Che Guevara as an icon.

If Dalton inevitably replicated the machistic dimension in the national poetic discourse, even as he radicalized class and other historical emphases, nevertheless, in the years just before his death, in relation to his critique of the ERP's *foquismo*, and his heightened awareness of the limits of constructed revolutionary subjectivity, he attempted (honestly, even if unsuccessfully) to incorporate a more positive feminist perspective. If, in the years after Dalton's death, Argueta's effort to ruralize and feminize the national voice (present in his poetry, but reaching a culmination in his novels of the 1970s and 1980s) was the most significant male contribution to the new orientation in literary and ideological production, nevertheless, in the feminization of Salvadoran literature, Alegría was clearly the most significant figure.

Of the few women in the prewar years able to follow Lars's lead and rise above class and sexual domination to write poetry, *Grupo Seis* poet Matilde Elena López and Liliam Jiménez were the best known. A writer of political verse, López expressed working class and women's perspectives over a period of several decades. So too did Jiménez, a Communist party militant imprisoned for her commitments and exiled in Mexico for many years, who wrote several volumes of very direct political verse.

Alegría is not a "people's poet," or even a political poet in the manner of these earlier "fellow travellers" or party women poets, or the middle-class revolutionary militant males like Rugama, Castillo, and Dalton. A woman of a prior generation, living abroad, her role and development cannot easily be likened to that of Najlis or Belli in Nicaragua. Deeply identified with the Salvadoran countryside of her youth, Alegría is a writer whose work has involved a constant projection from her initial subjectivity as a woman of her family and class position, toward a sense of herself as a modern woman with a growing consciousness of the problems of the poor and a solidarity with those fighting directly to change the basis of the Salvadoran world.

Beginning with the expressive system Alegría had developed outside of the overtly political realm, and with a very different life experience, she has managed, in a way parallel to but very different from Dalton's, to synthesize a point of view centered on the tensions between her own intimate value world and the sociohistorical forces generating popular struggle in El Salvador. The center of her work which seems somehow related to, or at least parallel with, Lars's feminized *regionalismo* is a deeply subjective, "magical realist" evocation of her smalltown, rural, childhood life, undoubtedly drawn from memories influenced by (as well as influencing) her personal and political experience. Drawing on provincial images from the perspective of her cosmopolitan apprenticeship, Alegría subsequently mediated her landowning-class, small town *poetisa* roots through political and testimonial currents—plotting through her writing how a woman with ties to the oligarchy could be transformed by history, how (again somewhat like Lars, whose political consciousness and sympathies grew in the very last years of her life) she could move from a comprehension of her own evolving sensibility and value world to giving voice to the many oppressed and poor (especially women) in relation to whom the Salvadoran struggle emerges and deepens.

Alegría's later transformations are unthinkable without the cultural ambiance and poetry of the 1960s. Nevertheless, she does not merely draw from the developing poetic system; instead she emerges as one of the essential forgers of the system, the one who most fully internalizes the work of the women writers who matured prior to the 1960s. This ripening takes place in relation to world feminist perspectives as essential dimensions of a poetic system that gradually begins to transcend a limited male-centeredness and moves toward expressing the total range of perspectives and aspirations essential to a popular and democratic national project.

As she began to focus on this project, Alegría also veered increasingly toward prose as an alternative expressive medium. Thus, often written with Darwin Flakoll, her politically informed novels and historical studies, as well as testimonials of working-class and peasant women. Thus, with respect to her continuing work in poetry, her pioneering of a new literary mode in which the transcribed testimonies of witness/participants (most of them poor women) in key events or in everyday life are cut as verse and inscribed within the poetic discourse system.

With regard, first, to Alegría's turn to prose fiction, it would be well to note the contribution of Ramón Luis Acevedo (1991) to the question of Alegría's achievement, as a kind of qualifying perspective with regard to Arias's placement of her as a major figure in the Central American "mini-boom." In his essay on the movement from poetry to fiction in the work of Guatemalan writer, Luis Alfredo Arango, Acevedo (1991, 139-54) suggests that what emerges is a special form of new narrative, the lyric novel whose specific Central American inflection is the maintenance and even a deepening of a political dimension, even though it portrays the subjective, interpersonal experience of one individual.

The fact, as McGowan suggests, that a woman's *künstlerroman* is so rare gives further strength to our evaluation of Alegría's achievement. So too our knowledge that the movement from poetry to prose is immediately a feminist achievement in itself, given the normative divisions of labor among Central American writer elites. Above all, however, the inference to be drawn from Acevedo is that Alegría's development of a lyric narrative marks her own particular contribution (her own particular bridge) to Central American fictional discourse, which then helped other writers (Roque, Argueta, Sergio Ramírez, Mario Roberto Morales, Arturo Arias, and, more recently, Gioconda, Belli) to develop the varying discursive strategies and texts which Arias refers to as the new narrative.

To be sure, Boschetto, Englebert, and others are right to point to the quasi-testimonial and poetic elements in *Luisa*. And in this sense, as Beverley and I note (1990, 195), Alegría's *Luisa* both anticipates and represents perhaps the "feminized" alternative to the collage metahistorical narrative form of Dalton's *Historias prohibidas.* Where Dalton was trying for his own Brechtian version of the objectivism and impersonalism of Ernesto Cardenal's exteriorism, Alegría's deeply personal book extends to the most minor details and anecdotes of her private and family life. But there is no question that her project, achieved before El Salvador's "Soccer War," is parallel to, and indeed anticipates Dalton's. Her project gives some sense, through a montage of different literary forms, of the overall historical and political process Central America has undergone, especially since 1932. She presents the process, however, from within the intimate world of a particular woman's memories and experience. Although *Luisa* is not testimonio, it is, like *Las historias,*

223

representative of a range of new postfictional, quasi-testimonial narrative forms that have appeared in the context of the Central American revolutionary struggle. It is an "effect," in other words, of the pressure of testimonio on the established genres and forms of the literary system.

In terms of other new tendencies in Salvadoran literature, Alegría's prose testimonial work is a major instance of the deconstruction of the bourgeois "I" in function of a new collective subjectivity. In relation to recent combat poetry and beyond, her major contribution has been the elaboration of a poetized testimonio (frequently involving elegy) in which the transcribed oral accounts of witness/participants in the war, in many cases peasant women, are edited and rearranged in verse form. "La mujer del Río Sumpul," which reconstructs in a series of voices the famous massacre of 1980, is her most powerful and influential effort in this vein. Clearly this development in one sense parallels but may also herald the greater voice and action of women, including younger women poets, in the overall struggle. But the full emergence of a more female-centered discourse system is signalled by its impact on all the writers, including the males, who contribute to the system—a matter which, of course, signals Alegría's overall contribution to Salvadoran and Central American literature, as well as to area feminism and revolutionary culture.

This then is the trajectory I would suggest in a mapping of Alegría's itinerary: from the inscribed feminine, lyric core to a confrontation with death and destruction and its historical sources, to the feminist, lyrical narrative inflected by testimonio, to fully testimonial discourse, back to a poetry that is now itself transformed by its contact with history and the figures who have tried to develop a literary system correlative to a new, modernized, and democratized national and regional universe. That this universe did not materialize in the 1980s and that the narrative and narrative-tending poetic forms were intervened and checked may be a reflection on the macro-story of male-centered imperialism, and the fact that the feminist intervention in textual production was ahead of the creation of a less authoritarian, male-centered, democratic socialist movement that was never accomplished at the level of revolutionary practice. The materialization of the feminist intervention and its effect in transforming the literary system, however, is indeed present in all of Alegría's work and marks her overall contribution to Central

American, Latin American, and now, through translation, overall American and world literature.

The trajectory specified and the issues related thereto should be considered clearly in relation to Ileana Rodríguez's exploration of nation/female body metaphors, to Doris Sommer's work (1990) on foundation narrations, to Fredric Jameson's suggestions about Third World national narratives (1986), and to Gayatri Spivak's work on subaltern representation (1987). If Alegría's turn to narrative is indeed rooted in the invasion of lyric purity by historical crisis and complication, then her writing may be seen in this context as an effort to "feminize" a Leninist male counterhistory, to transform it, if not replace it, by a new history in which lyric female subjectivity and its transformations are part of the new national and areawide narrative. This narrative, unlike Roque's objectivist *Historias prohibidas* and unlike the older and more "authoritarian," male master narratives that are part of a tradition fundamentally rooted in an older, communist-influenced, authoritarian Left political poetry (read Neruda), does not attempt to serve as a simulacrum for "totality," and seeks to maintain the personal, introspective, fragmentary, lyric, and feminist as basic to national becoming.

That the testimonialization of poetry, seen as a Left effort to destroy the "fragile vessel" of poetic form, is now under attack by the hegemonic Salvadoran writer of the Cristiani years, David Escobar Galindo, is an indication of our times and the threat to Alegría's standing, even as it may be indirect homage to her achievement as a writer, in the emergent "new world order."

On the other hand, the fact, revealed in her interview with McGowan, that Alegría finds herself now turning again to poetry and some of the earlier motifs in her work may also be a symptom of the decline of revolutionary (and narrative) energies, a symptom of Central America's contradictory and partial insertion as a peripheral formation in contemporary late capitalism and its postmodernist figuration. In this context I should stress my belief that Alegría's core qualities as a poet will protect her and the social values she represents from the full brunt of the reductive onslaught.

It would, of course, be a mistake to reify terms such as "lyric," "political," "feminist," "testimonial," "Third World" or "subaltern" as this essay runs the danger of doing. With all these caveats specified, let me now risk betraying Third Worldism and feminism today, by bemoaning the fact that until now Flakoll's role as Alegría's frequent coauthor and collaborator, and his possible weight in the constitution of her vision, are so unexplored.

To be sure, Acevedo (1991, 109) is sharp enough to suggest something special about the collaborative role; and, within this volume, Rodríguez points to "possibilities inherent in an erotic/patriotic international common front." This is clearly a difficult matter about which to speculate. But would it be so wrong to suggest that the transitions from private to public, from interpersonal to political, from feminine to feminist, from poetry to prose (Flakoll does not collaborate on Alegría's poetry) stem from, or rather are crystallized in part as a function of, the dynamism of their relationship? And does not this creative interaction (including all the terrible tensions and pain she admits to its involving) join with Alegría's direct U.S., Latin American, and world experience to give her work the richness that enables it simultaneously to confront and transcend regionalisms, and to stand as part of what is today being called "New World Writing?"

In any event, Bud Flakoll is himself a difficult-to-study but essential dimension of the creative synthesis which is Alegría's literary work. Is he the alternative example, the antithesis of the stultifying husbands and dictators who threaten Alegría's freedom-seeking women? Is he also a source of synthesis which, well rooted in Alegría's Central American experience (and U.S. interventions), promises to extend even beyond the New World and our recent historical conjunctures, to the point of contributing to a yet-to-be-configured counter- or subaltern culture able to bridge older divisions and dichotomies and find appropriate modes of struggle in relation to whatever that new world order may turn out to be?

The essays in this book constitute in themselves a bridge from the crisis years of Central America to a future in which the work of Claribel (*and Bud Flakoll*) will play a significant part. With this final thought, I now feel relieved of chauvinistic obligations and can say, with full awareness of consequences and limits, that this book indeed gives us . . . *Alegría*.

WORKS CITED

Acevedo, Ramón Luis. 1991. *Los senderos del volcán: Narrativa centroamericana contemporánea.* Guatemala: Editorial Universitaria.

Arias, Arturo. 1990. "Nueva narrativa centroamericana." In Liano, *Centroamericana,* 9-23.

————. 1991. "Literary Production and Political Crisis in Central America." *Revue internationale de science politique* 12/1 (January): 15-28.

Beverley, John, and Marc Zimmerman. 1990. *Literature and Politics in the Central American Revolutions.* Austin: University of Texas Press.

Dalton, Roque. 1975. *Las historias prohibidas del pulgarcito.* México: Siglo XXI.

Jakobson, Roman, and Morris Halle. 1980. *Fundamentals of Language.* The Hague: Mouton.

Jameson, Fredric. 1986. "Third-World Literature in the Era of Multinational Capitalism." *Social Text* 15 (Fall): 69-80.

Liano, Dante, ed. 1990. *Centroamericana* 1. Rome: Balzoni Editore.

Sommer, Doris. 1990. "Irresistible Romance: The Foundation Fictions of Latin America." In *Nations and Narrations,* ed. Homi K. Bhabha. London: Routledge.

Spivak, Gayatri. 1987. *In Other Worlds: Essays in Cultural Politics.* New York: Methuen.

Yúdice, George. 1985. "Letras de emergencia: Claribel Alegría." *Revista Iberoamericana* 51 (July-December): 953-64.

Zimmerman, Marc. 1988. *El Salvador at War: A Collage Epic.* Minneapolis: MEP.

Appendix A

CLOSING THE CIRCLE: AN INTERVIEW WITH
CLARIBEL ALEGRÍA

(Mystic, Connecticut, October 1991)

Marcia Phillips McGowan

McGowan. Claribel, do you feel a sense of solidarity with other women writers?

Alegría. Very much. I feel there is a sisterhood, and I am very happy when I read women's works that are really good. I also feel that I tend to be more critical of women than of men, mainly because I want them to be the best.

McGowan. Do you have a sense that your own voice speaks for a kind of collective consciousness?

Alegría. Well, sometimes. I do think that through my personal experience, I approach a collective consciousness. But not all the time.

McGowan. So you also have a sense of speaking in a very personal voice?

Alegría. A very private and personal voice.

McGowan. Is there a difference between the way you speak in your poetry, in your fiction, and in testimony?

Alegría. I think so. My poetry is subjective. I like to write testimony, because there I can jump to many solid facts. I can be more objective, and I don't have to wonder what is real.

McGowan. Do you feel more in testimony that you are speaking for a collective consciousness?

Alegría. Exactly. I think that is what testimonies are all about. So many things have happened that otherwise would not be

228

recorded or remembered. For instance, in El Salvador in 1932 a cultural lobotomy was performed on the entire nation by the dictator Martinez when he ordered the burning of all magazine and newspaper files dealing with the peasant massacre, and it was done. Our book, *Ashes of Izalco*, was the first historical novel written about the events of 1932. Later there was a documented study, *Matanza*, and Roque Dalton's testimonial book with Miguel Marmol. But I feel it was necessary to tell that story in order to fill a gap in historical memory.

McGowan. Claribel, many of your protagonists live with the pain of exile. In *Family Album*, for instance, all three female protagonists are or have been, in one way or another, exiled from their homelands. This is clearly an important theme in your work. To what degree does the experience of your women characters in exile differ because they are women?

Alegría. Usually, women depend on their men, and where the men want to live. If you remember in my three novellas in *Family Album*, for example, Karen is with her father, who wants to dictate to her that she stay in California, whereas she wants to return to Central America to stay with her grandmother. In Ximena's story, it's the same. Probably Ximena would have gone back to El Salvador, but her husband has his business in Paris, so she has to stay there. At the end of the novel she decides to work for the Nicaraguan revolution, but from Paris. In the third novella about Marcia, Slim was the one who wanted to go to Mallorca, so they went. Women are more dependent in that respect than men.

McGowan. When Ximena makes the choice to help the Nicaraguan guerrillas, do you envision that there will be some sort of trouble between her and her husband?

Alegría. I do. At least they are going to have lots and lots of discussions, because he doesn't really understand what is going on. He doesn't care what is happening, whereas she does very much.

McGowan. It is interesting that, in fact, she has remained with a husband who is not at all sympathetic with the cause.

Alegría. She wanted to live in naive innocence, ignoring what was happening in the real world so she could have a happy marriage, a happy life. She was simply sleeping and eating until her cousin came along and awakened her. Then she started remembering, and she made the decision: No, I have to help.

McGowan. It's very interesting after she awakens that she suddenly sees that Armando's picture is starting to disappear; the face in his photograph starts disappearing before her very eyes.

Alegría. Exactly. (Laughter.) Well, you know I believe in magic very much.

McGowan. Yes, I know. Let's talk about this examining of pictures in your fiction. Many of your characters keep family memories alive through telling stories and through examining pictures, as Ximena does. Can you comment on this as a recurring motif in your work?

Alegría. Well, Marcia, I think one of my pervasive themes is nostalgia. In another interview I even said that I deserve a Doctor Honoris Causa in Nostalgia. In *Family Album*, for instance, I remember stories that my nana or my mother told me in my childhood. I cling to my souvenirs; I feel there is a great deal of richness there. I keep going back to things like the family album, knowing they will trigger something inside me.

McGowan. You say that they are *your* memories, the things *your* mother and grandmothers and aunts would tell you, yet somehow they turn out be fictional, or at least fictionalized autobiography in your writing. (**Alegría.** That's right.) But are they, strictly speaking, transformed in some way when you tell the stories?

Alegría. Of course. They are transformed in many ways. I feel the writer takes one of these memories to serve as a bridge, a bridge over troubled waters, or perhaps as a diving board. This is what memory does for me; I depend on it a great deal. It is a great richness to recover memories, but I transform them in my fiction.

McGowan. Let's shift gears and talk a bit about your exile from your homeland. At what point did this occur, Claribel? And why?

Alegría. My real exile didn't start until 1980. Long before that, my parents sent me to the United States because I wanted to study. Then I got married, and because of my husband's work I could not return, so I stayed on in the States. Later, we travelled a great deal, but I always returned to El Salvador whenever I wanted to. I went back to see my people, visit my family.

But then, in March 1980, Archbishop Romero was assassinated. I was in Paris that day and had been invited to give a reading at the Sorbonne. I was preparing for that when a good friend, Roberto Armijo, a Salvadoran writer, phoned me to say that Monsignor Romero had been assassinated. I decided not to read my poetry. Instead, Bud and I stayed up all night to write about what Archbishop Romero signified as "the voice of the voiceless," and why they had to kill him for that. That was the origin of my protest writings, if you want to call them that.

At that time, my cousin was director of the National Guard, and later minister of defense. He sent word to me that I shouldn't return to El Salvador, because he would be unable to guarantee my personal safety.

Anyway, that was my awakening. I felt that I had to do something for my people, that I had to have the courage to speak out about what was happening. I was frequently invited to the United States and Europe, and I felt it would be a self-betrayal if I didn't speak out. So my exile truly began in 1980.

My mother died in 1982, but my brother phoned to say I mustn't come to the funeral or there would most likely be two burials.

McGowan. What is your situation now that a peace agreement has been signed?

Alegría. The agreement went into effect on February 1, and on March 1 Bud and I returned to El Salvador for the first time in twelve years. It was a very private family visit. My mother's birthday falls on 2 March and on that anniversary we went to lay flowers on her tomb, which I had not seen before, and on my father's who is buried beside her.

McGowan. Will you be returning to El Salvador more often now that there is peace?

Alegría. Possibly, if the agreement holds together and a firm peace is established. But at the moment nobody is celebrating peace as an accomplished fact. There are too many tensions that could pull it apart.

McGowan. During those years of exile was there ever any interference in your mail to or from your family?

Alegría. In my mail, no. There have been threatening letters. For instance I recall that I once received an anonymous letter that bore the letterhead of the Women's Auxiliary of ARENA, the death squad party in power. The writer told me I was completely crazy; one could see that from the expression in my eyes. It went on to say that I was already senile and they wouldn't bother to kill me, but they were going to take revenge on my children. They were simply advising me of that fact.

McGowan. Have any of your children gone back?

Alegría. Once my oldest daughter, Maya, took a bus from Nicaragua to Guatemala, and they assured her that they were not going to pass through El Salvador but via Honduras. She was reading a new book of mine when the bus turned off to El Salvador. A border guard checked the passengers, looked at the book and said: "Why are you reading that?"

She said: "It's a book somebody gave me."

"Do you know who that woman is?" he asked. She said no, because she realized the danger.

"Stop reading that crap," he told her, and he took the book away from her.

McGowan. That is horrifying. (Pause.) Tell me, Claribel, in what countries have you lived and worked? What conditions do you find particularly congenial for your writing?

Alegría. Well, I have lived and worked in many countries. I started in El Salvador, then in the United States, Mexico, Chile, Uruguay, Argentina, France, Mallorca, Spain, and now Nicaragua. In many of these places, we have lived for two years or more. I lived nearly eleven years in the United States and about twenty years in Europe. I agree completely with what Virginia Woolf said about a room of one's own. This is what I need: a room, a nook of my own. I need to close the door and lock it so I can talk aloud and pace back and forth. I require a sanctuary where no one can interrupt me.

McGowan. So it doesn't matter where in the world you are?

Alegría. It really doesn't matter as long as I have my little room where I can be comfortable and write.

McGowan. That's wonderful. Wherever you go. When you're travelling, do you find time to write? Say, on a lecture tour?

Alegría. Not when I am travelling. What I do then is take notes about things that impress me, people I meet. I have my seed book. I don't know if I ever told you about that; it's my treasure. If I read something that impresses me, if a thought comes to me during my travels, I write it down, and it is a source of richness.

From time to time I go through my seed book and find the germ of a new poem or story awaiting me.

McGowan. You call it your seed book rather than your journal?

Alegría. That's right. It contains little seeds that I can water.

McGowan. And you take it with you all over the world?

Alegría. Yes, I do.

McGowan. Are you very selective about what you take out of the seed book?

Alegría. It depends. Something I have forgotten completely suddenly impacts me when I reread it, as if it were waiting for me. Then I water it, so it will grow. That is my only selectivity. It happens when I feel the urge.

McGowan. Do you go back to your seed book frequently?

Alegría. Oh, yes. I couldn't live without it.

McGowan. So you take it with you when you travel, and then when you come back home and have more leisure to write, you look at it and see what seeds you planted when you were abroad?

Alegría. Exactly. The seeds might be planted either at home or abroad. A month or a year or two years might go by before something I had previously passed over calls my attention, and I discover that now I am ready for *that* seed.

McGowan. That is fantastic. Let's talk about some of the places you have travelled. What did you learn during your residence in Chile?

Alegría. It was a wonderful experience. We wrote *New Voices of Hispanic America* there. This is an anthology of then-young writers of Latin America. It was published in 1962 by Beacon Press. We are proud of that book because we "discovered" some wonderful writers who were little known, even in their own countries, and were completely unknown in the United States. For instance, Julio Cortázar by then had written three or four books, the most recent of which was *Bestiario*. We loved it, and we included him in the book. Juan Rulfo was another. He was a good friend of ours when we lived in Mexico and was working on his first book, *El llano en llamas*. He used to come to the house and read his unpublished stories to us. Mario Benedetti, Augusto Monterroso are others.

McGowan. Did you know all these people personally?

Alegría. Many of them. The rest we came to know through correspondence. For the first time I was in contact with a number of Latin America's finest writers, and many of them became lifelong friends. I am very grateful for that project, and I will never forget Chile. Besides, my son was born there.

McGowan. What years are we talking about?

Alegría. From 1954 to mid-1956. We were in Chile for two-and-a-half years, and we loved it.

McGowan. Did you receive books from women writers?

Alegría. Oh yes. As I recall, we included a total of about forty young writers, and roughly a quarter of them were women.

McGowan. Do you feel that the number of women writers has increased since you prepared that anthology?

Alegría. Most definitely. I feel that women are liberating themselves. The feminist movement has made them aware, and they are awakening and trying their wings. And very successfully. Let's take Nicaragua, for instance. I think that the women poets in Nicaragua of this generation—the Sandinista women—are better than their male contemporaries. Nicaragua is a land of poets, fantastic poets such as Ernesto Cardenal and Carlos Martínez Rivas, but until recently nearly all were men, men, men.

McGowan. Claribel, many women like Rigoberta Menchú, América Sosa, and Gloria Bonilla have given testimony about repression in Latin America. Is it particularly important for women writers to bear witness?

Alegría. I think so, Marcia. Latin America has always been a man's world, and men bear witness to *their* world. These women, though, are talking about their sisters, who until now were more or less ignored. We are letting the world know what is the position of women in Central America, about the importance of women in the liberation movements, about the many women who have died under torture.

Reality in Central America surpasses any kind of fiction; it is so gory, so horrible. And I think women, mothers, are more sensitive to this.

McGowan. So people not only within the country but outside the country can now understand the effects of war and repression, not just on the men but on women's lives as well.

Alegría. What it does to their lives; what happens when there are children to be raised or when husbands have disappeared. What

234

it is like to live in a brutal, machista world. Machismo is very much alive in Central America, all through Latin America.

McGowan. You see the testimony of women writers as being an effort, in part, to overcome that?

Alegría. I do. And I see it as an effort to liberate themselves from the idea that women cannot write about these things, that they are too terrible for women to write about, that women have too much sensitivity or that they are not intelligent enough to be objective. You know, all the testimonies of women like Rigoberta Menchú, Gloria Bonilla, and the rest are a liberating example.

McGowan. So machismo preserves the stereotypes that women have had to live with for ages. Stereotypes of not being able to be objective, for instance, of being subjective.

Alegría. Yes. Women are very, very objective, and at the same time I see in the testimonies of women a closer identification with the people they write about. Maybe that is because of motherhood. Maybe.

McGowan. You definitely see a kind of collective consciousness developing among these writers?

Alegría. Very much so, and I am happy about that.

McGowan. Claribel, in your work there is a very thin line between fiction and autobiography. In *Luisa*, for instance, and in *Family Album*, the situations of the characters closely parallel incidents in your own life. The gypsy in *Luisa*, you have told me, is *your* gypsy, and Luisa's husband's name is Bud. What is the place of autobiography in your fiction?

Alegría. It is very important, indeed. I think, as does García Márquez, that the most important years for a writer, or almost anyone, are the first eleven to thirteen years, and I find myself coming back to those years and to what happened to me then. I use my past as a stepping stone; these are the things that have happened to me. Anyone who wants to know my life story should just go to my books. I don't really need to write an autobiography. Someone with a little patience can find it in my poetry, but mostly in my books of narrative.

McGowan. "Village of God and the Devil" seems to be autobiographical in that it depicts the adventures of two characters who buy a house in Deyá, Mallorca, name it Ca'n Blau, and establish a relationship with Robert Graves, and yet you name the protagonists Marcia and Slim. Why do you alter some names and leave others intact in this story?

Alegría. Had I named them Claribel and Bud, the story would not have worked. I did that in order to achieve a certain distance, and it had to be done in the third person rather than in the first person. Besides, I wouldn't be able to sleep, because Bud has never freaked out, you know, or had electroshock treatments. So I wanted to protect him. (Laughter.) Many of the magical things that happened to me in that wonderful village of Deyá are the simple truth. I made very good friends there. It is a fisherman's town mostly, and some of the wives of the fishermen were my good friends. They would come to have a cup of tea with me, and they would tell me all these amazing stories. Like the one where everybody thought Manuela was a woman, and only when she died did they discover she was a man who had been married for thirty years to the village idiot. On the other hand, I invented the story about the Philosophers' Stone and Raimundo Lulio. (Laughter.) Bud and I invented it. We started out talking about what caused the Great Deyá Landslide and elaborating on that. But the stories of how Robert Graves exorcised village houses of poltergeists are absolutely true, and also the amazing number of John the Baptists who settled there.

McGowan. Well, I must say I'm relieved that the black hole is not real. It was terrifying. (Laughter.)

Alegría. I adore the works of Raimundo Lulio, you know, and that is how we started putting together this particular story.

McGowan. In addition to blurring the lines between fiction and autobiography, your writing defies categorization by genre. Lines are blurred among conversation and testimony and narrative, between short story and the novel. As a woman writer, do you consciously set out to defy these categories?

Alegría. I never set out on a writing project with categories in mind. Never. Each poem or short story or novel is a world of its own, and each new poem or short story, each novella always frightens me. With each one I feel that I am learning how to write all over again.

McGowan. So you don't consciously, as a part of your craft, set out to defy these traditional genres?

Alegría. No, I don't. But maybe I do so unconsciously, because some critics have told me that.

236

McGowan. Some critics have told you that, so it's plausible?

Alegría. But I myself am never conscious of it.

McGowan. Do you set out consciously in your writing to try to bring about change?

Alegría. Yes, I do sometimes, especially when I write testimony. Every writer likes to communicate, and sometimes I want to awaken the conscience of my reader, to make him aware of what has happened in my country. But it's dangerous to introduce politics into a poem, a novella, a work of creation. As Stendhal said, politics in a work of art is like a pistol shot in a concert hall: it startles without enlightening.

McGowan. In testimonials, though, you say you try to raise the consciousness of the readers and maybe to appeal to their conscience as well.

Alegría. I think so. I start writing a poem when something has moved me tremendously. "The Woman of Rio Sumpul," for example, is considered very political poetry. But I identified with what happened to that woman. Because it had such an impact on me and was such an obsession with me, I wrote the poem. But I did not write it with the intention of changing or raising the consciousness of people. However, you have to admit that in any story, in any novel, there is always the context: the social, political, and economic context. You cannot escape the context, can you?

McGowan. I absolutely agree. I think it is interesting that in the poetry, which many people interpret as being highly political, every time I have discussed it with you, you do not deny that there is a political reality there, but what you are saying, over and over again, is that it is personal. In the telling it becomes somehow political.

Alegría. In the telling it becomes political. Exactly. And, let's say, when you are writing a novel you have more freedom, you can sensitize the protagonists into making a difference. In a poem you cannot do that, but in a novel or a short story you can.

McGowan. You have liberties.

Alegría. You have more liberty than in a poem.

McGowan. And that is because of the distance that you try to draw between yourself and the novel or whatever fiction it is that you are writing?

Alegría. Yes. It is less dangerous than writing a poem. I don't want to write anything propagandistic, but it is easier in a novel or short story to say certain things through your protagonist that are at least plausible.

McGowan. Must the writer have a consciousness of class, race and gender issues, do you think?

Alegría. I don't think so. I don't bother about this very much. On the other hand, let me see. Maybe I am going to contradict myself here. Because I write testimony I do hope someone in my country, in my region—let's say a woman in my social class—is awakened by it. I am very depressed to see the rigid, stereotyped reactions within my class in El Salvador. Most of them are calloused about what has happened in my country. There are exceptions, of course, but very few. So it is true that when I have written testimonial books like *They Won't Take Me Alive*, I have been aware of class consciousness.

McGowan. What about the question of race? You say the people of your class, the women of your class, are not very conscious of these issues. Are they conscious of racial issues?

Alegría. No. In El Salvador, 95 percent of us are mestizos. But the majority of the women in my class, even though they look mestizo, are always talking as if they are Spanish. They completely forget their Indian mixture, and that irritates me, because being part Indian is a great richness. I am very proud to have Indian blood. These women also have it, but they deny it.

McGowan. Claribel, in her essay "Blood, Bread and Poetry," Adrienne Rich says that reading Margaret Randall's anthology of contemporary Cuban women poets was a powerful experience for her. She speaks of the consistently high level of poetry, the sense of the poets' connections with the world and community, and in their individual statements, the affirmation of an organic relation between poetry and social transformation. When I read your poetry, I also feel this affirmation. Is this an effect that you consciously strive to achieve?

Alegría. No, not in my poetry. But, as I have said, maybe I do it subconsciously. For many years, especially since the Nicaraguan revolution, I have been obsessed with and immersed in what is happening in Latin America. Because I have read so much about it, seen so much, acquired so much experience talking to other people, it's only natural that I write about it. I don't think I could consciously write poetry like that. Had I simply been existing, being very attentive to what is happening inside me, reading beautiful books and listening to beautiful music, probably I would be a total aesthete by now. But I did not let myself do that, and I became immersed in a civil war, as I have told you. That reality became woven into my fiction.

McGowan. Has there been any censorship of your writing in Latin American countries?

Alegría. No. Not officially. However, when the Army closed the National University of El Salvador in 1972, they burned an edition of my poetry along with other books. The book was called *Aprendizaje* (Apprenticeship), published by the University Press in 1970. *Ashes of Izalco* was published in El Salvador about ten years after I published it in Spain, but that was due to a special circumstance. The dictator, Molina, wanted to leave office with a liberal image so he decreed that some Salvadoran novels be published. A friend of mine, working in the Ministry of Education, slipped our book through. Amazingly enough, *Ashes* became required reading in secondary schools, and it has gone through more than twenty editions by now. It is even allowed in the prisons.

McGowan. That *is* ironic.

Alegría. About five years ago, the Jesuits at the "Universidad Centroamericana" started publishing some of my other books.

McGowan. Are they publishing testimony as well?

Alegría. Yes, they have published *They Won't Take Me Alive*, and they want to publish my last collection of poems that appeared in Nicaragua.

McGowan. Is this the same university where the six Jesuits were assassinated a few years ago?

Alegría. Yes. Over the past decade their University Press has been bombed at least four or five times. The death squads accuse them of publishing "subversive" literature, such as our books. As a matter of fact, Ignacio Ellacuria, the rector, invited me to come to the university and talk to the students in mid-1989, and he promised I would be protected. When Bud heard that, he snorted and asked: "How many divisions do the Jesuits have?" I decided not to go, and six months later Ellacuria and five other Jesuits, plus their housekeeper and her daughter, were pulled out of their dwelling on the campus and murdered by the army.

McGowan. That was a horrible crime. Tell me, Claribel, what is the obligation of those who have survived repression to those who have not survived?

Alegría. Let me quote Ernesto Cardenal on that. He has a beautiful poem, "For These Dead, Our Dead," which was an admonition to the Sandinista leaders of Nicaragua. He says, "When you receive the appointment, the award, the promotion, think of those who died in the struggle. You are their representatives." It is a beautiful poem, and Bud has translated it. Of course we have an obligation to remember those who died and why they died.

McGowan. Claribel, let's talk now about symbolism in your work. I notice that the ceiba tree keeps popping up in your poetry and in your fiction as well. Can you explain the importance of that tree to you?

Alegría. The ceiba tree is an ancient tree, a very Central American tree, a great symbol. To me, the ceiba is my childhood, and I am like the ceiba. When I learned that the ceiba I identified with in Santa Ana was broken apart and cut down, I cried and cried.

In one poem called "The Ceiba" I explain that its foliage is like the map of my country. So, yes, it is my symbol, my metaphor.

McGowan. In "Village of God and the Devil," Marcia is able to invoke the shamanic presence of Sea Eagle only after offering a libation to the giant tree which adopts her. The mythic and magical elements of your fiction seem to spring at least in part from a belief that spirits are always closely connected to the earth.

Alegría. I believe that, and if someone tells me that is very primitive and elemental, then I have to say that *I* am very primitive and elemental.

McGowan. Maybe even pagan. (Laughter.)

Alegría. Exactly. I agree that I have an element of paganism in me.

McGowan. Claribel, is it possible to establish a kind of mystical connection between the place of exile and the homeland through communing with these spirits?

Alegría. I think so. Ah yes, without them I would wither. I can't live without magic, you know. I think most people are like that but don't want to admit it for fear of being called superstitious. But all religions have magic in them and practically everyone practices some kind of religion, even these pagan rituals. There is something deep there, and to me it is very real. My dreams are clear cut, and in them I am frequently in communication with El Salvador.

McGowan. It is interesting that your tree functions in a very similar way in Mallorca.

Alegría. Yes, and I have another one in Nicaragua as well. And I never tell anyone, not even Bud, where my trees are. I can't live without my tree, and I communicate with my people through the tree. That's why Robert Graves told me I was a hamadryad.

McGowan. Is your tree in Nicaragua a ceiba tree as well?

Alegría. No, my ceiba was in El Salvador, and it was chopped down.

McGowan. And it can't be replaced?

Alegría. No.

McGowan. Let's talk a little more about spirits. In "Village of God and the Devil," particularly in the last section, poltergeists and exorcisms seem as real as Slim's overproductive but unprofitable garden. In Marcia's point of view, the houses in Deyá are haunted and their inhabitants are prone to drug-induced hallucinations. Spirits, objects like mirrors and bones become talismans, invested with terrific powers. Deyá even plays host to the philosopher's stone, a miniaturized black hole. Slim and Marcia are at home in this world, abandoning it only after the magic leaves. Claribel, why is it impossible for Marcia and Slim to live without magic?

Alegría. I told you before that I am elemental, very primitive, very pagan. Maybe it's because I'm from Central America, where so many things occur, and from my childhood I have been marked by that. I think magic surrounds me everywhere, and now it is surrounding me in Nicaragua as well. I find that strange things are always happening to me in the real world or in my dreams. I am sensitized to it, and I guess Bud has been very much influenced by it, because he was not like that when we got married. (Laughter). But now he has seen so many strange things happening that he is constantly overwhelmed. Okay, why not? Isn't magic just another way of looking at reality? Reality does not have to be circumscribed to just what we are touching and seeing. There are many other realities, and there *is* a magical reality. I feel sorry for people who do not sense that; I couldn't live without it.

241

McGowan. Would you say that you carry it with you wherever you go, or would you say that it is waiting for you when you get there?

Alegría. I think it is waiting for me. (Laughter.) Because no matter where I am, I sense it. I sensed it in Europe. I feel it *more* when I am in Central America and when I am in Deyá, especially during our first years in Deyá. When I was in Mexico, I felt it very strongly. In other countries, there is always magic waiting for me, but not as strongly.

McGowan. Do you find it even in England?

Alegría. Yes, I found it in Scotland, in Edinburgh, when I visited that wonderful castle and found voices waiting for me and telling me things. I would have loved to spend a night there. I found it in England more than in France.

McGowan. Maybe some day you should go to Glastonbury where all of the forces come together. I can imagine that would be a fantastic experience for you.

Alegría. Exactly. Do you know where I found it years ago? At Stonehenge. I was awed by that, and I felt the magic. I suppose I do take some of it with me.

McGowan. You take the susceptibility with you.

Alegría. And also the pull. In my case it is true that I am in virtually direct communication with my subconscious. That is part of it. My subconscious is very close to the surface, and I can fetch it.

McGowan. Do you think that is a quality of many poets?

Alegría. I think so.

McGowan. I know that you are fundamentally a poet, but it comes out strongly in your fiction, as well. It seems impossible to rid yourself of this sense of magic all around.

Alegría. When I think of my novellas, let's say, especially "The Talisman" and "Village of God and the Devil," I almost feel that they are poems in progress.

McGowan. Oh, I feel that too, very strongly. Where the magical elements are heightened, there is a kind of poetic power.

Alegría. Exactly, poetic power. And, as a matter of fact, I am returning more and more to my poetry these days.

McGowan. Claribel, what should your readers look forward to in the next couple of years? What kinds of things are you working on right now?

Alegría. Right now, Bud and I have recently finished another testimonial. It's the story of how the Peruvian Túpac Amaru Revolutionary Movement spent three years planning and excavating a 345-meter tunnel from a safehouse operational base to an exact point within the walls of the maximum security penitentiary of "Canto Grande," located outside Lima, Peru, on the edge of the Andean foothills.

On 9 July 1990, forty-eight political prisoners of the MRTA, including nine women and the leader of the organization, Victor Polay Campo, escaped cleanly through the tunnel and vanished into thin air. The single act of violence accompanying the escape occurred when one of the women prisoners was forced to bop a prison guard over the head with a bottle.

We were invited to go to Lima by some of the MRTA leaders who had read our other books of testimony, and we spent a week in a clandestine safehouse—the most hunted-for spot in Peru at that time—interviewing the people who had planned and dug the tunnel and the prisoners inside Canto Grande who had organized the escape.

As for my own work, I have recently completed a new book of poetry that will be called *Fugas* (Fugues). My main themes are love, death, and the encounter with old age. I also have a series of poems that are mythological: female mythology. I write about Penelope, Pandora, Persephone, and Demeter and relate them to contemporary psychology.

McGowan. So you are using fundamentally Greco-Roman mythology?

Alegría. In this volume, yes.

McGowan. You have used other mythologies in your poetry as well, but you have come to this particular mythology of late?

Alegría. That's right.

McGowan. And what are you working on currently?

Alegría. I am now working with Bud on a book of short stories, finishing my translation of Irish poets, and working with my son Erik on a translation of the Tao into Spanish. He translates directly from the Chinese, and I give it form. I am also waiting for the gypsy to dictate more poems to me.

McGowan. Are you in any hurry to complete these projects? Do you have book contracts for them?

Alegría. I am not in a hurry. Once you start publishing it becomes easier to find a publisher. I feel sorry for people who have not published yet. And it is always more difficult for a woman. If a woman has the same talent as a man, the man's work will be accepted more readily unless the woman has achieved a certain recognition.

McGowan. Do you think that maybe because of the worldwide recession and xenophobia, editors are being more selective and they are doing it in a sexist and racist way?

Alegría. I think there may be something to that: a lack of interest in writers outside one's own country. In Spain, there used to be great interest in Latin American writers, but that has diminished. I think the same thing has happened in France and Germany. I don't know about the United States. What do you say?

McGowan. In the United States I am seeing a kind of explosion of interest in ethnic literature *here*, so that Latina/Latino writers are very much in the forefront of publishing right now. Mexican-American writers, Chicana and Chicano writers, and certainly Asian-American writers are being published. I think that there is a kind of interest in our own ethnicity, though there is the acknowledgement that we have joined what everybody calls a global village and we are going to have to look to other cultures. In the academy, the push is certainly toward educating more people in languages. But it seems to me that when I go to academic conferences, the greater number of panels is focused on ethnic literatures of the United States.

Alegría. That is good, but then the people who write in other countries find it much more difficult to publish here.

McGowan. Yes, exactly. Will you publish your present work in Spanish first, then in English?

Alegría. Yes.

McGowan. Is *Luisa* the only work you published first in English?

Alegría. Yes. I gave *Luisa* to a Mexican editorial house before I gave it to the United States publisher, but the Mexican house delayed publication. The United States edition is a little longer, because I added two more episodes and a reprise of the seven key poems at the end.

McGowan. Does Bud always write in English first?

Alegría. He always does. And I always write in Spanish. I translate him, and he translates me.

McGowan. And what is Bud working on now?

Alegría. He has recently finished the testimonial with me. It is titled *Fuga de Canto Grande* in Spanish. My last book of poetry also was called *Fugas* because it is like a Bach fugue. I have a death theme, a mythological theme, and I go from love to death to mythology to growing old, to death, to love. To return to Bud, he is working with me on the book of short stories I have mentioned.

McGowan. When you are writing fiction, Claribel, or when you are working on testimony—when you are writing prose in general—do poems come to you at the same time, or do you set your poetry aside for a while?

Alegría. Sometimes I may be submerged in a testimonial or a fiction book when a poem comes to me insistently and I take time off to write it. But I write much less poetry when I am working with prose. That is why I have a feeling that I am returning more and more to poetry. I have a unique feeling that I would like to close the circle. I started with poetry, then reversed the tide, diversified, and now toward the end of the cycle I want to close the circle with poetry. That is my feeling, but I don't know. Something else can happen; you never know.

Appendix B

CHRONOLOGY OF CLARIBEL ALEGRÍA

1924   Born in Estelí, Nicaragua (12 May), daughter of Dr. Daniel Alegría and Ana María Vides.

1925   Family is forced into political exile in El Salvador following father's oppositionist activities during U.S. Marine occupation of Nicaragua. Claribel Alegría is only nine months of age.

1929   Family travels to Nicaragua for brief visit. Returns to El Salvador and Claribel enters José Ingenieros, progressive school named after renowned Argentine philosopher, and founded by her uncle, Ricardo Vides.

1932   The massacre of thirty thousand campesinos in Izalco, El Salvador, by members of the Salvadoran army headed by General Maximilano Hernández Martínez in retaliation for an uprising against the military dictatorship by Salvadoran revolutionary hero, Farabundo Martí.

1941   Alegría publishes her first poems in the Central American cultural supplement, *Repertorio Americano* (Costa Rica), edited by don Joaquín García Monge.

1943   José Vasconcelos arranges for Alegría to be admitted into girls' finishing school in Hammond, Louisiana, near New Orleans.

1944   Alegría is awarded a scholarship and spends the summer session at Loyola University, New Orleans. In September, by invitation from Juan Ramón Jiménez and his wife Zenobia, she travels to Washington, D.C., and registers for courses leading to the B.A. degree at George Washington University.

1947   In December Alegría marries Darwin (Bud) J. Flakoll (born February 20, 1923, in Wendte, South Dakota), former navy officer aboard destroyers during World War II, and a newspaperman in Washington, studying for his M.A. degree at George Washington University.

1948   Alegría graduates from George Washington University. *Anillo de silencio*, (Ring of silence), her first book of poetry, is published by Editorial Botas, Mexico.

1949   First daughter Maya is born in Washington, D.C.

1950   Twin daughters, Patricia and Karen, are born in Alexandria, Virginia. Alegría finishes book of short stories, *Tres cuentos* (three children's stories).

1951   Claribel and Bud move to Mexico after a short stay in El Salvador. They rent a house in Colonia Nueva Anzures, and are introduced to various writers, artists, and intellectuals, including, among others, Guatemalan writer August (Tito) Monterroso, living in political exile, Juan José Arreola, and Juan Rulfo, who frequent the house. In Mexico Alegría writes *Vigilias* (Vigils). *Suite* (poetry) is published by Editorial Brigadas Líricas in Argentina.

1953   Claribel and Bud arrive in Santiago, Chile, where they remain for nearly three years to work on a literary project funded by the Catherwood Foundation in Pennsylvania: an anthology of Latin American writers and poets, entitled *New Voices of Hispanic America*. Besides working on the anthology, Claribel writes a new book of poems, *Acuario*. *Vigilias* (poetry) is published by Editorial Poesía in América, México.

1954	Son Erik is born in January in Santiago, Chile.
1956	Bud and Claribel return to the United States. Bud submits application for appointment to Foreign Service.
1958	Bud appointed second secretary at the U.S. Embassy in Montevideo, Uruguay. Claribel writes another volume of poems, *Huésped de mi tiempo* (Guest of my time).
1960	Bud and Claribel are posted to Argentina. Claribel writes *Vía unica* (One-way traffic).
1961	The Casa de las Américas publishing house in Cuba is established, fostering stronger contact among Latin American writers. Claribel is invited to cultural events. *Huésped de mi tiempo* (Guest of my time) is published by Editorial Américalee, Argentina.
1962	*New Voices of Hispanic America* is published by Beacon Press. Claribel and Bud move to Paris, coming in contact with many Latin American writers living in exile at the time. Bud and Claribel collaborate on the writing of *Cenizas de Izalco* (Ashes of Izalco).
1965	*Vía unica* (poetry) is published by Editorial Alfa in Montevideo, Uruguay.
1966	*Cenizas de Izalco* (novel with Darwin J. Flakoll) is published by Seix-Barral in Barcelona. Publication is delayed by Spanish censorship. Bud and Claribel move to Palma Nova, Mallorca.
1968	Claribel and Bud move to Ca'n Blau Vell (the old blue house) in Deyá, Mallorca. Claribel writes *Pagaré a cobrar* (Installment payments), *Sobrevivo* (I survive), and three short novels: "El Detén" (The talisman), "Album familiar" (Family album), and "Pueblo de Dios y de Mandinga" (Village of God and the Devil). She also writes *Luisa in Realityland* at the urging of Julio Cortazar and his second wife, Carol Dunlap.

1970	*Aprendizaje* (poetry) is published by Editorial Universitaria in San Salvador. In 1972 the University is closed and the remaining editions are burned by the army.
1973	*Pagaré a cobrar* (poetry) is published by Editorial Ocnos, Barcelona.
1977	"El Detén" (novella) is published by Editorial Lúmen, Barcelona.
1978	*Sobrevivo* (poetry) is published by Editorial Cassa de las Américas in Habana, winning the Casa de las Américas Prize.
1979	The Sandinista rebels gain power in Nicaragua. On July 17, Anatasio Somoza II and his son (El Chiguín) flee Nicaragua for Homestead Air Force Base, Miami, in a Lear jet, taking with them the coffins of Anastasio Somoza I and his eldest son, Luis. Claribel and Bud arrive in Nicaragua in early September to research data for *Nicaragua: La revolución sandinista; Una crónica política, 1855-1979* (Nicaragua: The Sandinista Revolution; A Political Chronicle 1855-1979) (history).
1980	In March Monsigñor Oscar Arnulfo Romero, Archbishop of San Salvador, is assassinated while saying mass in a hospital chapel. Claribel Alegría delivers a poetic eulogy at the Sorbonne in Paris. By denouncing government atrocities there, she becomes a political exile from El Salvador.
1981	*Suma y sigue* (Add and carry; selected poetry anthology) is published by Editorial Visor, Madrid. *Nuevas Voces de Norteamérica* (New Voices of North America) (parallel text in English and Spanish) is published by Plaza y Janés in Barcelona. (With Flakoll) *Cien poemas de Robert Graves* (One Hundred Palms by Robert Graves) (anthology) is published by Lúmen, Barcelona.
1982	"Album familiar" (novella) is published by Editorial EDUCA, Costa Rica. *Nicaragua: La revolución sandini-*

sta (history) is published by Editorial ERA, Mexico. *Flowers from the Volcano*, translated by Carolyn Forché, is published by University of Pittsburgh Press.

1983   Claribel and Bud establish principal residence in Nicaragua. *No me agarran viva* (They won't take me alive) (testimony) is published by Editorial ERA, Mexico. *Poesía viva* (selected poetry) is published by Blackrose Press, London. *Karen en barque sur la mer* (French version of "El Detén") is published by Editorial Mercure de France in Paris. *Petit pays* (selected poetry) is published by Editorial Femmes in Paris.

1984   (With Flakoll) *Para romper el silencio* (To Break the Silence) (testimony) is published by Editorial ERA, Mexico.

1985   "Pueblo de Dios y de Mandinga" (novella) is published by Ediciones ERA, Mexico.

1986   *Pueblo de Dios y de Mandinga* (Village of God and the Devil) (three novellas) is published by Editorial Lúmen, Barcelona.

1987   *Luisa in Realityland* (prose/verse novel) is published by Curbstone Press, USA.

1989   *Woman of the River* (poetry) is published by University of Pittsburgh Press, USA. *Ashes of Izalco* (novel, with Darwin J. Flakoll) is published by Curbstone Press in September. *Y este Poema-río* (And this river-poem) (poetry) is published by Editorial Nueva Nicaragua.

1990   *On the Front Line* (anthology of Salvadoran guerrilla poetry edited and translated with Darwin J. Flakoll) is published by Curbstone Press. *Family Album* (three novellas) is published by Women's Press, England.

1991   *Family Album* (three novellas) is published by Curbstone Press.

Appendix C

THE PUBLICATIONS OF CLARIBEL ALEGRÍA

POETRY

Anillo de silencio (Ring of silence). Mexico: Botas, 1948.
Suite of Love, Anguish, and Solitude. Buenos Aires: Brigadas Líricas, 1951.
Vigilias (Vigils). Mexico: Ediciones Poesía de América, 1953.
Acuario (Aquarium). Santiago: Editorial Universitaria, 1955.
Huésped de mi tiempo (Guest of my time). Buenos Aires: Américalee, 1961.
Vía unica (One-way traffic; includes "Auto de fé" and "Comunicación a larga distancia"). Montevideo: Editorial Alfa, 1965.
Aprendizaje (Apprenticeship). El Salvador: Universitaria, 1970. Includes selections from *Anillo de Silencio, Vigilias, Acuario, Huésped de mi tiempo,* and *Vía Unica.*
Pagaré a cobrar y otros poemas (Installment payments). Barcelona: Ocnos, 1973.
Sobrevivo (I survive). Cuba: Casa de las Américas, 1978.
Tres Poemas (Three poems). Madrid: Papeles de Son Armadans, 1978.
Suma y sigue (Add and carry). Madrid: Visór, 1981. Anthology.
Flowers from the Volcano / Flores del volcán. Trans. Carolyn Forché. Pittsburgh: University of Pittsburgh Press, 1982. Anthology; parallel text in English and Spanish.
Poesía viva (Live poetry). London: Blackrose, 1983. Anthology.
Petit pays (Small country). Paris: Femmes, 1983. Anthology.
"Laughing to Death" and "Estelí." Trans. and ed. Doris Meyer and Margarite Fernández Olmos. In *Contemporary Women*

251

Authors of Latin America. Ed. Doris Meyer and Margarite Fernández Olmos. New York: Brooklyn College, 1983.
"Granny and the Golden Bridge." Trans. Darwin J. Flakoll. *The Massachusetts Review* 27 (Fall/Winter 1986): 503-5.
"The American Way of Life." Trans. Antonio Torres. *Index on Censorship* 5 (1988): 112-13.
"Summing Up." Trans. Darwin J. Flakoll. *The Paris Review* 30 (Fall 1988): 154.
"Little Cambray Tamales." Trans. Darwin J. Flakoll. *The Paris Review* 30 (Fall 1988): 155.
"Documentary." Trans. Darwin J. Flakoll. *The Paris Review* 30 (Fall 1988): 156-59.
Woman of the River / Mujer del río. Trans. Darwin J. Flakoll. Pennsylvania: University of Pittsburgh Press, 1989. Parallel text in English and Spanish.
Y este poema-río. Managua: Editorial Nueva Nicaragua, 1989.
"The Story of the Unhappy Willow." Trans. Darwin J. Flakoll. *Children's Literature* 17 (1989): 135-41.
"Little Cambray Tamales" (Five million bite-size tamales). Trans. Louise Popkin. *TriQuarterly* 77 (Winter 1989/1990): 273-74.
"Snapshots." Trans. Louise Popkin. *TriQuarterly* 77 (Winter 1989/1990): 275.

FICTION

Tres cuentos (Three stories). El Salvador: Ministerio de Cultura, 1958. Children's stories illustrated by Agustín Blancovaras.
Karen en barque sur la mer. Paris: Mercure de France, 1983. French version of "El Detén" (The talisman).
Familiealbum. Holland: Gennep Publishers, 1984. Dutch version of "Family Album."
"Boardinghouse." In *And We Sold the Rain: Contemporary Fiction from Central America.* Ed. Rosario Santos. New York: Four Walls, Eight Windows Press, 1988, 171-82.
"El detén" (The talisman). Barcelona: Editorial Lumen, 1977. Story novel.
"Albúm familiar" (Family album). San José, Costa Rica: Editorial Universitaria Centroamericana, 1982.

Family Album. Trans. Amanda Hopkinson. Willimantic, Conn.: Curbstone Press, 1991. Includes "The Talisman" and "Village of God and the Devil."

"Pueblo de Dios y de Mandinga: Con el asesoriamiento científico de Slim" (Village of God and the Devil: With Slim's scientific assessment). Mexico: Ediciones Era, 1985.

Despierta, mi bien, despierta (Awake, my love, awake). San Salvador, El Salvador: UCA Editores, 1986.

Luisa en el país de la realidad (Luisa in Realityland). Mexico: Universidad Autónoma de Zacatecas, 1987.

Luisa in Realityland. Trans. Darwin J. Flakoll. Willimantic, Conn.: Curbstone Press, 1987.

"The Awakening." In *Latin American Literary Review Special Issue: Short Stories by Latin American Women Writers*, ed. Kathleen Ross and Yvette Miller. 19/37 (Jan-June 1991): 30-33.

HISTORY AND *TESTIMONIO*

"Literatura y liberación nacional en El Salvador." *Casa de las Américas* 21/126 (May-June 1981): 12-16.

"The Writer's Commitment." In *Lives on the Line: The Testimony of Contemporary Latin American Authors*, ed. Doris Meyer. University of California Press, 1988, 306-11. Contributor.

EDITED TEXTS

Homenaje a El Salvador (Tribute to El Salvador). Madrid: Visor, 1981. Poetry anthology, prologue by Julio Cortázar.

On the Front Line: Guerilla Poetry of El Salvador. Willimantic, Conn.: Curbstone Press, 1989. Ed. and trans.

OTHER

"Redescubriendo América" (Rediscovering America) and "Managua." *Hispamérica* 12/36 (1983): 57-59.

"Para, de, con Julio Cortázar" (Far, by, with Julio Cortázar). *Casa de las Américas* 25 (July-Oct. 1984): 145-46.

"The Two Cultures of El Salvador." *The Massachusetts Review* 27 (Fall/Winter 1986): 493-502.

"Alliances—Alianzas." *Cahiers du Monde Hispanique et Luso-Brasilien/ Caravelle* 49 (1987): 43-61.

"The Work of Writing and Internal Exile" and "Six Poems." *The Sonoma Mandala Literary Review*. California: Sonoma State University Press, 1987, 20-46.

"The Politics of Exile." In *You Can't Drown the Fire: Latin American Women Writing in Exile*, ed. Alicia Partnoy. Pittsburgh: Cleis, 1988, 171-77.

"The American Way of Life." *Index on Censorship* (May 1988): 112-13.

"Carta a un desterrado (Letter to an outcast)." *Hispamérica* 18/52 (1989): 63-65.

"Las revoluciones son contagiosas" (Revolutions are contagious). *Barricada Internacional* (Managua, 8 July 1989): 45.

"Mi libro favorito: *Rayuela* " (My favorite book: *Hopscotch*). *Diario 16* (September 7, 1989): 8.

"Our Little Region." In *Being America: Essays on Art, Literature and Identity from Latin America*, ed. Rachel Weiss and Alan West. Fredonia, N.Y.: White Pine Press, 1991, 41-50.

"Latinidad and the Artist." In *Critical Fictions: The Politics of Imaginative Writing*, ed. Philomena Mariani. Seattle: Bay Press, 1991, 104-7.

"Not a Single Step Backwards." *Mayibuye* (Johannesburg, South Africa, March 1992): 33.

"¿Habrá paz en El Salvador?" (Will there be peace in El Salvador?). *Diario 16* (May 31, 1992): 68-72.

Contemporary Authors Autobiography Series 15. Detroit: Gale Research, 1992, 1-14. Contributor.

WITH DARWIN J. FLAKOLL

Fiction

Cenizas de Izalco (Ashes of Izalco). Barcelona: Seix Barral, 1966. Novel.

Cenizas de Izalco. San José: Editorial Universitaria Centroamericana, 1982.

Ashes of Izalco. Willimantic, Conn.: Curbstone Press, 1989. Novel.

History and Testimonio

La encrucijada salvadoreña (Salvadoran crossroads). Barcelona: Editorial Cidob, 1980. Historical essays.

Nicaragua: La revolución sandinista; Una crónica política, 1855-1979 (Nicaragua: The Sandinista Revolution; A Political Chronicle, 1855-1979"; history). Mexico: Ediciones Era, 1982.

No me agarran viva: La mujer salvadoreña en lucha (They won't take me alive: The Salvadoran woman in struggle). Mexico: Ediciones Era, 1983.

They Won't Take Me Alive. Trans. Amanda Hopkinson. London: Women's Press, 1987.

Para romper el silencio (To break the silence). Mexico: Ediciones Era, 1984. A history of El Salvador's political prisoners.

Edited Texts

New Voices of Hispanic America. New York: Beacon, 1962. Ed. and trans.

Nuevas Voces de Norteamérica. (Parallel text in English and Spanish.) Barcelona: Plaza y Janés, 1981.

Unstill Life: An Introduction to the Spanish Poetry of Latin America, ed. Mario Benedetti. New York: Harcourt, 1970. Trans.

Cien poemas de Robert Graves (One hundred poems by Robert Graves). Barcelona: Lumen, 1981. Anthology.

Translations

Chomsky, Noam. *On Power and Ideology (Sobre el poder y la ideología: Conferencias de Managua).* Madrid: Visor Distribuciones, 1989. Trans.

The Patient Impatience. Managua: Curbstone Press, 1992. Memoirs of Tomás Borge.

Appendix D

PUBLICATIONS AND INTERVIEWS CONCERNING CLARIBEL ALEGRÍA

JOURNAL ARTICLES AND REFERENCES

Acevedo, Ramón Luis. *Los senderos del volcán: narrativa centro-americana contemporanea.* Guatemala: Editorial Universitaria, 1991. Incorporates an essay on *Ashes of Izalco* (109-20) where he argues against an overly politicized interpretation of the novel.

———. *"Cenizas de Izalco* de Claribel Alegría y Darwin Flakoll o la armonización posible" (*Ashes of Izalco* or possible harmony). *Studi di letteratura ispanoamericana* 21 (1990): 77-88.

Arenal, Electa. "Two Poets of the Sandinista Struggle." *Feminist Studies* 7 (Spring 1981): 19-27. The article studies *Sobrevivo* by Claribel Alegría and *Línea de fuego* by Gioconda Belli.

Beverley, John, and Marc Zimmerman. *Literature and Politics in the Central American Revolutions.* Austin: Texas University Press, 1990. In the chapter "Salvadoran Revolutionary Poetry," editors discuss Alegría's "feminization of Salvadoran literature" (137) in the context of "The New Women's Poetry and Combat Poetry."

Cerna, Carlos. "Análisis de la novela *Cenizas de Izalco*" (Analysis of the novel *Ashes of Izalco*). *Taller de Letras* (Universidad Centroamericana José Simeon Cañas, San Salvador) 8/135:7-34.

Coronel Utrecho, José. *Líneas para un boceto de Claribel Alegría* (Lines for a sketch of Claribal Alegría). Managua: Editorial Nueva Nicaragua, 1989.

Crow, Mary. *Woman Who Has Sprouted Wings: Poems by Contemporary Latin American Women Poets.* Pittsburgh: Latin American Literary Review Press, 1987, 173-85.

Flores, Angel, and Kate Flores. *The Defiant Muse.* New York: Feminist Press, 1986, 92-96.

Forché, Carolyn. "The Ghosts of a Central American Girlhood." *Los Angeles Times* (15 November, 1987): 3-10.

Gallegos, Valdés, Luis y David Escobar Galindo. *Poesía femenina de El Salvador.* (Feminine Poetry of El Salvador). San Salvador: Ministerio de Educación, 1976, 137-44.

Hopkinson, Amanda. *Lovers and Comrades: Women's Resistance Poetry from Central America.* London: The Women's Press, 1989, 18-21, 26-28, 40-41, 100-103, 114-16.

Marting, Diane E. *Escritoras de Hispanoamérica* (Women writers of Spanish America). México: Siglo Veintiuno Editores, 1990, 10-20.

Papastamatiu, Basilia. "La sobrevida poética de Claribel Alegría" (Claribel Alegría's poetic survival). *Casa de las Américas* 110 (1978): n.p.

Rojas, Mario A. "Some Central American Writers of Liberation." In *Culture, Human Rights and Peace in Central America.* Ed. George F. McLean, Raul Molina, and Timothy Ready. Lanham, Md.: University Press of America, 1989, 128-32.

Sternbach, Nancy Saporta. "Remembering the Dead: Latin American Women's 'Testimonial' Discourse." *Latin American Perspectives* 18/3 (Summer 1991): 91-102. Article discusses Claribel Alegría's *No me agarran viva: La mujer salvadoreña en lucha* and *Flowers from the Volcano* .

———. "Claribel Alegría (1924): Nicaragua, El Salvador." In *Escritoras de Hispanoamérica: Una guía bio-bibliográfica* (Women writers of Spanish America: A bio-bibliographic guide), ed. Diane E. Marting. México: Siglo Veintiuno Editores, 1990, 10-20.

Shea, Maureen. "A Growing Awareness of Sexual Oppression in the Novels of Contemporary Latin American Women Writers." *Confluencia: Revista Hispánica de Cultura y Literatura* 4/1 (Fall 1988): 53-59. For a list of authors addressed in the essay, see Maureen Shea in DAI.

———. *Latin American Women Writers and the Growing Potential of Political Consciousness. Dissertation Abstracts International*

49/3 (September, 1988). Shea studies the following authors and their works: Dora Alonso, *Tierra inerme*; E. Poniatowska, *Hasta no verte Jesús mío*; Claribel Alegría, *Cenizas de Izalco*; and I. Allende, *La casa de los espíritus.*

Yúdice, George. "Letras de emergencia: Claribel Alegría" (Urgent letters: Claribel Alegría). *Revista Iberoamericana* 51/132-33 (July-December 1985): 953-64.

Zamora, Daisy. *La mujer nicaragüense en la poesía* (The Nicaraguan woman in poetry). Managua: Editorial Nueva Nicaragua, 1992, 107-55.

Zimmerman, Marc. *El Salvador at War: A Collage Epic.* Minneapolis: Marxist Educational Press, 1988. Discusses Alegría's poetry in the context of Salvadoran and Central American Left poetry.

Zoreda, Margaret Lee. "La función pública-política del escritor: Hannah Arendt y Claribel Alegría" (The public-political role of the writer: Hannah Arendt and Claribel Alegría). *Iztapalapa* (Mexico: Universidad Autonoma Metropolitana) 10/21 (1990): 145-54. Traces comparisons between the profile of the poet-politician as proposed by Hannah Arendt and its concrete expression in selected works by Claribel Alegría.

BOOK REVIEWS

Agosín, Marjorie. Review of *Luisa in Realityland* by Claribel Alegría. *The Christian Science Monitor* (March 1988): 20.

Belm, Dan. "'Woman of the River' by Claribel Alegría." *The Village Voice Literary Supplement* (April 1989):5.

Bushell, Agnes. Review of *Family Album* by Claribel Alegría. *Maine Progressive* (December 1991): 24.

Clausen, Jan. "*Flowers from the Volcano* by Claribel Alegría." In *Books & Life*, ed. Jan Clausen. Columbus: Ohio State University Press, 1989, 150-59.

Dalton, Roque. Review of *Huésped de mi tiempo* by Claribel Alegría. *Casa de las Américas* 15-16 (1962-63): 53-54.

Engelbert, Jo Anne. "*Flowers from the Volcano*, Claribel Alegría." *Latin American Review* 33 (September-December 1984): 75-76.

Ferrer-Vidal, Jorge. "La nueva poesía americana: nuevas voces de Norteamérica" (New American poetry: New voices of North America). *Jano* 557 (Barcelona, 1983): 143-45.

Fisher, Carl. Review of *Luisa in Realityland* by Claribel Alegría. *Small Press Book Review* (January/February 1989), n.p.

Handman, Fran. Review of *Ashes of Izalco* by Claribel Alegría and Darwin J. Flakoll. *New York Times Book Review* (5 November 1989): 25.

Kaganoff, Penny. Review of *Ashes of Izalco* by Claribel Alegría and Darwin J. Flakoll. *Publisher's Weekly* (11 August 1989): 450.

McGregor, Matt. "Novel of Vignettes and Poetry of El Salvador" (review of *Luisa in Realityland*). *The Chronicle* (Willimantic, Conn., 2 October 1987): 17.

Martínez, Manuel. "Sobrevivo entre la ironía y la ira" (I survive between irony and anger). *Ventana* (Manuaga, 29 April 1989): 5.

Menton, Seymour. Review of *Despierta, mi bien, despierta. World Literature Today* 62/2 (1988): 256-57.

Mitchell, Beverly. "Claribel Alegría—*Flowers from the Volcano.*" *Translation Review* 12 (1983):50-54.

Russo, Brian. Reviews *Ashes of Izalco, Woman of the River, On the Front Line. Mid-American Review* 10/2 (1990): 203-7.

Vollmer, Judith. Review of *Woman of the River* by Claribel Alegría. *The Women's Review of Books* (March 1990): 12-13.

Wright, Carolyne. "Flowers from the Volcano (Flores del volcán), Claribel Alegría." *Northwest Review* (University of Oregon) 21/2 and 3 (1983): 175-83.

SELECTED INTERVIEWS

Aguilera Diaz, Gaspar. "De Cronopios, desaparecidos, encuentros y poesía nicaragüense de hoy. Entrevista con Claribel Alegría." Mexico City: Universidad de Mexico, 1986.

Carney, Jeanne. "Visiting a Mythical Country: An Interview with Claribel Alegría." *Tidepools* (Anaheim, Calif.: Friends of the Humanities) 2/1: 36-38.

Forché, Carolyn. "Interview with Claribel Alegría." *Index on Censorship* 13/2 (April 1984): 11-13. In this interview Alegría discusses her values, works, politics, and the vitality of Latin American literature.

Graham-Yool, Andrew. "Claribel Alegría: The Smile Amid the Sadness." In *After the Despots: Latin American Views and Interviews.* London: Bloomsbury Press, 1991, 138-45.

McGowan, Marcia P. Interview with Claribel Alegría. Eastern Connecticut State University, Willimantic, Conn. October 1987. Radio station WECS.

Moraña, Mabel. "Desde las entrañas del monstruo" (From the entrails of the monster). *Brecha* 7/313 (29 November 1991): 20-21.

Perdomo, Miguel Anibal. "Obsesiones y conjuros en la obra de Claribel Alegría" (Obsessions and spells in the work of Claribel Alegría). *Hoy, Isla Abierta* (Santo Domingo, 26 August 1989): 16-18.

Rodríguez Sosa, Fernando. "No puedo tolerar la indiferencia" (I cannot tolerate indifference). *Revolución y Cultura* (Havana: September 1981): 20-21.

Taylor, Alexander. "Conversation in Managua: An Interview with Claribel Alegría and Darwin J. Flakoll" (Managua, 1987). Willimantic, Conn.: Curbstone Press, 1989.

Valenzuela, Luisa. "Dearest Friends: Claribel and Bud." *The Village Voice* (New York) 14 August 1984: 19-20.

"What Makes a Poem?" BBC Production (December 1991). Interview with Claribel Alegría and other poets.

CONTRIBUTORS

Marjorie Agosín is associate professor of Spanish at Wellesley College and author of numerous books of literary criticism. Among her most recent publications is *Mujer y literatura fantástica en el Cono Sur* (Santiago, Chile: Editorial Cuarto Propio, 1991). She is also a poet and human rights activist. Her work in this area includes *Circles of Madness: Mothers of the Plaza de Mayo* (Fredonia, NY: White Pine, 1992).

Arturo Arias is associate professor of humanities at San Francisco State University. Coauthor of the screenplay for the film *El Norte*, his most recent book in English is titled *After the Bombs* (Willimantic, Conn.: Curbstone Press, 1990). He is presently completing a novel and a book of Central American literary criticism.

Celia Catlett Anderson is associate professor of English at Eastern Connecticut State University where she teaches children's literature and directs the writing program. She has written a number of articles on children's literature and coauthored (with Marilyn Fain Aspseloff) a book entitled *Nonsense Literature for Children: Aesop to Seuss* (Hampden, Conn.: Library Professional, 1989).

Sandra M. Boschetto-Sandoval is associate professor of Spanish at Michigan Technological University, where she occasionally edits for *Reader: Essays in Reader-Oriented Theory, Criticism and Pedagogy.* Her articles on Hispanic literature have appeared in various critical anthologies and journals including *Crítica Hispánica, Discurso Literario*, and *Hispania.* Her research interests include Latin American women writers, literary and cultural theory, and intercultural communication.

Margaret B. Crosby is a Ph.D. candidate in the Department of Modern Languages at the University of New Mexico. She is currently writing her dissertation on the poetry, fiction, and *testimonios* of Claribel Alegría.

Jo Anne Engelbert is a professor of Latin American literature at Montclair State College in New Jersey, where she directs a program in translator training in Spanish. Her books include *Macedonio Fernández and the Spanish American New Novel* and the anthology *Macedonio*, both published in 1978 by New York Press. A literary translator, she is currently working on a bilingual anthology of Central American poetry under a Fulbright research grant.

Kathleen N. March is associate professor of Spanish at the University of Maine. She teaches Latin American literature, with particular emphasis on Central American women writers and testimonial writing. The founder of the Galician Studies Association, she has published numerous articles on Galician literature as well as on Latin American writers. She has been working on the presence of the Amazon in Latin American writing, and is completing a translation of Gioconda Belli's novel *La mujer habitada*.

Marcia Phillips McGowan is professor of English and director of women's studies at Eastern Connecticut State University. Her articles on women's studies curriculum development and women writers appear in such journals as *Frontiers* and *Letras Femeninas*. Her research interests include Hispanic women's fiction, Victorian and contemporary Anglophone women writers, and feminist pedagogy.

Nina L. Molinaro is assistant professor of Spanish at the University of Colorado at Boulder. The author of *Foucault, Feminism, and Power: Reading Esther Tusquets* (Cranbury, N.J.: Bucknell University Press, 1991), she has also published articles in *Revista de Estudios Hispánicos* and *Letras Femeninas*. Her research interests include the postwar Spanish novel, Hispanic women's fiction, and literary theory.

Cheryl H. Riess is assistant professor of Spanish at the University of South Dakota. She received her Ph.D. from the University of Kansas. Her research interests include contemporary Latin American literature, Argentine literature, and women's writing.

Ileana Rodríguez is associate professor of Spanish at The Ohio State University. She has written extensively on Caribbean and Central American literatures. Her most recent book is *House/Garden/Nation: Representation of Space, Ethnos, and Gender in Transitional Post-Colonial Literature by Women* (forthcoming). She is presently working on *The Constitution of the Social Subject and the Destruction of the Nation State*.

Jorge Ruffinelli is professor of Spanish at Stanford University. He is also editor-in-chief of the journal *Nuevo Texto Crítico*. He has published several books, among them *El lugar de Rulfo* (1980), *Literatura e ideología* (1982), *Poesía y descolonización* (1985), and *La escritura invisible* (1986).

Nancy Saporta Sternbach is assistant professor of Spanish at Smith College where she teaches courses on Latina/o and Latin American literature. She is the coeditor of *Breaking Boundaries: Latina Writing and Critical Readings* (Amherst: University of Massachusetts Press, 1989) and has published widely on Latin American women's writing. She is currently at work on Latin American women's essays and a feminist reading of Spanish American *modernismo.*

Mary Jane Treacy is professor of Spanish at Simmons College. After completing a doctoral dissertation on Golden Age comedy, she succumbed to the allure of Latin American and U.S. Hispanic women's writing and has stayed in this field ever since.

Marc Zimmerman is professor of Latin American Studies at the University of Illinois at Chicago. In addition to his work in Nicaragua's Ministerio de Cultura in 1979-80, he is the author of several books and editions-in-collaboration. These include *The Central American Trilogy* (1980, 1985, and 1988), *Literature and Politics in the Central American Revolution* (Austin: University of Texas Press, 1990) with John Beverley, and *U.S. Latino Literature: An Essay and Annotated Bibliography* (Chicago: March/Abrazo Press, 1992). He is completing a two-volume study of Guatemalan history and literature.

MONOGRAPHS IN INTERNATIONAL STUDIES

ISBN Prefix 0-89680-

Africa Series

38. Wright, Donald R. *Oral Traditions From the Gambia: Volume II, Family Elders*. 1980. 200pp.
084-9 $15.00

43. Harik, Elsa M. and Donald G. Schilling. *The Politics of Education in Colonial Algeria and Kenya*. 1984. 102pp.
117-9 $12.50

45. Keto, C. Tsehloane. *American-South African Relations 1784-1980: Review and Select Bibliography*. 1985. 159pp.
128-4 $11.00

46. Burness, Don, and Mary-Lou Burness, eds. *Wanasema: Conversations with African Writers*. 1985. 95pp.
129-2 $11.00

47. Switzer, Les. *Media and Dependency in South Africa: A Case Study of the Press and the Ciskei "Homeland."* 1985. 80pp.
130-6 $10.00

48. Heggoy, Alf Andrew. *The French Conquest of Algiers, 1830: An Algerian Oral Tradition*. 1986. 101pp.
131-4 $11.00

49. Hart, Ursula Kingsmill. *Two Ladies of Colonial Algeria: The Lives and Times of Aurelie Picard and Isabelle Eberhardt*. 1987. 156pp.
143-8 $11.00

51. Clayton, Anthony, and David Killingray. *Khaki and Blue: Military and Police in British Colonial Africa*. 1989. 235pp.
147-0 $18.00

52. Northrup, David. *Beyond the Bend in the River: African Labor in Eastern Zaire, 1864-1940*. 1988. 195pp.
151-9 $15.00

53. Makinde, M. Akin. *African Philosophy, Culture, and Traditional Medicine.* 1988. 175pp.
152-7 $13.00

54. Parson, Jack ed. *Succession to High Office in Botswana. Three Case Studies.* 1990. 443pp.
157-8 $20.00

55. Burness, Don. *A Horse of White Clouds.* 1989. 193pp.
158-6 $12.00

56. Staudinger, Paul. *In the Heart of the Hausa States.* Tr. by Johanna Moody. 1990. 2 vols. 653pp.
160-8 $35.00

57. Sikainga, Ahmad Alawad. *The Western Bahr Al-Ghazal Under British Rule: 1898-1956.* 1991. 183pp.
161-6 $15.00

58. Wilson, Louis E. *The Krobo People of Ghana to 1892: A Political and Social History.* 1991. 254pp.
164-0 $20.00

59. du Toit, Brian M. *Cannabis, Alcohol, and the South African Student: Adolescent Drug Use 1974-1985.* 1991. 166pp.
166-7 $17.00

60. Falola, Toyin, ed. *The Political Economy of Health in Africa.* 1992. 254pp.
168-3 $17.00

61. Kiros, Tedros. *Moral Philosophy and Development: The Human Condition in Africa.* 1992. 178pp.
171-3 $18.00

62. Burness, Don. *Echoes of the Sunbird: An Anthology of Contemporary African Poetry.* 1993. 198pp.
173-X $17.00

63. Glew, Robert S., and Chaibou Babalé. *Hausa Folktales from Niger.* 1993. 136pp.
176-4 $15.00

Latin America Series

9.   Tata, Robert J. *Structural Changes in Puerto Rico's Economy: 1947-1976.* 1981. xiv, 104pp.
107-1 $11.00

11.   O'Shaughnessy, Laura N., and Louis H. Serra. *Church and Revolution in Nicaragua.* 1986. 118pp.
126-8 $11.00

12.   Wallace, Brian. *Ownership and Development: A comparison of Domestic and Foreign Investment in Colombian Manufacturing.* 1987. 186pp.
145-4 $10.00

13.   Henderson, James D. *Conservative Thought in Latin America: The Ideas of Laureano Gomez.* 1988. 150pp.
148-9 $13.00

14.   Summ, G. Harvey, and Tom Kelly. *The Good Neighbors: America, Panama, and the 1977 Canal Treaties.* 1988. 135pp.
149-7 $13.00

15.   Peritore, Patrick. *Socialism, Communism, and Liberation Theology in Brazil: An Opinion Survey Using Q-Methodology.* 1990. 245pp.
156-X $15.00

16.   Alexander, Robert J. *Juscelino Kubitschek and the Development of Brazil.* 1991. 429pp.
163-2 $25.00

17.   Mijeski, Kenneth J., ed. *The Nicaraguan Constitution of 1987: English Translation and Commentary.* 1990. 355pp.
165-9 $25.00

18.   Finnegan, Pamela May. *The Tension of Paradox: José Donoso's The Obscene Bird of Night as Spiritual Exercises.* 1992. 179pp.
169-1 $15.00

19.	Sung Ho Kim and Thomas W. Walker, eds., *Perspectives on War and Peace in Central America.* 1992. 150pp.
	172-1	$14.00

20.	Becker, Mark. *Mariategui and Latin American Marxist Theory.* 1993. 214pp.
	177-2	$18.00

21.	Boschetto-Sandoval, Sandra and Marcia Phillips McGowan. *Claribel Alegria and Central American Literature: Critical Essays.* 1993. 263pp.
	178-9	$20.00

Southeast Asia Series

47.	Wessing, Robert. *Cosmology and Social Behavior in a West Javanese Settlement.* 1978. 200pp.
	072-5	$12.00

56A.	Duiker, William J. *Vietnam Since the Fall of Saigon.* Updated edition. 1989. 383pp.
	162-4	$17.00

64.	Dardjowidjojo, Soenjono. *Vocabulary Building in Indonesian: An Advanced Reader.* 1984. xviii, 256pp.
	118-7	$26.00

65.	Errington, J. Joseph. *Language and Social Change in Java: Linguistic Reflexes of Modernization in a Traditional Royal Polity.* 1985. xiv, 211pp.
	120-9	$20.00

66.	Binh, Tran Tu. *The Red Earth: A Vietnamese Memoir of Life on a Colonial Rubber Plantation.* Tr. by John Spragens. Ed. by David Marr. 1985. xii, 98pp.
	119-5	$11.00

68.	Syukri, Ibrahim. *History of the Malay Kingdom of Patani.* Tr. by Connor Bailey and John N. Miksic. 1985. xix, 113pp.
	123-3	$12.00

69.   Keeler, Ward. *Javanese: A Cultural Approach*. 1984. xxxvi, 522pp., Third printing 1992.
      121-7 $25.00

70.   Wilson, Constance M., and Lucien M. Hanks. *Burma-Thailand Frontier Over Sixteen Decades: Three Descriptive Documents*. 1985. x, 128pp.
      124-1 $11.00

71.   Thomas, Lynn L., and Franz von Benda-Beckmann, eds. *Change and Continuity in Minangkabau: Local, Regional, and Historical Perspectives on West Sumatra*. 1986. 363pp.
      127-6 $16.00

72.   Reid, Anthony, and Oki Akira, eds. *The Japanese Experience in Indonesia: Selected Memoirs of 1942-1945*. 1986. 411pp., 20 illus.
      132-2 $20.00

73.   Smirenskaia, Zhanna D. *Peasants in Asia: Social Consciousness and Social Struggle*. Tr. by Michael J. Buckley. 1987. 248pp.
      134-9 $14.00

74.   McArthur, M.S.H. *Report on Brunei in 1904*. Ed. by A.V.M. Horton. 1987. 304pp.
      135-7 $15.00

75.   Lockard, Craig Alan. *From Kampung to City. A Social History of Kuching Malaysia 1820-1970*. 1987. 311pp.
      136-5 $16.00

76.   McGinn, Richard. *Studies in Austronesian Linguistics*. 1988. 492pp.
      137-3 $20.00

77.   Muego, Benjamin N. *Spectator Society: The Philippines Under Martial Rule*. 1988. 232pp.
      138-1 $15.00

79.   Walton, Susan Pratt. *Mode in Javanese Music*. 1987. 279pp.
      144-6 $15.00

80. Nguyen Anh Tuan. *South Vietnam Trial and Experience: A Challenge for Development.* 1987. 482pp.
141-1 $18.00

81. Van der Veur, Paul W., ed. *Toward a Glorious Indonesia: Reminiscences and Observations of Dr. Soetomo.* 1987. 367pp.
142-X $16.00

82. Spores, John C. *Running Amok: An Historical Inquiry.* 1988. 190pp.
140-3 $13.00

83. Malaka. *From Jail to Jail.* Tr. and ed. by Helen Jarvis. 1990. 3 vols. 1,226pp.
150-0 $55.00

84. Devas, Nick. *Financing Local Government in Indonesia.* 1989. 344pp.
153-5 $16.00

85. Suryadinata, Leo. *Military Ascendancy and Political Culture: A Study of Indonesia's Golkar.* 1989. 250pp.
154-3 $18.00

86. Williams, Michael. *Communism, Religion, and Revolt in Banten.* 1990. 356pp.
155-1 $14.00

87. Hudak, Thomas John. *The Indigenization of Pali Meters in Thai Poetry.* 1990. 237pp.
159-4 $15.00

88. Lay, Ma Ma. *Not Out of Hate: A Novel of Burma.* Tr. by Margaret Aung-Thwin. Ed. by William Frederick. 1991. 222pp.
167-5 $20.00

89. Anwar, Chairil. *The Voice of the Night: Complete Poetry and Prose of Anwar Chairil.* 1993. Revised Edition. Tr. by Burton Raffel. 180pp.
                                                                       $17.00

90. Hudak, Thomas John, tr. *The Tale of Prince Samuttakote: A Buddhist Epic from Thailand.* 1993. 275pp.
174-8 $20.00

91. Roskies, D. M., ed. *Text/Politics in Island Southeast Asia: Essays in Interpretation.* 1993. 321pp.
175-6 $25.00

ORDERING INFORMATION

Orders for titles in the Monographs in International Studies series may be placed through the Ohio University Press, Scott Quadrangle, Athens, Ohio 45701-2979 or through any local bookstore. Individuals should remit payment by check, VISA, or MasterCard.* People ordering from the United Kingdom, Continental Europe, the Middle East, and Africa should order through Academic and University Publishers Group, 1 Gower Street, London WC1E, England. Orders from the Pacific Region, Asia, Australia, and New Zealand should be sent to East-West Export Books, c/o the University of Hawaii Press, 2840 Kolowalu Street, Honolulu, Hawaii 96822, USA.

Other individuals ordering from outside of the U.S. should remit in U.S. funds to Ohio University Press either by International Money Order or by a check drawn on a U.S. bank.** Most out-of-print titles may be ordered from University Microfilms, Inc., 300 North Zeeb Road, Ann Arbor, Michigan 48106, USA.

Prices are subject to change without notice.

* Please include $3.00 for the first book and 75¢ for each additional book for shipping and handling.

** Please include $4.00 for the first book and 75¢ for each additional book for foreign shipping and handling.